TEXTS IN GERMAN PHIL⌐

Ideas for a Philosophy of Nature

This is the first English translation of Schelling's *Ideas for a Philosophy of Nature* (first published in 1797 and revised in 1803), one of the most significant works in the German tradition of philosophy of nature and early nineteenth-century philosophy of science. It stands in opposition to the Newtonian picture of matter as constituted by inert, impenetrable particles, and argues instead for matter as an equilibrium of active forces that engage in dynamic polar opposition to one another. In the revisions of 1803 Schelling incorporated this dialectical view into a neo-Platonic conception of an original unity divided upon itself.

The text is of more than simply historical interest: Its daring and original vision of nature, philosophy, and empirical science will prove absorbing reading for all philosophers concerned with post-Kantian German idealism, for scholars of German Romanticism, and for historians of science.

TEXTS IN GERMAN PHILOSOPHY

General Editor: RAYMOND GEUSS

Advisory Board: RÜDIGER BUBNER, PETER HEATH,
GARBIS KORTIAN, WILHELM VOSSENKUHL, MARX WARTOFSKY

The purpose of this series is to make available, in English, central works of German philosophy from Kant to the present. Although there is rapidly growing interest in the English-speaking world in different aspects of the German philosophical tradition as an extremely fertile source of study and inspiration, many of its crucial texts are not available in English or exist only in inadequate or dated translations. The series is intended to remedy that situation, and the translations where appropriate will be accompanied by historical and philosophical introductions and notes. Single works, selections from a single author, and anthologies will all be represented.

Friedrich Nietzsche *Daybreak*
J. G. Fichte *The Science of Knowledge*
Lawrence S. Stepelevich (ed.) *The Young Hegelians: An Anthology*
Wilhelm von Humboldt *On Language*
Heinrich Rickert *The Limits of Concept Formation in Natural Science*
Friedrich Nietzsche *Untimely Meditations*
Friedrich Nietzsche *Human, All Too Human*
Friedrich Wilhelm Joseph von Schelling *Ideas for a Philosophy of Nature*

FRIEDRICH WILHELM JOSEPH VON SCHELLING

Ideas for a
Philosophy of Nature

as
Introduction to the Study of This Science
1797
Second Edition 1803

Translated by
Errol E. Harris and Peter Heath
with an Introduction by Robert Stern

CAMBRIDGE
UNIVERSITY PRESS

CAMBRIDGE UNIVERSITY PRESS

Cambridge, New York, Melbourne, Madrid, Cape Town,
Singapore, São Paulo, Delhi, Tokyo, Mexico City

Cambridge University Press
The Edinburgh Building, Cambridge CB2 8RU, UK

Published in the United States of America by
Cambridge University Press, New York

www.cambridge.org
Information on this title: www.cambridge.org/9780521357333

First published 1988
Reprinted 1995

A catalogue record for this publication is available from the British Library

Library of Congress Cataloguing in Publication data

ISBN 978-0-521-32102-0 Hardback
ISBN 978-0-521-35733-3 Paperback

Contents

Book II

Introduction

When it first appeared at Easter in 1797, Schelling's *Ideas for a Philosophy of Nature* marked the real beginning of a new phase in his philosophical development. Two years before its publication Schelling had left the Tübingen theological seminary, where he had met and made friends with Hegel and Hölderlin, and had taken up a post as private tutor to an aristocratic family; in 1796 he moved with the family to Leipzig. There he plunged into a study of medicine, physics and mathematics, and arrived at a picture of nature that emphasized its polarity and dynamism. This new attention to nature led Schelling to break away from the Fichtean themes that had dominated his previous writings. It is true that he retained elements of his previous outlook, and tried to fit his conception of nature into the framework of the Fichtean idealism of his early works; nonetheless, Schelling's discovery of nature represents the start of a fresh phase in his philosophical career. The *Ideas* of 1797 came out of these new reflections on nature, to be followed a year later by *On the World Soul*, the second of Schelling's major works on *Naturphilosophie*. These works at once brought him fame, as well as the support of Goethe, who secured for him a professorship at Jena in 1798.

Six years after its first publication, in 1803, Schelling brought out a second edition of this work, in which he added extensive supplements to the original text. By this time, however, the philosophical background to Schelling's dynamic conception of nature was no longer that of Fichte's dialectic of subject and object, but was now that of his own neo-Platonic philosophy of the absolute. This introduction will begin by explaining Schelling's dynamic conception of nature, and will then examine the effect on this conception of Schelling's change in philosophical outlook between the two editions of the *Ideas*.

I

In *On the World Soul* Schelling declares that "it is the first principle of a philosophical doctrine of nature to *go in search of polarity and dualism throughout all nature.*"[1] As with Heraclitus, this emphasis on polarity was associated by Schelling with a conception of nature as a balance of opposed forces or tendencies, a balance that when disrupted leads to strife and activity. In particular, Schelling argues in the *Ideas* that matter, which appears to be dead and inert, is in fact nothing more than an equilibrium of these opposed forces, and that it may be "brought to life" when this equilibrium is disturbed and a conflict of forces ensues:

In the *dead object* everything is *at rest*–there is in it no conflict, but eternal equilibrium. Where physical forces divide, living matter is gradually formed; in this struggle of divided forces the living continues, and for that reason alone we regard it as a visible analogue of the mind. (p. 177)[2]

Schelling, therefore, stands opposed to the Newtonian picture of matter as made up of hard, impenetrable, inert particles that are acted on by forces external to them. He claims that "absolute inertness . . . is a concept without sense or significance" (p. 165), and argues instead that matter is an equilibrium of active forces that stand in polar opposition to one another.

As Schelling acknowledges (cf. pp. 184–5), this notion of matter is derived in large part from Kant's "construction" of matter in the *Metaphysical Foundations of Natural Science* (1786).[3] There, in the chapter entitled "Dynamics," Kant argues that the apparent solidity and impenetrability of material nature are in fact derived from a repulsive force that must be balanced by an attractive force if matter is not to "disperse itself to infinity."[4] Kant insists that *both* these opposed forces are essential for the construction of matter, and material bodies should be seen as arising from the union of the two:

That property upon which as a condition even the inner possibility of a thing rests is an essential element of its inner possibility. Therefore, repulsive force belongs just as much to the essence of matter as attractive force; and one cannot be separated from the other in the concept of matter.[5]

---

[1] F. W. J. Schelling, *Sämmtliche Werke*, edited by K. F. A. Schelling; 14 vols. (Stuttgart, 1856–61), II, p. 459.

[2] All references, other than those given in footnotes, are to the translation of the *Ideas* in this volume.

[3] In his *Lectures on the Method of University Studies* (1803) Schelling comments that "the Kantian construction of matter first led to a higher view directed against the materialistic approach." He adds, however, that "all its positive elements remained at too low a level" (F. W. J. Schelling, *On University Studies*, translated by E. S. Morgan, edited and with an introduction by N. Guterman [Athens, Ohio, 1966], p. 130).

[4] I. Kant, *Metaphysical Foundations of Natural Science*, translated with an introduction and essay by J. Ellington (Indianapolis, 1970), p. 57.

[5] *Ibid.*, p. 60.

In opposition to the "mathematico-mechanical" approach of atoms and the void, therefore, Kant had argued for a "metaphysico-dynamical" conception of matter as made up of a balance of opposed forces.

Kant's "metaphysico-dynamical" conception clearly forms the background to Schelling's account of matter given in the first six chapters of Book II of the *Ideas*. These chapters form the central core of the work. Like Kant, Schelling argues that attractive and repulsive forces are "conditions of the *possibility* of matter" (p. 154): "Matter and bodies, therefore, are themselves nothing but products of opposing forces, or rather, are themselves nothing else but these forces" (p. 156). Like Kant also, Schelling contrasts his understanding of matter with that of the Newtonian atomists, who treat matter as if it were independent of force by allowing "reflection" to separate the latter from the former (cf. p. 18).

Schelling therefore begins from the presupposition (which, as we shall see, he thinks can only be grounded *philosophically*) that "attractive and repulsive forces constitute the *essence* of matter itself" (p. 165). As a result Schelling claims to be able to dispense with all the efforts of a purely *mechanistic* physics, to explain the gravitational attraction of matter in mechanical terms. In particular, in Chapter 3 of Book II, Schelling sets out to refute the explanation of gravitation offered by the French-Swiss theorist Georges-Louis le Sage, who had postulated an ether of minute particles (*particules ultramondaines*) moving in all directions at high velocity in all parts of space. Le Sage then explained the phenomenon of gravitational attraction by arguing that two ordinary spherical bodies would screen each other from the bombardment of these particles, so that on the side of each body facing the other the impact of particles would be less than that on the other side, and the resulting disequilibrium of force would impel the bodies towards each other. Schelling dismisses this hypothesis, not only on the grounds that it still leaves the motion of the minute particles unexplained (p. 164), and that the idea of indivisible primary particles is absurd (pp. 161–2), but also because his (or Kant's) dynamical conception of matter renders le Sage's mechanistic hypothesis redundant (pp. 166–7).

In the following three chapters of Book II Schelling then goes on to give an explanation of the chemical properties of bodies and chemical processes on the basis of the dynamical account of matter. In the first of these chapters on chemistry he takes up the question of the *qualitative* determination of matter. He argues that although matter in general is constructed from an equilibrium of the "basic forces" (*die Grundkräfte*) of attraction and repulsion, particular qualities of matter in fact derive from an upsetting of this equilibrium, and a predominance of one of these forces over the other; otherwise, Schelling maintains, the forces would simply cancel each other out, in which case neither force would be present in matter to any determinate degree:

> Thus force as such can affect us only insofar as it has a particular degree. But so long as we think of these dynamical forces quite generally – in a wholly indeterminate relationship – neither one of them has a particular degree. We can picture this relationship as an absolute *equilibrium* of these forces, in which the one always cancels out the other, and neither allows the other to grow up to a particular degree. So if *matter* as such is to acquire *qualitative* properties, its forces will have to have a particular degree, i.e., they will have to depart from the generality of the relationship in which the mere understanding thinks of them – or more plainly – they will have to deviate from the equilibrium in which they are originally and necessarily conceived. (p. 216)

From this argument Schelling derives what he calls the "principle of dynamical chemistry" (p. 221): "*All quality of matter rests wholly and solely on the intensity of its basic forces*" (p. 216; cf. also p. 233). The qualities Schelling is referring to here are essentially those of elasticity and mass, where the former is associated with the repulsive force, and the latter with the attractive force (p. 253). Other properties, such as colour and temperature, are dependent on these primary qualities, especially on the quality of elasticity (cf. pp. 224–5 on the colour of light, and p. 226 on the heating of bodies).

Using this principle of dynamical chemistry, Schelling then goes on to give his account of chemical processes and chemical affinity. As one might expect, he rejects any attempt (e.g., by le Sage or Georges-Louis Leclerc, Comte de Buffon) to offer a Newtonian explanation of chemical affinities in terms of an ether or gravitational attraction (although he grants that these conceptions may have some value as hypotheses, insofar as they help to turn chemistry into a mathematical science [p. 210]). Instead he argues that chemical affinity occurs between bodies with opposite degrees of basic forces (i.e., a high degree of repulsive force and a low degree of attractive force on the one hand, and a low degree of repulsive force and a high degree of attractive force on the other); such bodies, he maintains, will enter into chemical reactions in order to restore their imbalance of basic forces to an equilibrium (cf. p. 264). Schelling goes on to argue that as a result the way to set a chemical reaction into motion is to upset this equilibrium between the basic forces of two bodies, so that they are forced into combination if a balance of forces is to be restored (pp. 253–4). The chemical product that results from this combination will be a median of the basic forces of the two opposed bodies (p. 255). (It has to be said that this conception of the chemical process led Schelling into some strange views: For example, he seems to have held that the paradigm of a chemical reaction is that between a solid and a fluid body, where the former has a high degree of attractive force, and the latter has a high degree of repulsive force [cf. pp. 133, 254 and 268]. Nonetheless, though the terms and concepts he employs are rather different, Schelling's account is in some respects closer than that of the Newtonians to an account of chemical affinity in terms of opposed electrical charge.)

Now that we have seen how for Schelling matter only enters into chemical interaction when the balance of attractive and repulsive forces within "dead matter" is disturbed, we can look more profitably at Book I of the *Ideas*, where he discusses combustion, light, air, electricity and magnetism.

Schelling's theory of heat and combustion rests on his dynamic conception of matter. On the one hand, he rejects absolutely the caloric theory of heat, which treats heat as an imponderable fluid that enters into chemical combination with the body when it is warmed: Schelling observes that "to postulate a heat-matter as the cause of heat is not to explain the situation, but to pay oneself with words" (p. 228; cf. also p. 4). On the other hand, although he appears to go along with the kinetic theory in accepting that heat is a "mere modification of matter as such" (p. 231), he still rejects any *mechanical* explanation of the expansion of a heated body as being caused by vibrating atoms that push one another apart (p. 246). In opposition to both these current explanations of heat, Schelling develops a theory more in line with his dynamical explanation of matter, arguing that heat is simply a particular degree of repulsive or expansive force possessed by a heated body, which may be communicated to another body until equilibrium is restored (p. 226). Nonetheless, although Schelling insists that heat itself does not enter into chemical combination with the heated body (pp. 228 and 263), he argues that heat may be the cause of chemical combinations, as occurs, for example, in combustion: In increasing the degree of repulsive force within the body, heating enables it to combine chemically with oxygen, which is "charged" with the opposite attractive force.

In his treatment of light, Schelling is also unwilling to allow the existence of a special "light-stuff" or substance, which can enter into chemical combinations with other forms of matter (although he allows that this view of light may have some value as a scientific *fiction*) (p. 78; cf. also pp. 73–4). Rather, he argues that light is nothing more than "the highest degree known to us of the expansive force" (p. 224); it differs from heat in that whereas *any* state of matter (gas, liquid or solid) can possess that degree of expansibility or repulsive force felt as heat, only air is capable of that degree of expansive force required in order to be a medium for light (cf. pp. 226–8).

Air interests Schelling, however, not simply because it is the "medium that conducts to earth the higher forces (light and heat)" (p. 133) but also because the atmosphere displays an equilibrium and interaction of opposed moments. Air is therefore an important instance of the balance of polarity in nature, where the vital air (oxygen) given off by the vegetable kingdom is balanced by the exhalation into the atmosphere of "mephitic gas" (carbon dioxide) by the animal kingdom: "The collectively uniform distribution of substances, which dispenses ever new materials in nicely calculated proportions into the atmospheric cycle, never lets it reach the point where a perfectly pure air would exhaust our vital forces, or a mephitic gas would stifle all seeds of life" (p. 88). Atmospheric air also displays a polar opposition of life-giving oxygen on the one hand, and azotic air (nitrogen) on the other, which in contrast to the former is damaging to all living beings.[6] Schelling rejects absolutely the suggestion of Christoph Girtanner that the elements of atmospheric air are separated into layers, and argues strongly that they must be chemically mixed (pp. 88–9).

From this account of the duality of air Schelling moves on in the next chapter to a discussion of that polar phenomenon *par excellence,* that favourite of all the Romantics and *Naturphilosophen,* which so excited the popular and scientific imagination throughout the period: electricity. Given that Schelling's philosophy of nature as a whole places such an emphasis on polarity and the basic forces of attraction and repulsion, it is not really surprising that electricity so fascinated him, and his account of it is very much determined by his general dynamic conception of matter as I have analysed it. This conception leads him to reject Benjamin Franklin's picture of electricity as a subtle elastic fluid, arguing that the postulation of such a fluid is nothing but a "*lazy Philosophy of Nature,* which believes it has explained everything if it postulates the causes of phenomena as basic materials in the bodies, from which they then emerge (*tamquam Deus ex machina*) only when needed to explain some phenomenon in the shortest and most convenient way" (p. 101). Instead Schelling argues that positive electricity is the result of the elasticity of matter, while negative electricity is the result of its cohesion. He then goes on to suggest that this cohesion of matter is caused by oxygen, which he characterizes as a

---

[6] The etymology of azote is ἀ (without) and ξωή (life).

"cohesion-intensifying principle" (p. 67). Schelling brings together both these points in the second-edition supplement to this chapter.

We can accordingly state the general law of the electrical relation of bodies thus: *That one of the two which enhances its cohesion in opposition to the other will have to appear negatively electric, and that one which diminishes its cohesion, positively electric.* It is evident from this how the electricity of every body is determined, not only by its own quality, but equally by that of the other. As is shown in the foregoing chapter, though very incompletely, the bearing which the electric relationship of bodies has upon that of their oxidizability is intelligible, since this too is determined by cohesion-relationships. (p. 118)

This account of oxygen as causing cohesion in matter, and thereby giving rise to negative electricity, explains Schelling's curious-looking claim in the first edition that *"the basis of negative electrical matter is either oxygen itself or some other basic substance wholly homogeneous with it"* (p. 102). Given this account of oxygen, Schelling is able to arrive at a dynamical picture of electricity, explaining the negative pole in terms of an increased attractive force caused by oxidation, while at the same time being able to dispense with a unique electrical matter or fluid to account for the presence of this negative electrical charge.

Schelling displays a similar reluctance to allow the existence of imponderable fluids in his discussion of magnetism. While he grants that the one-fluid theory of Franz Aepinus has considerable value as a *hypothesis*, he does not accept that this magnetic fluid is any more than "a (*scientific*) *fiction*, on which to base *experiments* and *observations* (as *regulative*), but not *explanations* and *hypotheses* (as *principle*). For if we speak of a magnetic matter, we have in fact said nothing more by this than what we knew anyway, namely, that there has to be *something* which makes the magnet magnetic" (p. 125). In the case of magnetism, however, Schelling offers little by way of an alternative explanation of the magnetic properties of bodies, although he hints that a chemical explanation may be the most fruitful path to follow (p. 127).

Now there is no doubt that one major reason for Schelling's hostility towards the postulation of special fluids and matters to account for phenomena like light, heat, electricity and magnetism in Book I of the *Ideas* is his conception of matter as essentially constructed from the polar opposition of dynamical forces, forces that can be used to account for these phenomena, and which need no *further* explanation in terms of matters and fluids. The only explanation that Schelling feels *can* be offered for this polarity of basic forces cannot in fact be given at the level of empirical science at all, but rather must come from outside our possible experience; "we are therefore obliged to ascend to philosophical axioms" (p. 172), to the "higher science" of philosophical explanation.

II

In the first edition of the *Ideas,* by a philosophical explanation of the dynamic polarity of nature Schelling primarily means a *transcendental* account, which like Kant's should be based on an examination of the possibility of our experience (cf. pp. 155–6). Thus, in Chapter 4 of Book II Schelling sets out to show that "these concepts of universal attraction and repulsion" must be *"conditions* for the possibility of all objective knowledge" (p. 171); thereby he hopes to demonstrate, as the title of this chapter claims, the "First Origin of the Concept of Matter, from the Nature of Perception and the Human Mind."

However, Schelling's transcendental deduction of the forces of attraction and repulsion, and with them matter, departs considerably from the Kantian picture, as developed by the latter in the *Critique of Pure Reason,* of a transcendental ego which employs the categories to synthesize and structure an atomistic manifold given to it by the transcendental object. Schelling rejects this Kantian picture quite forcefully in the Introduction to the *Ideas,* on the grounds that it rests on a mistaken form-matter distinction,[7] that it requires the dogmatic postulation of the nonsensical things-in-themselves, and that it cannot explain how the postulated things-in-themselves cause representations in us (pp. 25–7).

Rather than base his transcendental deduction of the basic forces and matter on this Kantian conception, therefore, Schelling develops his deduction along more Fichtean lines, as set out by the latter in his *Foundations of the Entire Science of Knowledge* (1794).[8] Schelling did not work out the full details of this Fichtean deduction until his *System of Transcendental Idealism* of 1800,[9] but the beginnings of such an attempt can be seen in the first edition of the *Ideas.*

Fichte had begun his *Science of Knowledge* with the aim of discovering the "primordial, absolutely unconditioned first principle of all

---

[7] Donald Davidson has more recently attacked the clearly Kantian doctrine of "conceptual schemes" on similar grounds, arguing that the "dualism of scheme and content, of organizing system and something waiting to be organized, cannot be made intelligible and defensible" (D. Davidson, "On the Very Idea of a Conceptual Scheme," in his *Inquiries into Truth and Interpretation* [Oxford, 1975], p. 189).

[8] English translation in J. G. Fichte, *The Science of Knowledge, with the First and Second Introductions,* translated by P. Heath and J. Lachs (Cambridge, 1982).

[9] F. W. J. Schelling, *System of Transcendental Idealism,* translated by P. Heath, with an introduction by M. Vater (Charlottesville, Va., 1978).

human knowledge."[10] Taking as his starting point the "perfectly certain and established"[11] proposition A *is* A, or A = A, he then argues that this proposition requires a necessary connection or bond (which he calls X) between A as subject and A as predicate. Fichte then argues that this connection must be present in the judging self, along with the A that forms the subject and predicate of the judgement. Finally, just as Kant had argued that all connection of the manifold by the understanding rests on the original unity of the "I think" or consciousness,[12] so Fichte argues that this connecting link (X) between the two sides of the judgment of identity also requires the unity of the self that makes the judgment: He thereby arrives at the principle I *am* I, or I = I. The unity and identity of self-consciousness therefore form the "absolutely unconditioned first principle of all human knowledge," as all knowledge must fall under the rule A = A, and this rule itself rests on that unity of consciousness which Fichte has deduced.

He then moves on to a second "perfectly certain and established" proposition: that "not-A is not equal to A."[13] This positing of not-A, Fichte argues, requires the original positing of A, and is therefore materially conditioned by this original positing. At the same time he argues that the act of counterpositing rests on the second principle of human knowledge, which states that a not-self must be opposed to the self; and just as the not-A was conditioned by the original positing of the A, so the not-self must be conditioned by the original positing of the self.[14]

Fichte next goes on to argue that this counterpositing of the not-self by the self in fact leads into contradiction as it stands. For if the not-self is posited, the self is negated; but on the other hand, the not-self can only come to be if it is posited by the self; so if the former is to be posited, the latter cannot be negated. A way must therefore be found whereby the positing of the not-self does not absolutely negate and eliminate the self, and *vice versa*. The question therefore is, "How can A and not-A, being and non-being, reality and negation, be thought

---

[10] Fichte, *The Science of Knowledge*, p. 93.

[11] *Ibid.*, p. 94.

[12] I. Kant, *Critique of Pure Reason*, translated by N. Kemp Smith, second impression (London, 1933), pp. 151–8 (B130–40).

[13] Fichte, *The Science of Knowledge*, p. 102.

[14] "As surely as the absolute certainty of the proposition 'not-A is not equal to A' is unconditionally admitted among the facts of empirical consciousness, *so surely is a not-self opposed absolutely to the self*. Now all that we have just said concerning opposition in general is derived from this original opposition, and thus holds good of it from the start; it is thus absolutely unconditioned in form, but conditioned as to matter. And with this we have also discovered the second basic principle of all human knowledge" (*ibid.*, p. 104).

together without mutual elimination and destruction?" The answer Fichte gives is that "they will mutually *limit* one another," where "to *limit* something is to abolish its reality, but not *wholly* but in *part* only, by negation."[15] Thus, he argues, the only way in which the contradictory nature of the second principle of human knowledge can be overcome is in the following third principle: "*In the self I oppose a divisible not-self to the divisible self.*"[16] In this way Fichte arrives at a pair of opposed moments that nonetheless require one another for their determination,[17] and which can therefore be conjoined in a synthesis.

The way in which Fichte came to this unity of apparently absolutely opposed moments is of the utmost importance as a foreshadowing of Hegel's later development of the dialectic, and the similarity between the two is clear: Just as Fichte begins from the one-sided identity of the self, so Hegel's dialectic of categories begins from the simply self-identical categories of the understanding; and just as Fichte proceeded to deduce from this the necessity of a not-self, so for Hegel the one-sided categories pass over into their opposite or other; and just as for Fichte this apparently absolute opposition of self and not-self can in fact be unified in a higher synthesis once the mutual determination of the apparent opposites is seen, so for Hegel the opposition of categories must be overcome by reason, while their difference is preserved.[18]

It is also clear that in his early writings, and in the first edition of the *Ideas*, this Fichtean dialectic of the self and the not-self had a great influence on Schelling. For example, in his work of 1795, *Of the I as the Principle of Philosophy, or On the Unconditional in Human Knowledge,*[19] Schelling begins like Fichte with an absolutely self-identical I, which is then opposed by a not-I which stands outside it. Also like Fichte, Schelling then argues that this absolute oppositing must be overcome, and that the two opposed moments must in fact mutually determine each other through negation, so that in the final synthesis a finite I is limited by a finite not-I:

---

[15] *Ibid.*, p. 108.

[16] *Ibid.*, p. 110.

[17] Fichte's argument here rests on Spinoza's dictum "*determinatio negatio est*" ("determination is negation"). Hegel also made extensive use of this principle in constructing his dialectic.

[18] These three phases of the dialectic are most clearly presented by Hegel in his *Logic*, §§79–82; English translation in G. W. F. Hegel, *Hegel's Logic*, translated by W. Wallace with a foreword by J. N. Findlay; 3rd ed. (Oxford, 1975), pp. 113–21.

[19] English translation in F. W. J. Schelling, *The Unconditional in Human Knowledge: Four Early Essays (1794–1796)*, translated and commentary by F. Marti (Lewisburg, Pa., 1980).

The absolute I describes an infinite sphere which includes all reality. Counter to that another infinite sphere is set up (not only excluded) which includes all negation (absolute not-I). . . . The absolute sphere of the not-I, if it were simply posited absolutely, would have to cancel the I altogether, because one infinite sphere does not tolerate another. On the other hand, the sphere of the I would cancel the sphere of the not-I, insofar as the latter is posited as infinite. And yet both are supposed to be posited. There is no remedy but the striving of the I to draw into its own sphere the sphere of the not-I, for the latter is to be posited, and positing is possible only in the I. But this possibility is denied by the negation which is the nature of the sphere of the not-I. Consequently, this latter negation can be posited only in contrast to the sphere of the I. If it is to be posited inside the sphere of reality, the infinite sphere of negation turns into a finite sphere of reality, i.e., it can be posited only as reality necessarily connected with negation. And by that the I becomes restricted.[20]

This "progression from thesis to antithesis and from there to synthesis"[21] clearly has the character of Fichte's dialectic of self and not-self.

It is this dialectic that forms the background of Schelling's transcendental deduction of the basic forces of matter as it is presented in Chapter 4 of Book II in the first edition of the *Ideas*. Schelling begins this deduction by arguing that insofar as matter is real, it must be given to us in intuition. In contrast to much empiricist psychology, however, he maintains that intuition cannot be a merely passive reception of impressions, for otherwise no explanation can be offered of the *consciousness* we have of these impressions (p. 173).[22] Schelling argues instead that the apparent passivity of intuition is in fact nothing more than a limitation of a primary *activity*, in contrast to which the passivity is determined. This pure activity is for Schelling (as it was for Fichte) the essential attribute of the self, and it is only in dialectical contrast to this activity that the passivity induced in us by the intuition of the not-self can arise; conversely, only through this opposition of the not-self can the activity of the self be determined, making the dialectical dependence of these apparent opposites complete:

All *thinking* and presentation in us is therefore necessarily preceded by an *original activity*, which, *because it precedes* all thinking, is to that extent absolutely *undetermined* and *unconfined*. Only once an opposing element is present does it become *restricted*, and for that very reason a *determinate* (thinkable) activity. If this activity of our mind were *originally* restricted (as is imagined by the philosophers who reduce everything to thinking and presentation), the mind could never *feel* itself to be *confined*. It *feels* its *confinement* only insofar as it feels at the same time its original *lack of confinement*.

[20] *Ibid.*, p. 92, footnote in the first edition.
[21] *Ibid.*, p. 90, footnote.
[22] Schelling makes a similar point in the *System of Transcendental Idealism*, pp. 61–2.

Now upon this original activity there *works* (or so at least it seems to us, from the standpoint we here occupy) an activity *opposed* to it, which has hitherto been no less completely undetermined, and thus we have *two mutually contradictory activities, as necessary conditions for the possibility of an intuition.* (p. 175)

Now, from this dialectical account of the mutual dependence of the unrestricted and restricted activities of the self, and thus of the self and the not-self, Schelling argues that *"the product of intuition is necessarily a finite one, which proceeds from opposing, mutually restricting activities"* (p. 177). In other words, the object of intuition must itself be constructed from the opposition of forces that make possible the consciousness of this object. In this way, Schelling claims to have derived the polarity of forces within matter from the transcendental polarity of self and not-self, by giving a transcendental deduction of the opposition of basic forces in the object, beginning from the original dialectic of opposed activities within the knowing mind. According to Schelling, it is this dialectic that makes experience of the object possible, but which itself can only be grounded at the transcendental level, not at the level of experience.

In the object, however, those *opposing activities,* from which it emerged in intuition, have at the same time become permanent. The mental origin of the object lies beyond consciousness. For with it consciousness first arose. It therefore appears as something that exists quite independently of our freedom. So those opposing activities, which intuition has united in it, appear as *forces* attaching to the object in itself, without any reference to a possible cognition. For the *understanding* they are something merely *excogitated* and found by inference. But it presupposes them to be *real*, since they necessarily proceed from the *nature* of our mind, and of intuition itself. (p. 182)

III

Schelling's philosophical thought, though not without a degree of continuity, is nonetheless notoriously protean, and his outlook changed a good deal between the two editions of the *Ideas.* By 1803 Schelling had worked out his so-called philosophy of identity, most notably in his *Exhibition of My System of Philosophy* (1801) and *Further Exhibitions from the System of Philosophy* (1802), as well as in his dialogue *Bruno, or Concerning the Divine and Natural Principle of Things* (1802). In these writings Schelling no longer explained the fundamental phenomenon of difference and polarity in the Fichtean way, as the dialectical positing by a one-sided moment of its opposite; rather, Schelling's philosophy now encompassed the absolute, and duality was now understood as the division of a primordial neo-Platonic unity. Thus, whereas in the first edition of the *Ideas* Schelling's deduction of the polarity of nature had been purely dialectical—as the transition of one moment into its opposite or other—in the second edition this polarity is conceived as the unfolding into difference of an original unity. This new conception is neatly summed up in the following passage from Giordano Bruno, which Schelling presents as giving the "creed of true philosophy" towards the end of his eponymous dialogue: "To penetrate into the deepest secrets of nature, one must not tire of inquiring into the opposed and antagonistic extremes or end points of things. To discover their point of union is not the greatest task, but to do this and then develop elements out of their point of union, this is the genuine and deepest secret of art."[23]

The point of union from which Schelling's identity philosophy begins is the absolute, which is utterly homogeneous and undifferentiated, a Parmenidean One. Now, whereas on a purely dialectical approach this empty absolute would inevitably give rise to its opposite,[24] thereby introducing duality and opposition into the picture, Schelling's identity philosophy is not dialectical in this way; rather, he posits duality as arising *within the absolute itself,* as a "self-division of the undivided absoluteness into subject and object" (p. 47), opposites that must then be brought back to unity, while preserving their difference. This movement gives rise to Schelling's doctrine of three levels or potencies (*die Potenzen*),[25] as a hierarchy of structures that must be repeated by each finite thing or class of things. The first potency is that of relative identity, which involves the transition of unity into difference; the second potency is that of relative difference, which involves the opposite and complementary movement of difference into unity; and both these potencies are encompassed by a third potency of absolute identity, which is the identity of identity and difference. Schelling insists, however, that this third potency, of absolute identity, is in fact primary (cf. pp. 180–1), and that the other two emerge from it only after the "eternal self-division of the absolute into subject and object" (p. 150), which brings about the introduction of difference into this unity.

In the supplementary Introduction he wrote for the second edition of the *Ideas*, Schelling presents these three levels or potencies using the scholastic terminology of form and essence:

[23] F. W. J. Schelling, *Bruno, or On the Natural and the Divine Principle of Things*, edited and translated with an introduction by M. G. Vater (Albany, N.Y., 1984), note 110, p. 260, and p. 222.

[24] As occurs, for example, in Hegel's well-known dialectic of Pure Being, Not-Being, and Becoming; see Hegel, *Logic*, §§86–88, pp. 124–33.

[25] This term was first used in print by Schelling's fellow *Naturphilosoph* Karl Eschenmayer, and was taken from the theory of powers in mathematics.

In this absoluteness and in the eternal act, it [the absolute] is utterly one, and yet, in this unity, again immediately a totality of the three unities, namely, that in which the essence is absolutely shaped into form, that in which the form is absolutely shaped into essence, and that in which both these absolutenesses are again one absoluteness. (p. 48)

Schelling does nothing to explain his use of this terminology here, but a fuller (though by no means unproblematic) account is given by the character called Alexander in the *Bruno*. From this account it is clear that Schelling conceives of a thing's essence as infinite and undifferentiated, whereas its form constitutes the element of limitation and determination; and the absolute, as the form of all forms, unifies this limitation and finiteness with the infinite essence, thereby bringing together both unity and multiplicity in an absolute unity.[26] Moreover, even when in the *Ideas* Schelling uses the different terminology of universal and particular (p. 48) and infinite and finite (p. 49), the point he is making is basically the same: The absolute is the unity of the twofold movement of unity into difference (or universal into particular, or infinite into finite) and difference into unity (or particular into universal, or finite into infinite).

From this Schelling argues that there must be three levels or potencies in Nature-philosophy (pp. 51 and 137–9). The first potency is the movement of the infinite into the finite, in which the unity of the former gives rise to the spatially differentiated material bodies that make up the world. The second level is made up of the "reverse embodiment of the particular into the universal or essence" (p. 51), in which the universal is given its highest expression in the phenomenon of light. Finally, both these movements are brought together in the primary unity of the third potency, which is represented in the natural world by the organism, as the "perfect mirror-image of the absolute in Nature and for Nature" (p. 51).

In addition, Schelling not only uses this doctrine of potencies to give an account of magnetism (as the transition of identity into difference), electricity (as the transition of difference into unity) and chemistry (as the union of this twofold movement) (cf. pp. 137 and 268); he also deduces from it the construction of matter that he puts forward in the second edition of the *Ideas*. As in the first edition, he constructs matter from the opposed basic forces of attraction and repulsion; but instead of deducing these forces *dialectically*, as opposites requiring each other in order to come into being, he now simply derives them from the twofold movement of the absolute, as an

---

[26] Schelling, *Bruno*, pp. 206–7.

original unity that produces difference out of unity and unity out of difference (cf. pp. 158 and 192).[27]

It should now be clear how in the second edition Schelling's whole philosophy of nature has been rethought against the background of his identity philosophy, in the context of his neo-Platonic meditations on the relation of the one to the many. As a result, nature's polarity is no longer seen as a purely dialectical positing of contraries, but rather as the division of an original unity. "Matter, too, like everything that exists, streams out from the eternal essence, and represents in appearance an effect, albeit indirect and mediate only, of the eternal dichotomizing into subject and object, and of the fashioning of its infinite unity into finitude and multiplicity" (p. 179). With this new philosophy of nature Schelling incorporated the dialectic of contraries into his account of the transition of the one into the many; he thereby succeeded in making the dialectic part of his neo-Platonic conception of reality, an aspect of the dialectic that was only really lost when Hegel managed to break away from Schelling's doctrine of the absolute.[28]

IV

Schelling's *Ideas for a Philosophy of Nature* is a work of considerable historical interest: It offers many insights into the development of Schelling's thought and of post-Kantian German idealism, into the history and philosophy of science of the period, and into the whole intellectual phenomenon of *Naturphilosophie*, which is represented here by one of its most forceful and influential proponents. Moreover, the *Ideas* is of more than merely historical interest. The view of nature, of philosophy and of empirical science that it puts forward is both daring and all-embracing, and as such it should be admired as one of the most startling and original attempts of human speculation to provide us with a total account of the nature of what is.

ROBERT STERN

[27] Schelling also departs from the first edition by adding *gravity* to attraction and repulsion as the third principle of the construction of matter which brings together the other two.

[28] In his early works Hegel was clearly greatly influenced by Schelling's doctrine of the absolute, and therefore followed him in viewing dialectical opposition as the division of an original unity: "An authentic speculation, even when it does not succeed in constructing itself completely into a system, necessarily begins from the absolute identity. The dichotomy of the absolute identity into subjective and objective is a production by [or of] the Absolute" (G. W. F. Hegel, *The Difference between Fichte's and Schelling's System of Philosophy*, translated by H. S. Harris and W. Cerf [Albany, N.Y., 1977], pp. 114–15). Only later, when he had rejected Schelling's neo-Platonic absolute, did Hegel return to a more Fichtean model of the dialectic, as the transition from a one-sided moment into its other, through which the former is determined. Hegel makes this contrast clear in G. W. F. Hegel, *Lectures on the History of Philosophy*, translated by E. S. Haldane and F. H. Simson, 3 vols. (London, 1896; reprinted 1974), III, pp. 525–6.

Translators' Note

The text of this translation is that of the second edition, of 1803, in which often quite lengthy, if at times arcane, supplements were added to each chapter. Their purpose was not so much to update the scientific matter under discussion but rather to bring the original content into line with the latest developments in the author's own philosophical views. There were also some changes of wording between the first and second editions, reported in the Collected Edition of K. F. A. Schelling (1856ff.), and in most of its successors. These have been incorporated, in square brackets, in the footnotes to each chapter, the rest of which are virtually all by Schelling himself. In addition, we have provided, in the Appendix, some biographical details of the numerous but now little-remembered scientific writers of the period, to whom Schelling frequently refers. The aim here is merely to identify these figures, not to give any full account of their work. Under the circumstances, it seemed otiose to include such familiar names as those of Descartes, Spinoza, Newton, Bacon, or Kant; but we have in fact made room for some others equally famous – Franklin, Lavoisier and Volta, for example – where it seemed not unlikely that the reader might welcome a brief reminder of what they are famous for.

The translation of Book I has been made in the first instance by Harris; Book II, and the rest of the editorial matter, are attributable to Heath. Each, however, has revised the work of the other, not only to eliminate errors but also to secure a measure of uniformity in the rendering of technical terms. Our preferred versions are recorded in the Glossary; but where more than one option is given there, it should not be supposed that this reflects unreconciled disagreement between the translators. It is simply that – as we see it – the same German word cannot always be suitably – or even intelligibly – translated by a single English equivalent. Our aim, in other words, has been to provide, so far as possible, a clear and idiomatic translation which is nevertheless as close to the original as we can make it. It goes without saying that we may not always have succeeded, and that others, more perceptive or

better informed, may be able to set us right. Corrections or sugges-
tions will therefore be welcome, and will be duly acknowledged and
adopted, should there be any later opportunity for improving the
text.

PLH
EEH

Glossary

Anschauung	Intuition, perception
Atmospherische Luft	Atmospheric air
Aufheben	Remove, abolish, cancel
Auflösung	Dissolution
Azotische Luft	Azotic air, azote (nitrogen)
Begriff	Concept, notion
Beschaffenheit	Constitution, characteristic
Bestimmen	Determine, define, specify
Brennbare Luft	Inflammable air (hydrogen)
Darstellung	Presentation, account
Differenz	Difference
Eigenschaft	Property, attribute
Einbildung	Embodiment
Element	Element
Erregung	Excitation
Erscheinung	Phenomenon, appearance
Gegensatz	Opposite, contrary
Gleichgewicht	Equilibrium
Grundstoff	Basic material, basic substance
Hervorbringen	Produce, engender, create
Idee	Idea
Indifferenzierung	Indifferencing
Kapacität	Capacity (heat, etc.)
Körper	Body, substance
Lebensluft	Vital air (oxygen)
Luft	Air
Materie	Matter
Organisation	Organism, organization
Potenz	Potency, power
Salpeterluft	Nitrous air, nitrogen
Sauerstoff -gas	Oxygen
Stoff	Substance, stuff, material
Subject-objectivierung	Division into subject and object
Trennung	Separation
Verbindung	Combination, bonding
Verbrennung	Combustion
Verhältnis	Relationship, proportion, ratio
Vorstellung	Idea, presentation, conception
Wärmestoff	Heat-stuff, caloric
Wirksamkeit	Efficacy
Zerlegung	Disintegration
Zersetzung	Decomposition

Ideas for a Philosophy of Nature

FRIEDRICH WILHELM JOSEPH VON SCHELLING

Preface to the First Edition[1]

What the previous philosophical speculation of our age has left us as its net result is briefly the following: "The former theoretical philosophy (under the name of metaphysics) was a mixture of quite heterogeneous principles. One part of it contained laws, which pertain to the possibility of *experience* (general *natural laws*), another, fundamental principles which extend over all experience (essentially metaphysical principles).

"Now, however, it has been established that only a *regulative* use can be made of the latter in theoretical philosophy. Only our moral nature raises us above the phenomenal world, and laws which, in the realm of ideas, are of *constitutive* use are for that very reason *practical* laws. So nothing remains hereafter of what was previously metaphysical in theoretical philosophy, except the practical alone. What are left to theoretical philosophy are only the general principles of a possible experience, and instead of being a science which *follows* physics (metaphysics), it will in future be a science which *precedes* physics."

But now theoretical and practical philosophy (which in deference to the schools perhaps we may separate, but which are originally and necessarily united in the human mind) fall apart as *pure* and *applied*.

The *pure* theoretical philosophy concerns itself only with the investigation into the reality of our knowledge *as such;* it belongs, however, to the *applied,* under the name of a Philosophy of Nature, to derive from principles a *determinate* system of our knowledge (that is, the system of experience as a whole).

What *physics* is for *theoretical* philosophy, *history* is for the *practical,* and so the two main branches of our empirical knowledge develop out of these two main parts of philosophy.

Thus in working out the *Philosophy of Nature* and the *Philosophy of Man,* I hope to embrace the whole of *applied* philosophy. From the

[1] [The title of the first edition was *Ideas for a Philosophy of Nature,* The subtitle *as Introduction to the Study of This Science* was added in the second edition.]

3

former natural science, from the latter history, should receive a scientific foundation.

The following essay is intended only to be the beginning of an execution of this plan. I shall explain in the Introduction the *idea* of a Philosophy of Nature on which this essay is based. So I must expect that the test of the philosophical principles of this work will issue from this Introduction.

But so far as the *execution* is concerned, as the title already indicates, this work contains no scientific system, but only *ideas* for a Philosophy of Nature. One may regard it as a series of individual discussions on this subject.

The present first part of this work divides into two, the empirical and the philosophical. I considered it necessary to begin with the first, because what follows in the text very often takes cognizance of more recent discoveries and investigations in physics and chemistry. However, this involved the inconvenience that much had to remain in doubt which I believed myself able to decide, on philosophical principles, only at a later stage. With regard to many statements of the first Book, therefore, I must refer to the second (especially the eighth chapter). With respect to questions as yet still to some extent in dispute concerning the nature of heat and the phenomena of combustion, I have followed the basic rule of admitting absolutely no hidden elemental substances in bodies, the reality of which can in no way be established by experience.

In all these investigations concerning heat, light, electricity and the like, writers have recently mingled more or less philosophical principles without first distancing themselves from the empirical context, principles which are already alien to the experimental sciences in and for themselves, and usually so indefinite that intolerable confusion arises as a result. In physics nowadays the concept of force is played with in this way more frequently than ever, especially since doubts have begun to be entertained about the materiality of light, etc.; the question has already several times been raised whether electricity might not perhaps be *life-force*. All these vague ideas introduced illegitimately into physics I have had, in the first part of the work, to leave in their indefiniteness, since they can be rectified only philosophically. Otherwise I have sought to keep myself always within the limits of physics and chemistry in this part – and therefore also to speak their picture-language.

In the section on light (pp. 68–82), I wished especially to give opportunity for inquiries into the influence of light on our atmosphere. That this influence is not merely of the mechanical kind is already inferrable from the relationship of light to vital air. Further investigations into this topic could perhaps produce more detailed conclusions even about the nature of light and its propagation in our atmosphere. The matter is doubly important since we now know indeed that the atmospheric air is a mixture, but do not know how Nature can maintain this relation of different kinds of air constant, despite the innumerable changes in the atmosphere. What I have said about this, in the section on the kinds of air, is far from sufficient to afford a final conclusion on this point. The hypothesis which I have proposed concerning the origin of electrical phenomena, and have supported with evidence, I should like all the more to see tested, since if it is true, it must extend its influence still further (for instance, to physiology).

The *philosophical* part of this work is concerned with *dynamics* as the basic science of a theory of Nature, and *chemistry* as following from it. The part which follows next will include the principles of the theory of organic nature, or so-called physiology.[2]

It will be apparent from the Introduction that my purpose is not to *apply* philosophy to natural science. I can think of no more pitiful, workaday occupation than such an application of abstract principles to an already existing empirical science. My object, rather, is first to allow natural science itself to *arise* philosophically, and my philosophy is itself nothing else than natural science. It is true that chemistry teaches us to *read* the *letters,* physics the *syllables,* mathematics *Nature;* but it ought not to be forgotten that it remains for philosophy to interpret what is read.

[2] [This sentence reads, in the first printing of this Preface: "The part which follows next will include general kinematics, statics, and *mechanics,* the principles of natural science, theology and physiology." Cf. the remark on p. 272.]

Preface to the Second Edition

In this work, which appears here in a new edition, the residual problems are undoubtedly due chiefly to the circumstance that it contained the author's first ideas and reflections on the Philosophy of Nature. Since then, the objective range of this science has been enhanced from without by the enrichments which have accrued to it from several admirable intellects, as also from application to almost every branch of natural science; internally, as I believe I may assume, its relation to philosophy in general has been established. All the greater had the effort to be to remove as much as possible from the later version of this work the deficiencies of the earlier, of which I, perhaps least of all, could remain unaware.

To this end not only have the corrections that seemed necessary been made in the text of the first edition, but an attempt has also been made to indicate the present degree of completion of the science, in supplements to each chapter, and to couple the later fruits to the seedlings of the first rough sketch. In this connection two objects have been kept in view, first to set forth for the friends of philosophy, in the supplement to the Introduction and scattered intermittently elsewhere, the position reached through progressive development of the Philosophy of Nature in its relation to speculation in general, but secondly, in the supplements to the first and the second Books, to convey to the natural scientists, who have bestowed upon this work more attention than on any of my others, a conspectus of current views in the Philosophy of Nature on all the subjects touched upon in the present work.

So considered, it will justify itself in its new form as an introduction to the study of the Philosophy of Nature, inasmuch as it constitutes at the same time a transition to a second part, which would include organic physics and a critique of the most outstanding learned opinions so far offered on this subject.

Jena, 31st December 1802

Introduction

What philosophy is as such cannot just be answered immediately. If it were so easy to agree about a definite concept of philosophy, one would only need to analyse this concept to see oneself at once in possession of a philosophy of universal validity. The point is this: Philosophy is not something with which our mind, without its own agency, is originally and by nature imbued. It is throughout a work of freedom. It is for each only what he has himself made it; and therefore the idea of philosophy is also only the result of philosophy itself, which, as an infinite science, is at the same time the science of itself.[1]

Instead, therefore, of prescribing an arbitrary concept of philosophy in general or of the Philosophy of Nature in particular, in order thereafter to resolve it into its parts, I shall endeavor to let such a concept itself first *come into being* before the eyes of the reader.

Meanwhile, as one must, after all, have some starting point, I shall provisionally presuppose that a Philosophy of Nature *ought* to deduce the possibility of Nature, that is of the all-inclusive world of experience, from first principles. But I shall not deal with this concept analytically, or presuppose that it is correct and derive consequences from it, but before all else I shall investigate whether reality belongs to it as such, and whether it expresses anything that admits of *development*.

ON THE PROBLEMS WHICH A PHILOSOPHY OF NATURE HAS TO SOLVE

Whoever is absorbed in research into Nature, and in the sheer enjoyment of her abundance, does not ask whether Nature and experience be possible. It is enough that she is there for him; he has made her real by his very *act*, and the question of what is possible is raised only by one who believes that he does not hold the reality in his *hand*.

---

[1] [First edition]: the idea of philosophy [is] only the result of philosophy itself, a universally valid philosophy, however, [is] an inglorious fantasy.

Whole epochs have been spent in research into Nature, and yet one does not weary of it. Some have devoted their entire lives to this avocation and have not ceased to pray to the veiled goddess. Great spirits have lived in their own world, untroubled about the principles of their discoveries; and what is the whole reputation of the shrewdest doubter against the life of a man who has carried a world in his head and the whole of Nature in his imagination?

How a world outside us, how a Nature and with it experience, is possible – these are questions for which we have *philosophy* to thank; or rather, *with* these questions philosophy came to be. Prior to them mankind had lived in a (philosophical) state of nature. At that time man was still at one with himself and the world about him. In obscure recollection this condition still floats before even the most wayward thinker. Many never lose it and would be happy in themselves, if the fateful example did not lead them astray; for Nature releases nobody willingly from her tutelage, and there are no *native* sons of freedom.[2] Nor would it be conceivable how man should ever have forsaken that condition, if we did not know that his spirit, whose element is *freedom*, strives to make *itself* free, to disentangle itself from the fetters of Nature and her guardianship, and must abandon itself to the uncertain fate of its own powers, in order one day to return, as victor and by its own merit, to that position in which, unaware of itself, it spent the childhood of its reason.

As soon as man sets himself in opposition to the external world (how he does so we shall consider later), the first step to philosophy has been taken. With that separation, reflection[3] first begins; he separates from now on what Nature had always united, separates the object from the intuition, the concept from the image, finally (in that he becomes his own *object*) himself from himself.

But this separation is only *means*, not *end*. For the essence of man is action. But the less he reflects upon himself, the more active he is. His noblest activity is that which is not aware of itself. As soon as he makes himself object, the *whole* man no longer acts; he has suspended one part of his activity so as to be able to reflect upon the other. Man is not born to waste his mental power in conflict against the fantasy of an imaginary world, but to exert all his powers upon a world which has influence upon him, lets him feel its forces, and upon which he can react. Between him and the world, therefore, no rift must be estab-

---

[2] The greatest philosophers were always the first to return to it, and Socrates (as Plato relates), after he had stood throughout the night sunk in contemplation, prayed in the early morning to the rising sun. [Note to the first edition.]

[3] [Here and on the following pages, as well as later on, "speculation" occurred in the first edition, instead of "reflection," and "to speculate" instead of "to reflect."]

lished; contact and reciprocal action must be possible between the two, for only so does man become man. Originally in man there is an absolute equilibrium of forces and of consciousness. But he can upset this equilibrium through freedom, in order to reestablish it through freedom. But only in equilibrium of forces is there health.

Mere reflection, therefore, is a spiritual sickness in mankind, the more so where it imposes itself in domination over the whole man, and kills at the root what in germ is his highest being, his spiritual life, which issues only from Identity. It is an evil which accompanies man into life itself, and distorts all his intuition even for the more familiar objects of consideration. But its preoccupation with dissection does not extend only to the phenomenal world; so far as it separates the spiritual principle from this, it fills the intellectual world with chimeras, against which, because they lie beyond all reason, it is not even possible to fight. It makes that separation between man and the world permanent, because it treats the latter as a thing in itself, which neither intuition nor imagination, neither understanding nor reason, can reach.4

In contrast to this stands the true philosophy, which regards reflection as such merely as a means. Philosophy *must* presuppose that original divorce, because without it we should have no need to philosophize.

Therefore it assigns to reflection only *negative* value. It proceeds from that original divorce to unite once more, through freedom, what was originally and *necessarily* united in the human mind, i.e., forever to cancel out that separation. And so far as philosophy itself was made necessary only by that separation – was itself only a necessary evil, a discipline of errant reason – so it works in this respect for its own destruction. That philosopher who might employ his life, or a part of it, in pursuing the philosophy of reflection in its endless dichotomizing, in order to eliminate it in its ultimate ramifications, would earn

---

4 [The last passage reads in the first edition]: *Mere* speculation, therefore, is a spiritual sickness of mankind, and moreover the most dangerous of all, which kills the germ of man's existence and uproots his being. It is a tribulation, which, where it has once become dominant, cannot be dispelled – not by the stimulation of Nature (for what can that do to a dead soul?), nor by the bustle of life.

> Scandit aeratas vitiosa naves
> Cura nec turmas equitum relinquit.

Every weapon is justifiable against a philosophy which makes speculation not a *means* but an *end*. For it torments human reason with chimeras which, because they lie beyond all reason, it is not even possible to combat. It makes that separation between man and the world *permanent*, because it treats the latter as a *thing-in-itself*, which neither intuition nor imagination, neither understanding nor reason, can reach.

for himself the most worthy place by this service, which, although it remains negative, may be respected equally with the highest, even if he were not himself to have the satisfaction of seeing philosophy in its absolute form resurrect itself self-consciously out of the dismembering activities of reflection.⁵ The simplest expression of complicated problems is always the best. He who first attended to the fact that he could distinguish himself from external things, and therewith his ideas from the objects, and conversely, the latter from the former, was the first philosopher. He first interrupted the mechanics of his thinking, upset the equilibrium of consciousness, in which subject and object are most intimately united.

In that I envisage the object, object and idea are one and the same. And only in this inability to distinguish the object from the idea during the envisaging itself lies the conviction, for the ordinary understanding, of the reality of external things, which become known to it, after all, only through ideas.

This identity of object and idea the philosopher now does away with, by asking: How do ideas of external things arise in us? By this question we displace the things *outside* of ourselves, suppose them to be independent of our ideas. At the same time there ought to be connection between them and our ideas. But we are acquainted with no *real* connection between *different* things other than that of *cause* and *effect*. So the first endeavor of philosophy is to put object and idea into the relationship of cause and effect.

But now we have expressly posited things as *independent of ourselves*. On the other hand, we feel *ourselves* to be dependent upon the objects. For our idea is itself only *real* insofar as we are compelled to assume agreement between it and the things. So we cannot make the things the effects of our ideas. Nothing remains, therefore, but to make the ideas dependent upon the things and to regard the latter as causes, the former as effects.

Now, however, one can see at first glance that by this move we essentially cannot achieve what we wanted. We wanted to explain how it comes about that in us the object and the idea are inseparably united. For only in this union lies the reality of our knowledge of external things. And it is just this reality that the philosopher is sup-

---

⁵ The philosopher who spends his life, or part of it, pursuing speculative philosophy into its bottomless abysses, in order there to dig out its deepest foundation, brings to humanity an offering which, because it is the sacrifice of the noblest that he has, may perhaps be respected as much as most others. It is fortunate enough if he brings philosophy to the point at which even the ultimate necessity for it as a special science, and therewith his own name, vanishes forever from the memory of mankind. [First edition.]

posed to establish. But if the things are *causes* of ideas, then they *precede* the ideas. Consequently the separation between the two becomes permanent. But we wanted, after we had separated object and idea through freedom, to unite them again through freedom, we wanted to know that, and why, there is *originally* no separation between them.

Further, we know the things only through and in our ideas. Therefore, what they are, insofar as they precede our ideas, and so are not presented – of that we have no conception whatever.

Again, in asking: How does it come about that I have ideas? I raise myself *above* the idea and become, *through* this very question, a being that feels itself to be *free ab origine* with respect to all ideation, who surveys the ideation itself and the whole fabric of his ideas *beneath* him. Through this question itself I become an entity which, independent of external things, has *being in itself*.

Thus, with this question itself, I step out of the series of my ideas, release myself from connection with the things, adopt a position where no external force can reach me any longer; now, for the first time, the two hostile beings *mind* and *matter* separate. I place each of them in different worlds, between which no further connection is possible. In that I step out of the series of my ideas, even *cause* and *effect* are concepts which I survey from above. For they both arise only in the necessary succession of my ideas, from which I have released myself. How, then, can I subordinate myself again to these concepts, and allow things external to me to affect me?[6]

Or let us make the attempt the other way round, allow external things to affect us, and now explain how, despite this, we come to the question how ideas are possible in us.

Indeed, how things affect *me* (a free being) is not at all conceivable. I conceive only how things affect things. So far as I am *free*, however (and I *am* free, in that I raise myself above the interconnection of things and ask how this interconnection itself has become possible), I am not a *thing* at all, not an *object*. I live in a world entirely my own; I am a being that exists, not for other beings, but *for itself*. There can be only deed and act in me; from me effects can only *proceed;* there can be no *passivity* in me, for there is passivity only where there is effect and countereffect, and this is only in the interconnection of things, above which I have raised myself. But let it be the case that I am a

---

[6] Some ingenious members of the Kantian school have opposed this from the start. This philosophy allows all concepts of cause and effect to arise only in our minds, in our ideas, and yet the ideas themselves again, to be *caused* in me, according to the law of causality, by external things. Nobody wanted to hear of it at the time; but now surely it must be heard.

thing, which is itself caught up in the series of causes and effects, and is itself, together with the entire system of ideas, a mere result of the manifold effects which impinge upon me from without; in short, suppose I am myself a mere piece of mechanism. But what is caught up in mere mechanism cannot step out of the mechanism and ask: How has all this become possible? *Here,* in the midst of the series of phenomena, absolute necessity has assigned to it its place; if it leaves this place, it is no longer this thing. It is inconceivable how any external cause whatsoever could affect this self-dependent being, whole and complete in itself.

In order to be able to philosophize, therefore, one must be capable of asking that very question with which all philosophy begins. This question is not such as one can, without further ado, address to others. It is one brought forth freely, a problem self-given. *That* I am capable of posing this question is proof enough that I am, as such, independent of external things; for how otherwise could I have asked how these things themselves are possible *for me,* in my consciousness? One would therefore have to think that anyone who so much as raises this question is by that very fact refusing to explain his ideas as effects of external things. But this question has fallen among those who were completely incapable of devoting themselves to it. As it passed into their mouths, it also took on another sense, or rather, it lost all sense and meaning. *They* are beings who know themselves in no other way than so far as laws of cause and effect have power and dominion over them. *I,* in that I raise this question, have exalted myself above these laws. *They* are caught up in the mechanism of their thinking and representing; *I* have broken through this mechanism. How would they wish to understand me?

One who for himself is nothing other than what things and circumstances have made him, who, without dominion over his own ideas, is seized by, and dragged along with, the stream of causes and effects – how will he wish to know whence he comes, or whither he goes, or how he has become what he is? Does the wave know this, that drives hence in the stream? He has not even the right to say that he is a result of the collective effect of external things; for in order to be able to say this, he must presuppose that he knows *himself,* that he is therefore also something *for himself.* But this he is not. He exists only for other rational beings – not for himself – is a mere *object* in the world; and it is advantageous for him and for science that he should never hear of anything else or imagine anything other.

From time immemorial the most ordinary people have refuted the greatest philosophers with things understandable even to children and striplings. One hears, reads, and marvels that such common things were unknown to such great men and that people admittedly so insignificant could master them. It does not occur to anybody that perhaps the philosophers were also aware of all that; for how else could they have swum against the stream of evidence? Many are convinced that Plato, if he could only have read Locke, would have gone off ashamed; many a one believes that even Leibniz, if he arose from the dead to go to school for an hour with him, would be converted, and how many greenhorns have not sung triumphal songs over Spinoza's grave?

What was it, then, you ask, that drove all these men to forsake the common ways of thinking of their age and to invent systems opposed to everything that the great mass of people have always believed and imagined? It was a free inspiration, which elevated them into a sphere where *you* no longer even understand their task, while on the other hand many things became inconceivable to them, which seem very simple and understandable to you.[7]

It was impossible, for them, to join and bring into contact things which, in you, Nature and mechanism have always united. They were also unable to deny the world outside them, or that there was a mind within them, and yet there appeared to be no possible connection between the two. To you, if you ever think about these problems, there can be no question of converting the world into a play of concepts, or the mind within you into a dead mirror of things.[8]

Long since, the human spirit (still youthful, vigorous and fresh from the gods) had lost itself in mythology and poetic fictions about the origin of the world. The religions of entire peoples were founded on that conflict between spirit and matter, before a happy genius – the first philosopher – discovered the concepts in which all succeeding ages grasped and held firm both ends of our knowledge. The greatest thinkers among the ancients did not venture beyond this contradiction. Plato still sets matter, as an other, over against God.[9] The *first* who, with complete clarity, saw mind and matter as one, thought and extension simply as modifications of the same principle, was *Spinoza*. His system was the first bold outline of a creative imagination, which conceived the finite immediately in the idea of the infinite, purely as such, and recognized the former only in the latter.[10] *Leibniz* came, and

---

[7] It was a free inspiration which they gave *themselves,* and which raised them to where the leaden wings of your imagination are unable to carry you. After they had raised themselves thus above the course of Nature, much became inconceivable to them, which to you is all too intelligible. [First edition.]

[8] to transform mind into matter [First edition.]

[9] as a self-subsistent being [First edition.]

[10] of a creative imagination, which went over from the infinite in idea to the finite in intuition. [First edition.]

went the opposite way. The time has come when his philosophy can be re-established. His mind despised the fetters of the schools; small wonder that he has survived amongst us only in a few kindred spirits and among the rest has long become a stranger. He belonged to the few who also treat science as a free activity.[11] He had in himself the universal *spirit of the world,* which reveals itself in the most manifold forms; and where it enters, life expands. It is therefore doubly insufferable that only now are the right words for his philosophy supposed to have been found, and that the Kantian school should force its inventions upon him—alleging that he says things the precise opposite of everything he taught. There is nothing from which Leibniz could have been more remote than the speculative chimera of a world of *things-in-themselves,* which, known and intuited by no mind, yet affects us and produces all our ideas. The first thought from which he set out was: "that the ideas of external things would have arisen in the soul by virtue of her own laws *as in a particular world,* even though nothing were present but God (the infinite) and the soul (the intuition of the infinite)." He still asserted in his latest writings the absolute impossibility that an external cause should produce an effect upon the inwardness of a mind; he asserted, accordingly, that all alterations, all change of perceptions and presentations in a mind, could proceed only from an inner principle. When Leibniz said this, he spoke to philosophers. Today some people have intruded into philosophizing, who have a feeling for all else, but not for philosophy. Accordingly, if among ourselves it is said that no ideas could arise in us through external causes, there is no end of astonishment. Nowadays it is valid in philosophy to believe that the monads have windows, through which things climb in and out.[12]

It is quite possible to drive even the most convinced adherent of things-in-themselves as the causes of our ideas into a corner by all sorts of questions. One can say to him, I understand how matter affects matter, but neither how one in-itself affects another, since there can be no cause and no effect in the realm of the intelligible, nor how this law of one world extends into another altogether different from it, in fact completely opposed to it.[13] You would then have to admit, if I am dependent on external impressions, that I myself am nothing more than matter—as it were, an optical glass, in which the light-ray of the world refracts. But the optical glass does not itself see; it is merely an instrument in the hand of a rational being. And what is that in me which judges it to be an impression that has impinged upon

---

[11] who see everything, and even the truth *beneath* them [First edition.]

[12] Leibnitii Princip. Philosoph. #7.

[13] ["but neither how an in-itself. . . . opposed to it" is lacking in the first edition.]

me? Again, my own self, which surely, insofar as it judges, is not passive, but active – and thus something in me which feels itself free from the impression, and which nevertheless knows about the impression, apprehends it, raises it to consciousness.

Further, during the intuiting, no doubt arises concerning the reality of the external perception. But now comes the understanding and begins to divide and divides endlessly. Is matter outside you real? If so, it must *consist* of infinite parts. If it consists of infinitely many parts, it must have been put together out of these parts. But for this assembling our imagination has only a finite measure. Therefore an endless putting together must have occurred in finite time. Or the putting together must have begun somewhere, which means there are ultimate parts of matter, so I must (in the dividing) encounter such ultimate parts; but I only ever find bodies of the same kind and never penetrate beyond the surface; the real seems to flee before me, or to vanish under my hand, and matter, the first foundation of all experience, becomes the most insubstantial thing we know.

Or does this conflict exist simply to enlighten us about ourselves? Is perception, as it were, only a dream, which mirrors reality in front of all rational beings, and is understanding given to them only in order to awaken them from time to time – to remind them what they are, so that their existence (for obviously enough we are intermediate beings) may thereby be divided between sleeping and waking? But I cannot understand any such primordial dream. All dreams are but shadows of reality, "recollections from a world, which previously was actual." If one wished to assume that a higher Being was causing these shadow-images of actuality in us, even here the question would recur as to the real possibility of the concept of such a relationship (since I know of simply nothing in this sphere, which would follow according to cause and effect); and since that Being surely produced what it imparted to me out of itself, then presuming, as is necessary, that it can have no transitive effect on me, there would be no other possibility than that I had received that shadow-show merely as a limitation, or modification, of its absolute productivity, and thus again, within these limits, always through production.[14]

Matter is not insubstantial, you say, for it has original *forces*, which cannot be annihilated by any subdivision. "Matter has forces." I know that this expression is very common. But how? "Matter has" – here

---

[14] Even on the assumption that a higher Being mocked us with such shadow-images, yet I cannot conceive how it could awaken even a mere image of reality in me, without my having been acquainted with reality itself beforehand – the whole system is too fantastical for it to have been maintained in earnest by anybody. [First edition.]

then it is presupposed as something that exists for itself and independently of its forces. So would these forces be merely accidental to it? Because matter is at hand *outside you*, so also it must owe its forces to an external cause. Are they, as it were, as some Newtonians say, implanted in it by a higher hand? But you have no conception of influences by which forces are *implanted*. You know only how matter, i.e., force itself, works against force; and how effects can be produced on something which originally is not *force*, we have no conception at all. One may say something of the sort; it can pass from mouth to mouth; but never yet has it actually entered any human head, because no human head can think any such thing. Therefore, you cannot conceive matter at all without force.

Further: Those forces are forces of attraction and repulsion. "Attraction and repulsion"–do these, then, take place in empty space? Do they not themselves already presuppose occupied space, that is, matter? So you must admit that neither forces without matter nor matter without forces can be conceived. But now matter is the final substratum of your knowledge, beyond which you cannot go; and as you cannot explain those forces *from* the matter, so you cannot explain them at all empirically, that is, by something *outside yourself*, as surely you must do according to your system.

Irrespective of this it is asked in philosophy how matter *is possible* external to us, thus also, how those forces are possible outside us. One can abjure all philosophizing (would to God those who do not understand it would be pleased to do so), but if you do wish to philosophize, you cannot neglect those questions. Now, however, you can in no way make intelligible what a force might be independent of you. For force as such makes itself known only to your *feeling*. Yet feeling alone gives you no objective concepts. At the same time you make objective use of those forces. For you explain the movement of celestial bodies–universal gravitation–by forces of attraction and maintain that in this explanation you have an absolute principle of these phenomena. In your system, however, the force of attraction ranks as nothing more or less than a *physical* cause. For as matter independent of you exists outside you, so likewise you can only know what forces belong to it through experience. As physical ground of explanation, however, the force of attraction is nothing more and nothing less than an occult quality. All the same, let us first see whether empirical principles can be adequate at all to explain the possibility of a world system. The question answers itself in the negative; for the ultimate knowledge from experience is this, that a universe exists; this proposition is the limit of experience itself. Or rather, that a universe exists is itself only an *idea*. Even less, therefore, can the universal equilibrium of world forces be anything that you could have concocted from experience. For you could not even extract this idea from experience for the individual system if it is everywhere idea; but it is transferred to the whole only by analogical inferences; such inferences, however, give no more than probability. Whereas ideas like that of a universal equilibrium, true in themselves, must for that reason be products of something, or must be grounded in something, which is itself absolute and independent of experience.[15]

Accordingly, you would have to admit that this idea itself reaches over into a higher region than that of mere natural science. Newton, who never wholly abandoned himself to that, and himself still sought after the *effective cause of attraction,* saw only too well that he stood at the frontier of Nature and that here two worlds diverge. Seldom have great minds lived at the same time without working from altogether different angles towards the same objective. Whereas Leibniz based the system of the spiritual world on the pre-established harmony, Newton found the system of a material world in the equilibrium of world forces. But if, after all, there is unity in the system of our knowledge, and if we ever succeed in uniting the very last extremes of that system, we must hope that even here, where Leibniz and Newton diverged, an all-embracing mind will at some time find the midpoint round which the *universe of our knowledge* moves – the two worlds between which our knowledge is at present still divided; and Leibniz's pre-established harmony and Newton's system of gravitation still appear as one and the same, or merely as different aspects of one and the same totality.[16]

I go farther. Raw matter, that is, matter insofar as it is thought of as merely filling space, is only the firm ground and basis on which the edifice of Nature is first constructed. Matter has to be something real. But what is real only permits of being sensed. How then is sensation possible in me? As you say, it is not enough that I should be affected from without. There must be something in me which *senses,* and between this and what you assume to be outside me no contact is possible. Or, if this external thing works on me as matter on matter, then I can only react upon this externality (as it were, by repulsive force), but not *upon myself.* And yet this has to occur, for I have to *sense,* have to raise the sensation to consciousness.

What you sense of matter you call *quality,* and only insofar as it has a determinate quality is it said to be real for you. That it has quality *at all* is *necessary,* but that it has this *determinate* quality appears to you as

---

[15] Ideas, like that of a universal equilibrium, are only products of a creative faculty in us. [First edition.]

[16] ["and Leibniz's . . . one and the same totality" is lacking in the first edition.]

contingent. If so, then matter as such cannot have one and the same quality: There must, therefore, be a multiplicity of *determinations* with all of which you are nevertheless acquainted through mere sensation. What then is it that causes sensation? "Something *internal,* an inner constitution of matter." These are words, not facts. For where then is the inside of this matter? You can divide endlessly and yet come no farther than to the surfaces of bodies. All this has long been obvious to you; so you have long since explained what is merely sensed as something which has its basis only in the manner of your sensing. But this is the very least. For it does not make sensation any more intelligible that nothing which exists outside of you should be in itself sweet or sour; in any case, you always assume a *cause* actually outside you, which produces these sensations in you. But suppose we allow you the inner effects of outer causation, what then have colours, scents, and the like, or the causes external to you of these sensations, in common with your mind? You investigate very meticulously how light reflected from bodies affects your optical nerves, also indeed how the inverted image on the retina is not inverted in your soul, but appears upright. But then again what is that in you which sees this image on the retina itself, and investigates how indeed it can have come into the soul? Obviously it is something which to this extent is completely independent of the external impression, and to which nevertheless this impression is not unknown. How then did the impression reach *this* region of your soul in which you feel wholly free and independent of impressions? However many intervening factors you insert between the effects on your nerves, brain, etc., and the idea of an external thing, you only deceive yourself; for the transition from the body to the soul, according to your own submissions, cannot occur continuously, but only by a leap, which you profess you would rather avoid.

Moreover, that one mass works upon another by virtue of its mere motion (by impenetrability) is what you call impact or *mechanical* movement.

Or else, one material thing works on another without the condition of a previously received motion, so that movement proceeds from rest[17] through attraction, and this is your *gravity.*

You conceive of matter as *inert,* that is, as something which does not move self-actively, but can only be moved by external causes.

Again, the gravity which you ascribe to bodies, you set equal to the quantity of matter (irrespective of its volume) as specific weight.[18]

---

[17] ["without the condition . . . proceeds from rest" is lacking in the first edition.]

[18] Again, specific gravity belongs to bodies, that is, the quantity of attraction is equal to the quantity of matter (irrespective of their volume). [First edition.]

Now you find, however, that one body can impart motion to another without being moved itself, that is, *without* acting upon it by *impact*.

You observe, further, that two bodies can mutually attract one another altogether independent of the relation of their masses, that is to say, *independent* of the laws of *gravity*.

You therefore assume that the ground of this attraction can be sought neither in the weight nor on the surface of the body so moved; the ground must be something internal and must depend on the *quality* of the body. Only you have never yet explained what you understand by the *inner nature* of a body. Moreover, it has been demonstrated that quality has legitimate sense only in relation to your sensation. But here we are speaking, not of your sensation, but of an objective fact, which occurs outside you, which you apprehend with your senses, and which your understanding seeks to translate into intelligible concepts. Now, assume that we admit quality to be something which has a ground, not merely in your sensation, but in the body outside you; what then do the words mean: One body attracts another by virtue of its qualities? For what is *real* in this attraction, that is, what enables you to perceive it, is merely – the motion of the body. Motion, however, is a pure mathematical magnitude, and can be defined purely phoronomically. How then does this external movement combine with an inner quality? You are borrowing pictorial expressions, which are taken from living natures, for example, family relationship. But you would be very hard put to convert this image into an intelligible concept. Further, you heap elementary stuff on elementary stuff, but these are nothing else than just so many refuges of your ignorance. For what do you think of under these terms? Not matter itself, e.g., carbon, but something that is contained in this matter, as if hidden, and first imparts these qualities to it. But where then is this elementary stuff in the body? Has anyone ever found it by division or separation? As yet there is not one of these stuffs which you could present to the senses. But even if we presume their existence, what do we gain? Is the quality of matter somehow explained thereby? I conclude thus: Either the quality which they impart to the body belongs to the elementary stuffs themselves, or it does not. In the first case, you have explained nothing, for the question was just that, how do qualities arise? In the other case, again nothing is explained, for I understand how one body could (mechanically) strike the other and so impart motion to it; but how a body completely devoid of qualities could impart quality to another, this nobody understands, and nobody can make it intelligible. For quality as such is something of which so far you have been in no position to give any objective conception, and yet of which you make objective use (in chemistry, at least).

These are the elements of our empirical knowledge. For if we may once presuppose matter and with it forces of attraction and repulsion, besides an endless multiplicity of kinds of matter, which are all distinguished from another by qualities, we have, according to the guidance of the table of categories:

1. *Quantitative* motion, which is proportional only to the quantity of matter – *gravity;*
2. *Qualitative* motion, which is appropriate to the inner constitution of matter – *chemical* motion;
3. *Relative* motion, which is transmitted to bodies by influence from without (by impact) – *mechanical* motion.

It is these three possible motions from which natural science engenders and develops its entire system.

The part of physics which is concerned with the *first* is called *statics*. That which is concerned with the *third* is called *mechanics*. This is the main part of physics; for basically the whole of physics is nothing but applied mechanics.[19] That part, which is concerned with the *second* kind of motion, serves in physics only as ancillary, namely *chemistry,* whose object is essentially to trace the specific difference of matter; it is the science which first creates for mechanics (in itself a wholly formal science) content and diverse application. It requires, that is to say, very little trouble to derive from the principles of chemistry the main objects which physics (with respect to its mechanical and dynamical motions)[20] investigates; for example, for chemical attraction between bodies to take place, one may say, there must be a matter which extends them, which works against inertia – light and heat – also substances which mutually attract one another and, so that there may be the greatest simplicity, *one* fundamental substance, which all others attract. And, as Nature itself requires many chemical processes for its continuance, these conditions of chemical processes, and so vital air, as the product of light and that fundamental stuff, must be present everywhere. And as this air would promote the violence of combustion all too readily and exhaust the strength of our organs excessively,

---

[19] In mechanics the universal properties of bodies, like elasticity, solidity, density, etc., insofar as they have influence on *mechanical* movement, can likewise be included. However, *universal* kinematics does not at all belong among the empirical sciences – I believe that, according to this division, physics acquires a far simpler and more natural coherence than it has hitherto received in most textbooks.

[20] ["and dynamical" is added in the second edition.]

a mixture of it with another kind of air directly opposed to it is needed – atmospheric air, and so forth.

This is more or less the way in which the theory of Nature attains completeness. But our present concern is not how we might present such a system, once it exists, but how in general such a system could exist. The question is not whether and how that assemblage of phenomena and the series of causes and effects, which we call the course of Nature, has become actual *outside us*, but how they have become actual *for us*, how that system and that assemblage of phenomena have found their way to our minds, and how they have attained the necessity in our conception with which we are absolutely compelled to think of them. For it is presupposed, as undeniable fact, that the representation of a succession of causes and effects external to us is as necessary for our mind as if they belonged to its very being and essence. To explain this necessity is a major problem of all philosophy. The question is not whether this problem as such ought to exist, but how, once it exists, it must be solved.

First of all, what does it mean to say: We must think of a succession of phenomena, which is absolutely *necessary?* Obviously this: These phenomena could follow one another only in this *particular* succession, and *vice versa*, only in these *particular* phenomena can this succession proceed.

For that our ideas follow one another in this precise order, that for example the lightning precedes the thunder, does not follow it, and so on, for this we do not seek the reason *in us;* it does not matter *to us* how we let the ideas follow one another; the reason must, therefore, lie in *the things*, and we declare that this particular succession is a succession of the *things themselves*, not merely of our ideas of them. Only insofar as the phenomena *themselves* follow one another thus and not otherwise are we compelled to represent them in this order; only because and insofar as this succession is *objectively* necessary is it also *subjectively* necessary.

Now from this it follows further that this particular succession cannot be divorced from these particular phenomena; the succession must thus come to be and arise together with the phenomena, and conversely the phenomena must come about and arise together with the succession; therefore, both succession and phenomenon are in mutual relation, both are mutually necessary in regard to each other.

One has only to analyse the commonest judgments that we pass at every moment about the connection of phenomena, in order to discover that the above presuppositions are contained in them.

Now, if neither the phenomena can be separated from their succession nor the succession from its phenomena, only the two following cases are possible:

Either succession and phenomena both arise together and inseparably *outside* us.

Or succession and phenomena both arise together and inseparably
within us.

Only in these two cases is the succession, which we represent to
ourselves, an actual succession of things, not merely an ideal sequence
of our presentations one after another.

The first assertion is that of the common human understanding,
and even of philosophers formally opposed to Hume's scepticism,
Reid and Beattie, among others. In this system the things in themselves follow one another; we have only to look at them; but how the
representation of them got into us is a question pitched much too high
for this system. But we do not want to know how the succession is
possible outside us, but how this particular succession, since it proceeds quite independently of us, yet is represented *as* such by us, and
insofar as it is so, with absolute necessity. Now of this question that
system takes no account. It is therefore not susceptible of any philosophical critique; it has not one point in common with philosophy,
from which one could proceed to investigate, test or contest it, for it is
altogether oblivious of the question which it is the essential business of
philosophy to solve.

That system should first be made philosophical before one could
even test it. But then one runs the risk of fighting against a mere
fabrication, for the common understanding is not so consistent, and
such a system as that consistent with common sense has in fact never yet
existed in any human head; for as soon as one seeks to give it philosophical expression, it becomes wholly unintelligible. It speaks of a succession, which, *independently* of me, is supposed to take place *outside* me. I
understand how a succession (of ideas) takes place *within* me; but a
succession which goes on in the things themselves, independent of the
finite ideas, is wholly unintelligible to me. For if we were to posit a Being
who was not finite, and accordingly not bound to the succession of
presentations, but who grasped everything, present and future, together in one intuition, for such a Being there would be no succession
in the things external to him: It is therefore a succession as such, only
under the condition of the finitude of the representation. But if the
succession were also grounded in the things-in-themselves, independently of all presentation, there would have to be a succession for such a
Being as we have assumed as well, which is self-contradictory.

For this reason, all philosophers up to the present have unani-
mously declared that succession is something which cannot be conceived at all apart from the presentations of a finite mind. Now we
have established that, if the presentation of a succession is to be neces-

sary, it must arise together with the things, and *vice versa;* the succession must be as little possible without the things as the things without the succession. If, therefore, succession is something possible only in our ideas, there is a choice between only two alternatives.

Either one insists that things exist outside us independently of our ideas. Then, by so doing, the objective necessity, with which we represent to ourselves a particular succession of *things,* is explained away as mere illusion, inasmuch as one denies that the succession takes place in the things themselves.

Or one adheres to the assertion that the very phenomena themselves, together with the succession, come to be and arise only in our ideas, and that only to that extent is the order in which they follow one another a genuinely objective order.

Now the first assertion obviously leads to the most fantastical system that has ever existed, and which even today would be maintained only by a handful, without their even knowing it. *Here* now is the place to dispose completely of the axiom that things affect us from without. For let us just ask what things outside us and independent of these ideas might be. First we must divest them of everything that belongs only to the peculiarities of our faculty of representation. To that belongs, not only succession, but also all conception of cause and effect and, if we wish to be consistent, also all representation of space and extension, both of which are utterly inconceivable without time, from which we have removed the things-in-themselves. Nevertheless these things-in-themselves, although altogether inaccessible to our faculty of intuition, must still be actually present—one knows not how or where—probably in the *twilight worlds* of Epicurus—and these things have to *affect* me in order to occasion my ideas. True it is that nobody has ever yet entered into the question what idea we actually frame of such things. To say that they are not conceivable is one way out, but that is soon cut off. If we speak of them, we must have an idea of them, or else we speak as we should not. One has, indeed, an idea even of nothing; one thinks of it at least as the absolute void, as something purely formal, and so on. One might think that the idea of things-in-themselves were a similar notion. But the idea of nothing can, after all, still be made palpable through the schema of empty space. Things-in-themselves, however, are expressly excluded from space and time, for the latter belong, of course, only to the peculiar form of representation of finite beings. So nothing is left but an idea which floats midway between something and nothing, i.e., which does not even have the virtue of being absolutely nothing. It is, in fact, scarcely credible that such a nonsensical conglomeration of things, which, bereft of all sensible characteristics, are nevertheless supposed to function as sensible things, should ever have come into anybody's head.[21]

Indeed, if everything that belongs to the presentation of an objective world is eliminated beforehand, what is there left for me to understand? Clearly, only *myself*. So all ideas of an external world would have to develop out of *me*, myself. For if succession, cause, effect, and the rest, first attach to things in my representation of them, one can as little conceive what those concepts could be without the things, as what the things could be without the concepts. Hence the venturesome explanation which this system is constrained to give of the origin of representation. In opposition to things-in-themselves it sets up a mind, and this mind contains in itself certain *a priori* forms, which have only this advantage over things-in-themselves, that one can at least represent them as something absolutely empty. In representing the things, we apprehend them in these forms. Thereby the formless objects acquire structure; the empty forms, content. How it happens that things come to be represented at all, about that there is the deepest silence. It is enough that we represent things as external to us. Only in the representation, however, do we first carry space and time over to them, and further, the concepts of substance and accident, cause and effect, and so on. Thus the succession of our ideas arises in us, and indeed a necessary succession; and this self-made succession, first brought forth in consciousness, is called the course of Nature.

This system requires no refutation. To propound it is to overturn it from the bottom up. In fact, the *Humean* scepticism is vastly superior and not at all comparable to it. Hume (faithful to his principles) leaves it altogether undecided whether our ideas correspond to things outside us or not. In every case, however, he has to assume that the *succession* of appearances takes place only in our ideas; but that we take just this *particular* succession as *necessary* he declares to be pure illusion. But what one can justly demand of Hume is that he at least explain the source of this *illusion*. For that we do actually think of a sequence of causes and effects as necessary – that thereon rest all our empirical sciences, theory of Nature and history (in which he was himself so great a master), he cannot deny. But whence this illusion itself? Hume answers: "From custom; *because hitherto the appearances have followed one another in this order,* the imagination has accustomed itself to expect the same order also in the future, and this expectation has, like every long habituation, ultimately become for us a *second*

---

[21] The truth is that the idea of things-in-themselves had come down to Kant through the tradition and had lost all meaning in the course of inheritance. [This note is lacking in the first edition.]

nature." But this explanation turns in a circle, for the very thing that had to be explained was *why things have hitherto followed one another in this order* (which Hume does not deny). Was this sequence perhaps something in the things outside us? But apart from our ideas there is no succession. Or, if it was merely the succession of our ideas, then a reason for the persistence of this succession must also be given. What exists independent of me I am unable to explain; but for what goes on only *in me* the reason must be found also in me. Hume can say: It is so, and that satisfies me. But this is not to philosophize. I do not say that a Hume *ought* to philosophize, but once a man *proclaims* that he wants to philosophize, he can no longer dismiss the question, Why?

So nothing remains but the attempt to derive the necessity of a succession of presentations from the *nature* of our mind, and so of the finite mind as such, and, in order that this succession may be genuinely *objective*, to have the things themselves, together with this sequence, arise and come into being in it.

Among all previous systems I know only two—the Spinozistic and the Leibnizian—which not only undertook this attempt, but whose entire philosophy is nothing else but this attempt. Now because there is still at present much doubt and discussion about the relation of these two systems—whether they contradict each other, or how they cohere—it seems useful to say something about them at the outset.

Spinoza, as it seems, was worried at a very early stage about the connection of our ideas with things outside us, and could not tolerate the separation which had been set up between them. He saw that ideal and real (thought and object) are most intimately united in our nature. That we have ideas of things outside us, that our ideas even reach out *beyond* the things, he could explain to himself only in terms of our *ideal nature;* but that these ideas correspond to actual *things,* he had to explain in terms of the *affections* and *determinations* of the ideal in us. Therefore we could not become aware of the real, save in contrast to the ideal, or of the ideal, save in contrast to the real. Accordingly, no separation could occur between the actual things and our ideas of them. Concepts and things, thought and extension, were, for this reason, one and the same for him, both only modifications of one and the same ideal nature.

However, instead of descending into the depths of his self-consciousness and descrying the emergence thence of the two worlds in us—the ideal and the real—he passed himself by; instead of explaining from our nature how finite and infinite, originally united in us, proceed reciprocally from each other, he lost himself forthwith in the idea of an infinite outside us. In this infinity there arose, or rather originally were—one knows not whence—affections and modifications, and with these an endless series of finite things. For, because there was no transition in his system from infinite to finite, a beginning of *becoming* was for him as inconceivable as a beginning of *being*. Yet that this endless succession is envisaged by me, and is envisaged with *necessity,* followed from the fact that the things and my ideas were originally one and the same. I myself was only one of the Infinite's thoughts, or rather just a constant succession of presentations. But Spinoza was unable to make it intelligible how I myself in turn become aware of this succession.

For, generally speaking, as it came from his hand, his system is the most unintelligible that ever existed. One must have taken this system up into oneself, have put oneself in the place of his infinite Substance, in order to know that infinite and finite – do not *arise,* but – *exist* originally together and inseparably, not *outside us,* but *in us,* and that the nature of our mind and of our whole mental existence rests on just this original union. For we know immediately only our own essence, and only ourselves are intelligible to us. How affections and determinations are and can exist in an Absolute external to me, I do not understand. But I do understand that even within me there could be nothing *infinite* unless there were at the same time a *finite.* For that necessary union of ideal and real, of the absolutely active and absolutely passive (which Spinoza displaced into an infinite Substance outside me) exists *within me* originally without my co-operation, and that is just what *my* nature consists in.[22]

Leibniz followed this route, and here is the point where he diverges from Spinoza and connects with him. It is impossible to understand Leibniz without having stationed oneself at this point. *Jacobi* has shown that his whole system sets out from the concept of *individuality* and reverts to it. In the concept of individuality alone, there is an original union of what all other philosophy separates, the positive and the negative, the active and the passive in our nature. How there can be *determinations* in an infinite external to us, Spinoza knew no way of making intelligible, and he sought in vain to avoid a transition from the infinite to the finite. This transition is absent only where finite and infinite are *originally* united, and this *original* union exists nowhere except in the essence of an individual nature. Leibniz, therefore, went over neither from the infinite to the finite nor from the latter to the former, but both were made actual for him at the same time – as if through one and the same unfolding of our nature – through one and the same operation of the mind.

----

[22] But closer consideration will at once teach anyone that every positing-in-me of the absolute identity of finite and infinite, like the positing-outside-me, is again only *my* positing, so that the former *in itself* is neither an in-me nor an outside-me. [This note is added in the second edition.]

That ideas in us *follow* one another is the necessary consequence of our finitude, but that this series is *endless* proves that they proceed from a being in whose nature finitude and infinity are united.

That this succession is *necessary* follows, in Leibniz's philosophy, from the fact that the things together with the ideas arise by virtue of the mere laws of our nature, according to an inner principle in us, as in a world of its own. What alone Leibniz held to be originally real and actual *in themselves* were *perceptual beings;* for in these alone was that *unification* original, out of which everything else that is called actual *develops* and *goes forth.* For everything which is actual outside us is finite, and so not conceivable without a positive, which gives it reality, and a negative, which sets its limit. This unification of positive and negative activity, however, is nowhere *original* except in the nature of an individual. External things *were* not actual *in themselves,* but have only *become* actual through the mode of presentation of spiritual natures; but that from whose nature all existence first *emerges,* that is, the ideating being alone, would have had to be something which bears the source and origin of its existence in itself.

If now the whole succession of ideas springs from the *nature* of the finite mind, so likewise the whole series of our experiences must be derivable from it. For that all beings like ourselves perceive the phenomena of the world in the same necessary serial order is conceivable only and solely from our common nature. To explain this agreement of our nature, however, by a pre-established harmony is actually not to explain it. Because this word only says *that* such agreement occurs, but not how and why. It is, however, implicit in Leibniz's system itself that this agreement should follow from the *essence* of finite natures as such. Because if this were not so, the mind would cease to be absolutely *self-explanatory* of its knowledge and cognition. Nevertheless it would still have to seek the ground of its ideas *outside itself.* We should have reverted once again to the same point from which we began; the world and its order would be *contingent* for us, and the representation thereof would come to us only from without. But with that we are inevitably swept beyond the limits within which alone we understand ourselves. For if a superior hand had so contrived us in the first place that we were compelled to envisage such a world and such an order of phenomena, then, discounting the fact that this hypothesis is wholly unintelligible to us, this whole world is once again an illusion: One thrust of that hand is able to wrest it from us, or to translate us into an entirely different order of things; it is then wholly doubtful even that beings of our own kind (with similar ideas to ours) exist outside us. Leibniz, therefore, could not have associated with the pre-established harmony the idea that one usually couples with it. For he explicitly asserts that no mind could have *come to be;* that is, the concepts of cause and effect are altogether inapplicable to a mind. It is, therefore, absolutely self-explanatory of its being and knowing, and just because it exists at all, is also *what it is,* i.e., a being to whose *nature* this particular system of ideas of external things also belongs.

Philosophy, accordingly, is nothing other than a *natural history of our mind.* From now on all dogmatism is overturned from its foundations. We consider the system of our ideas, not in its *being,* but in its *becoming.* Philosophy becomes *genetic;* that is, it allows the whole necessary series of our ideas to arise and take its course, as it were, before our eyes. From now on there is no longer any separation between experience and speculation. The system of Nature is at the same time the system of our mind, and only now, once the great synthesis has been accomplished, does our knowledge return to analysis (to *research* and *experiment*). But this system does not yet exist. Many faint-hearted spirits have misgivings at the outset, for they speak of a system of *our nature* (the magnitude of which they do not know), no otherwise than as if they were speaking about a *syllabus*[23] of our *concepts.*

The dogmatist, who assumes everything to be originally *present* outside us (not as *coming to be* and *springing forth from* us) must surely commit himself at least *to this:* that what is *external* to us is also to be explained by *external* causes. He succeeds in doing this, as long as he remains within the nexus of cause and effect, despite the fact that he can never make it intelligible how this nexus of causes and effects has *itself* arisen. As soon as he raises himself above the individual phenomenon, his whole philosophy is at an end; the limits of mechanism are also the limits of his system.

But now mechanism alone is far from being what constitutes Nature. For as soon as we enter the realm of *organic nature,* all mechanical linkage of cause and effect ceases for us. Every organic product exists *for itself;* its being is dependent on no other being. But now the cause is never the *same as* the effect; only between quite *different* things is a relation of cause and effect possible. The organic, however, produces *itself,* arises *out of itself;* every single plant is the product only of an individual *of its own kind,* and so every single organism endlessly produces and reproduces only *its own species.* Hence no organization progresses *forward,* but is forever turning back always into *itself.* Accordingly, an organization as such is neither *cause* nor *effect* of anything outside it, and so is nothing that intrudes into the nexus of mechanism.

---

[23] In the writings and translations from the earliest times of German purism one finds the expressions: *Syllabus of essences, Syllabus of Nature.* It is a shame that our modern philosophers have allowed this expression to go out of use.

Every organic product carries the reason of its existence in *itself*, for it is cause and effect of itself. No single part could *arise* except in this whole, and this whole itself consists only in the *interaction* of the parts. In every other object the parts are *arbitrary;* they exist only insofar as I *divide*. Only in organized beings are they *real;* they exist without my participation, because there is an *objective* relationship between them and the whole. Thus a *concept* lies at the base of every organization, for where there is a necessary relation of the whole to the part and of the part to the whole, there is *concept*. But this concept dwells in the *organization itself*, and can by no means be separated from it; it *organizes itself*, and is not simply, say, a work of art whose concept is to be found *outside* it in the understanding of the artist. Not only its form but its *existence* is purposive. It could not organize itself without already being organized. The plant nourishes itself and subsists through assimilation of external matter, but it can assimilate nothing to itself unless it is already organized. The maintenance of the living body depends on respiration. The vital air it inhales is decomposed by its organs in order to flow through the nerves as electric fluid. But to make this process possible, organization must already have been present, which yet, on the other hand, does not survive without this process. Thus organization constructs itself only out of organization. In the organic product, for this very reason, form and matter are inseparable; this particular matter could only arise and come to be along with this particular form, and *vice versa.* Every organization is therefore a *whole; its unity lies in itself;* it does not depend on our choice whether we think of it as one or as many. Cause and effect is something evanescent, transitory, mere *appearance* (in the usual sense of the word). The organism, however, is not mere appearance, but is *itself* object, and indeed an object subsisting through itself, in itself whole and indivisible, and because in it the form is inseparable from the matter, the *origin* of an organism, as such, can no more be explained mechanically than the origin of matter itself.

So if the purposiveness of the organic product is to be explained, the dogmatist finds himself completely deserted by his system. Here it no longer avails to separate concept and object, form and matter, as it pleases us. For *here,* at least, both are originally and necessarily united, not in our idea, but in the *object* itself. I should like one of those who take playing with concepts for philosophy, and fantasies of things for real things, to venture with us into *this* field.

First of all you must concede that here the talk is of a *unity,* which is absolutely inexplicable in terms of *matter,* as such. For it is a unity of the *concept,* a unity that exists only in relation to an intuiting and reflecting being. For that there is absolute individuality in an organism, that its parts are possible only through the whole, and the whole is possible, not through assembling, but through interaction, of the parts, is a *judgement* and cannot be judged at all save only by a mind, which relates whole and part, form and matter, reciprocally one to another, and only through and in this relation does all purposiveness and attunement to the whole arise and come to be in the first place. What indeed have these parts, which are but matter, in common with an *Idea*, which is originally alien to matter, and to which they are nevertheless attuned? Here no relation is possible except through a third thing, to whose ideas both, matter and concept, belong. Such a third thing, however, is only an intuiting and reflecting mind. So you have to admit that organization as such is conceivable only in relation to a *mind*.

Even those who will have it that the organic product itself arises from a wonderful collision of atoms admit this. For in that they derive the origin of these things from blind chance, they also promptly abolish all purposiveness in them and with it all conception of organization itself – that is to say, if consistently thought out. For since purposiveness is conceivable only in relation to a judging intellect, the question must be answered how the organic products arise independently *of me*, as if there were no relation at all between them and a judging intelligence, that is, as if there were no purpose in them anywhere.

Hence the first thing that you grant is this: Any conception of purpose can arise only in an intelligence, and only in relation to such an intelligence can anything be called purposive.

At the same time, you are no less compelled to concede that the purposiveness of natural products dwells in *themselves,* that it is *objective* and *real,* hence that it belongs, not to your *arbitrary,* but to your *necessary* representations. For you can very easily distinguish what is arbitrary and what is necessary in the conjunction of your concepts. Whenever you conjoin things which are separated in space in *a single* aggregate, you act quite freely; the unity which you bestow on them you transfer to them simply from your thoughts; there is no reason residing in the *things themselves* which required you to think of them as one. But when you think of each plant as an individual, in which everything concurs together for one purpose, you must seek the reason for that in the *thing outside you:* you feel yourself constrained in your judgement; you must therefore confess that the unity with which you think it is not merely *logical* (in your thoughts), but *real* (actually outside you).

It is now incumbent upon you to answer the question, how it happens that an idea, which obviously exists merely in you, and can have reality only in relation to yourself, must yet be actually intuited and represented by you, as itself outside you.

Certainly there are philosophers who have *one* universal answer to all these questions, which they repeat at every opportunity and cannot repeat enough. That which is form in the things, they say, we initially impose on the things. But I have long sought to know just how you could be acquainted with what the things are, without the form which you first impose on them, or what the form is, without the things on which you impose it. You would have to concede that, *here* at least, the form is absolutely inseparable from the matter, and the concept from the object. Or, if it rests with your choice whether or not to impose the idea of purposiveness on things outside you, how does it come about that you impose this idea only on *certain* things, and not on *all*, that further, in this representing of purposeful products, you feel yourself in no way *free*, but absolutely constrained? You could give no other reason for either than that this purposive form just belongs to certain *things* outside you, originally and without assistance from your choice.

This granted, what was valid before is also valid here: The form and matter of these things could never be separated; both could come into being only together and reciprocally, each through the other. The concept which lies at the base of this organization has no reality *in itself*, and, conversely, this particular matter is not *organized matter, qua* matter, but only because of the indwelling *concept*. This particular object, therefore, could arise only together with this concept; and this particular concept, only together with this particular object.

All previous systems must be judged according to this principle.

In order to comprehend this union of concept and matter, you assume a higher divine intelligence, who designed his creations in ideal forms and brought forth Nature in accordance with these ideals. But a being in whom the concept *precedes* the act, the design the execution, cannot *produce*, but can only form or model, matter already there, can only stamp the impress of the understanding and of purposiveness upon the matter from without. What he produces is purposive, not *in itself*, but only in relation to the understanding of the artificer, not *originally* and *necessarily*, but only contingently. Is not the understanding a dead faculty? And has it any other use than to grasp and apprehend the actual when it is present? And, instead of creating the actual, does it not borrow its own reality from actuality itself? And is it not merely the slavishness of this faculty, its capacity for describing the *outlines* of the real, which sets up an accommodation between itself and the reality? But here the question is how the *actual* arises, and with it the ideal (the purposive), which is simply inseparable from it. Not that the things of Nature, as such, are purposive, as every work of art is also purposive, but that this purposiveness is something which could not be imparted to them at all from without, that they are purposive originally *through themselves* – this is what we want to see explained.

You therefore take refuge in the *creative* power of a divinity, from which the actual things together with their ideas proceeded and sprang forth. You realized that you had to allow the actual to arise together with the purposive, the purposive together with the actual, if you wished to assume something outside you that is purposive in and through itself.

But let us assume for a moment what you allege (although you yourself are in no position to make it intelligible); let us assume it is through the creative power of a divinity that the whole system of Nature arose and with it all the diversity of purposive products external to us. Have we in fact advanced even a single step farther than before, and do we not find ourselves once again at the same point from which we set out at the beginning? How organic products external to, and independent of, me have actually come to be was not at all what I required to know; for how could I even form a clear idea of that for myself? The question was: how the *representation* of purposive products outside me has got *into me,* and how, *although it pertains to things only in relation to my understanding,* I am nevertheless compelled to think of this purposiveness as *actually outside me* and necessary. This question you have not answered.

For as soon as you regard the things of Nature as actual outside you and hence as the work of a creator, no purposiveness can inhere in them, because this is of course valid only in relation to *your* understanding. Or do you also wish to presuppose concepts of purpose and the like in the creator of the things? But as soon as you do this, he ceases to be a creator and becomes merely an artificer, he is at most the architect of Nature. However, you *destroy* all idea of *Nature* from the very bottom, as soon as you allow the purposiveness to enter her from without, through a transfer from the intelligence of any being whatever. As soon as you make the idea of the creator *finite,* therefore, he ceases to be creator; extend it to *infinity,* and you then lose all conception of purposiveness and understanding, and only the idea of an absolute power remains. From now on everything finite is merely a modification of the infinite. But you no more comprehend how a modification may be possible in the infinite as such, than you comprehend how this modification of the infinite, that is, how the whole system of finite things, could have got into your consciousness, or how the unity of things, which can only be *ontological* in the Infinite Being, can have become *teleological* in your understanding.

You could, of course, seek to explain this by the peculiar nature of a finite mind. But if you do that, you no longer need the infinite as something external to you. You could, from now on, allow everything to arise and come to be simply in your mind. For if you also presuppose things *outside* and independent of you, which *in themselves* are purposive, you must nevertheless still explain how your *ideas* agree with these external things. You would have to take refuge in a preestablished harmony, would have to assume that a mind, analogous to your own, reigns in the very things outside you. For only in a mind able to create can concept and actuality, ideal and real, so interpenetrate and unite that no separation is possible between them. I cannot think otherwise than that Leibniz understood by substantial form a mind *inhering in* and regulating the organized being.

This philosophy must accept, therefore, that there is a hierarchy of life in Nature. Even in mere organized matter there is *life*, but a life of a more restricted kind. This idea is so old, and has hitherto persisted so constantly in the most varied forms, right up to the present day — (already in the most ancient times it was believed that the whole world was pervaded by an animating principle, called the world-soul, and the later period of Leibniz gave every plant its soul) — that one may very well surmise from the beginning that there must be some reason latent in the human mind itself for this natural belief. And so it is. The sheer wonder which surrounds the problem of the origin of organic bodies, therefore, is due to the fact that in these things necessity and contingency are most intimately united. *Necessity*, because their very *existence* is *purposive*, not only their form (as in the work of art), *contingency*, because this purposiveness is nevertheless actual only for an intuiting and reflecting being. For that reason, the human mind was early led to the idea of a *self*-organizing matter, and because organization is conceivable only in relation to a mind, to an original union of mind and matter in these things. It saw itself compelled to seek the reason for these things, on the one hand, in Nature herself, and on the other, in a principle exalted above Nature; and hence it very soon fell into thinking of mind and Nature as one. Here for the first time there emerged from its sacred obscurity that ideal being in which the mind supposes concept and deed, design and execution, to be one. Here first a premonition came over man of his own nature, in which intuition and concept, form and object, ideal and real, are originally one and the same. Hence the peculiar aura which surrounds this problem, an aura which the philosophy of mere reflection, which sets out only to *separate*, can never develop, whereas the pure intuition, or rather, the creative imagination, long since discovered the symbolic language, which one has only to construe in order to discover that Nature speaks to us the more intelligibly the less we think of her in a merely reflective way.

No wonder that language, used dogmatically,[24] soon lost sense and meaning. So long as I myself am *identical* with Nature, I understand what a living nature is as well as I understand my own life; I apprehend how this universal life of Nature reveals itself in manifold forms, in progressive developments, in gradual approximations to freedom. As soon, however, as I separate myself, and with me everything ideal, from Nature, nothing remains to me but a dead object, and I cease to comprehend how a *life outside* me can be possible.

If I question the common understanding, it believes that *life* is to be seen only where there is *free movement*. For the capacities of animal organs – sensibility, irritability, and the like – themselves presuppose an impulsive principle, without which the animal would be incapable of reacting to external stimulation, and only through this free reactivity of the organs does the stimulus from without become excitation and impression. Here the most complete reciprocity prevails: Only through excitation from without is the animal determined to movement, and conversely, only through this capacity to produce movement in itself does external impression become a stimulus. (Hence there can be neither irritability without sensibility nor sensibility without irritability.)

But all these functions of the organs, purely as such, are insufficient to explain *life*. For we could very well imagine an arrangement of fibres, nerves, and so on, in which (as, for example, in the nerves of a dissected organic body, by electricity, metallic stimulation, etc.) free movements could be produced by external stimuli, without our being able to attribute *life* to this composite thing. One might perhaps retort that nevertheless the coordination of *all* these movements would bring about life; but that involves a higher principle, which we can no longer explain in terms of matter alone, a principle that orders all individual movements, holds them together, and so first creates and brings forth a whole out of a multiplicity of motions which agree with one another, and mutually produce and reproduce themselves. So here again, we meet that absolute unification of Nature and Freedom in one and the same being. The living organism is to be a product of *Nature:* but in this natural product an ordering and coordinating *mind* is to rule. These two principles shall in no way be separated in it, but most intimately united. In intuition the two are not to be distinguishable at all; there must be neither *before* nor *after,* but absolute simultaneity and reciprocity between them.

As soon as philosophy removes this internal conjunction, two systems arise directly opposed to each other, of which neither can refute

---

[24] scientifically and dogmatically used [First edition.]

the other, because both entirely destroy all idea of life, which flees all the farther from them the nearer they think to approach it.

I am not speaking of that so-called philosophy of those who would hold that even thought, imagery and will spring up in us, now from a chance collision of already organized particles, now through an actually artificial conjunction of muscles, fibres, membranes and ligaments which hold the body together, and fluid substances which flow through it, and so on. I maintain, however, that we as little understand empirically a life *outside us* as we do a consciousness *outside us*, that neither the one nor the other is explicable from physical causes, that in this respect it is completely indifferent whether the body is regarded as an accidental aggregate of organized particles, or as a hydraulic machine, or as a chemical laboratory. Assume, for instance, that all the movements of a living body were explicable by changes in the composition of its nerves, its sinews, or the fluid that is taken to circulate in them; then not only is it a question of how those changes are caused, but also of what principle holds all these changes harmoniously together.

Or if at last a philosophical purview of Nature as a system, which nowhere stands still but progresses, discovers that with living matter Nature oversteps the limits of inorganic chemistry, so that (because otherwise chemical processes in the body would be unavoidable and because the dead body is destroyed by genuine chemical dissolution) there must be in the living body a principle which exempts it from chemical laws, and if this principle is now called *Life-force*, then I maintain on the contrary that Life-force, taken in this sense (and however prevalent this expression may be), is a completely self-contradictory concept. For we can think of force only as something finite. But no force is finite by *nature* except insofar as it is limited by one opposing it. Where we think of force (as in matter), therefore, we must also presume a force *opposed* to it. Between opposing forces, however, we can only conceive a double relationship. Either they are in *relative* equilibrium (in absolute equilibrium they would both be completely eliminated); then they are thought of as at *rest*, as in matter which is therefore said to be inert. Or one thinks of them as in perpetual, never-settled conflict, where each in turn prevails and submits; but then, again, a third must be present which keeps this conflict going and maintains the work of Nature in this conflict of alternately prevailing and submissive forces. Now this third cannot itself be a force, for otherwise we should return to the previous alternative. So it must be something that is higher than just *force;* yet *force* is the ultimate (as I shall prove) to which all our physical explanations must return; so that third would have to be something which lies right outside the limits of empirical research into Nature.

But now beyond and above Nature, in the ordinary notion of it, nothing higher is acknowledged than mind.[25] However, if we now want to conceive the Life-force as a spiritual principle, then we totally abolish that concept in so doing. For *force* means what, at least as a *principle,* we can put at the apex of natural science, and what, although not itself presentable, yet, in the *way it works,* is definable by physical laws. But how a mind can act physically we have not the slightest idea; for that reason also, a mental principle cannot be called *Life-force,* an expression by which one always at least suggests the hope of allowing that principle to work according to physical laws.[26]

But if we forgo, as we are then compelled to do, this concept (of a Life-force), we are now obliged to take refuge in a completely antithetical system, in which at once mind and matter stand opposed to each other, regardless of the fact that we now understand how mind affects matter as little as we could previously understand how matter affects mind.

Mind, considered as the principle of life, is called *soul.* I shall not repeat the objections that have long since been brought against the philosophy of the dualists. It has hitherto been contested for the most part from principles which had as little content as the contested system itself. We do not ask how in general a connection is possible between soul and body (a question to which one is not entitled, because the questioner himself does not understand it) but rather – what one can understand and must answer – how the idea of such a connection has arisen *in us.* That I think, imagine, will, and that this thinking, etc., can so little be a result of my body, that on the contrary the latter only becomes *my* body through these capacities to think and to will, I know full well. Let it meanwhile be permitted, moreover, for the sake of speculation, to distinguish the principle of motion from the moved, the soul from the body, despite the fact that as soon as the talk is of action we completely forget this distinction. Now with all these assumptions, at least this much is obvious, that if there is in me life and soul, the last as something distinct from the body, I can become aware of either only through *immediate* experience. That I *am* (think, will, etc.) is something that I must know, if I know anything at all. Thus I

---

[25] Now we know nothing higher, for which forces as such could exist, than Spirit; for only Spirit can represent to itself forces and equilibrium or conflict of forces. [First edition.]

[26] This one sees very clearly from the utterances of many defenders of the *Life-force.* Herr Brandis, for example (in his *Experiments on the Life-force,* #81), asks, "Should electricity (which seems to cooperate in phlogistical processes generally) also participate in the phlogistical life-processes (which the author assumes), or *might electricity be the life-force itself?* I consider it *more than likely.*"

understand how an idea of my own being and life arises in me, because if I understand anything whatsoever, I must understand this. Also, because I am immediately aware of my own being, the inference to a soul in me, even if the conclusion should be false, at least rests on *one* indubitable premise, that I *am, live, imagine, will.*

But how do I now come to transfer *being, life,* etc., to things *outside* me? For just as soon as this happens, my immediate knowledge is converted into *mediate.* But now I maintain that there can be only an *immediate* knowledge of being and life, and that what *is* and *lives* only is and lives insofar as it first and foremost exists *for itself,* is aware of its life through being alive. Suppose, then, that there appears to me in my perception an organic being, freely self-moving, then I certainly know that this being *exists,* that it is *for me,* but not that it *exists for itself* and *in itself.* For life can as little be represented outside life as consciousness outside consciousness.[27] So even an empirical conviction[28] that something lives outside me is absolutely impossible. For the Idealist can say that your representing to yourself organized, free, self-moving bodies can just as well belong simply to the necessary peculiarities of your faculty of representation; and even the philosophy which bestows life on everything external to me does not permit the idea of this life outside me to come into me from *outside.*

But if this idea arises only *in me,* how can I be persuaded that anything corresponds to it outside me? It is also obvious that I am persuaded of a life and self-existence outside me only *practically.* I must in practice be *compelled* to acknowledge beings outside me, who are like me. If I were not compelled to enter into the company of people outside me and into all the practical relationships associated with that; if I did not know that beings, who resemble me in external shape and appearance, have no *more* reason to acknowledge freedom and mentality in me than I have to acknowledge the same in them; in fine, if I were not aware that my moral existence only acquires purpose and direction through the existence of other moral beings outside me, then left to mere speculation, I could of course doubt whether humanity dwelt behind each face and freedom within each breast. All this is confirmed by our commonest judgements. Only of beings external to me, who put themselves on an equal footing with me in life, between whom and myself giving and receiving, doing and suffering, are fully reciprocal, do I acknowledge that they are spiritual in character. On the other hand, if the rather curious question is brought up, whether animals also have souls, a person of common

---

[27] Jacobi's *David Hume* [Breslau, 1787], p. 140.
[28] theoretical [First edition.]

sense is at once taken aback, because, with the affirmation of that, he would consider himself committed to something he cannot immediately know.[29]

If in the end we go back to the original source of the dualistic belief, that a soul distinct from the body dwells at least in *me*, then what is it in me which itself in turn judges that I consist of body and soul, and what is this *I* which is supposed to consist of body and soul? Here, clearly, there is something still higher, which, freely and independently of the body, gives the body a soul, conceives body and soul together, and does not itself enter into this union – a higher principle, as it seems, in which body and soul are themselves again identical.

Finally, if we persist in this dualism, we now have close at hand the antithesis from which we began: mind and matter. For the same incomprehensibility, as to how connection is possible between matter and mind, continues to oppress us. One can conceal from oneself the finality of this antithesis by deceptions of all kinds, can insert between mind and matter any number of physical intermediaries, which come to be ever more and more tenuous. But sometime, somewhere, a point must surely come where mind and matter are one, or where the great leap we have so long sought to avoid becomes inevitable; and in this all theories are alike.

Whether I allow animal spirits, electrical fluids, or types of gas to suffuse or fill the nerves, and thereby to propagate impressions from outside into the sensorium, or whether I pursue the soul into the uttermost (and still more problematical) humours of the brain (a project which at least has the merit of having done the *uttermost*) is, with respect to the *matter in hand*, altogether indifferent. It is clear that our critique has come full circle, but not that we have become in any degree wiser than we were to begin with, about that antithesis from which we started. We leave behind man, as evidently the most devious problem of all philosophy, and our critique ends here in the same extremity with which it began.

If, finally, we gather up Nature into a single Whole, *mechanism*, that is, a regressive series of causes and effects, and *purposiveness*, that is, independence of mechanism, simultaneity of causes and effects, stand confronting each other. If we unite these two extremes, the idea arises in us of a purposiveness of the whole; Nature becomes a circle which returns into itself, a self-enclosed system. The series of causes and effects ceases entirely, and there arises a reciprocal connection of

---

[29] which he has the right and authority to assert only of himself and those like him. [First edition.]

means and *end;* neither could the individual become *real* without the whole, nor the whole without the individual.

Now this absolute purposiveness of the whole of Nature is an Idea, which we do not think arbitrarily, but *necessarily*. We feel ourselves forced to relate every individual to such a purposiveness of the whole; where we find something in Nature that seems purposeless or quite contrary to purpose, we believe the whole scheme of things to be torn apart, or do not rest until the apparent refractoriness to purpose is converted to purposiveness from another viewpoint. It is therefore a necessary maxim of the reflective reason, to presuppose everywhere in Nature a connection by end and means. And although we do not transform this maxim into a constitutive law, we still follow it so stead-fastly and so naïvely that we openly assume that Nature will, as it were, voluntarily come to meet our endeavour to discover absolute pur-posiveness in her. Similarly, we proceed with complete confidence in the agreement of Nature with the maxims of our reflective reason, from special subordinate laws to general higher laws; nor do we cease to assume *a priori*, even of phenomena which still stand isolated in the series of our perceptions, that *they* too are interconnected through some common principle. And we only believe in a Nature external to us where we discern multiplicity of effects and unity of means.[30]

What then is that secret bond which couples our mind to Nature, or that hidden organ through which Nature speaks to our mind or our mind to Nature? We grant you in advance all your explanations of how such a purposive Nature has come to be actual *outside us*. For to explain this purposiveness by the fact that a divine intelligence is its author is not to philosophize, but to propound pious opinions. By that you have explained to us virtually nothing; for we require to know, not how such a Nature arose outside us, but how even the very *idea* of such a Nature has got *into us;* not merely how we have, say, arbitrarily generated it, but how and why it originally and *necessarily* underlies everything that our race has ever thought about Nature. For the exis-tence of such a Nature *outside me* is still far from explaining the exis-tence of such a Nature *in me;* for if you assume that a predetermined harmony occurs between the two, indeed that is just the object of our question. Or if you maintain that we simply *impose* such an idea on Nature, then no inkling of what Nature is and ought to be for us has ever entered your soul. For what we want is not that Nature should coincide with the laws of our mind *by chance* (as if through some *third* intermediary), but that *she herself*, necessarily and originally, should

---

[30] where we discern an *infinity* of effects and a *finitude* of means. [First edition.]

not only *express*, but *even realize*, the laws of our mind, and that she is, and is called, Nature only insofar as she does so.

Nature should be Mind made visible, Mind the invisible Nature. Here then, in the absolute identity of Mind *in us* and Nature *outside us*, the problem of the possibility of a Nature external to us must be resolved. The final goal of our further research is, therefore, this idea of Nature; if we succeed in attaining this, we can also be certain to have dealt satisfactorily with that problem.

*   *   *

These are the main problems, whose solution is to be the purpose of this essay.

But this essay does not begin *from above* (with the establishment of principles), but *from below* (with experimental findings and the testing of previous systems).

Only when I have reached the goal which I have set myself will it be permissible for me to retrace in reverse the course which has been run.

Supplement to the Introduction: Exposition of the General Idea of Philosophy as Such, and of the Philosophy of Nature in Particular, as a Necessary and Integral Part of It

Against the empirical realism, which, before Kant, had become a general system of thought and was even dominant in philosophy, in consequence of the necessity with which every one-sidedness immediately calls up another opposed to it, only an equally empirical idealism could at first arise and be accredited. In Kant himself, of course, it was not so fully elaborated in its entire empirical character as it appeared among his followers, but it was, in germ, implicit in his writings. Those who had not laid empiricism aside, before they encountered him, would also not have acquired it through him. It remained quite the same, only translated into another, idealistic-sounding language, and returned in an altered form all the more obstinately the more certainly those, who had taken it in this form from Kant, were persuaded that they had in every respect freed themselves from it and risen superior to it. That the determinations of things by and for the understanding in no way bear upon things *in themselves*, this they accepted; meanwhile, these things-in-themselves still had the same relation to the conscious mind as had previously been ascribed to empirical things, the relation of affecting, of cause and effect. The foregoing Introduction is in part directed against empirical realism in itself, in part against that absurd combination of the crudest empiricism with a kind of idealism, which had developed out of the Kantian school.

Both are in certain measure smitten with their own weapons. Against the first, those concepts and ways of thinking, which it uses itself, as derived from experience, are exploited only inasmuch as it is shown that they are degenerate and misused ideas. Against the second, all that was needed was the eviction of the first contradiction which lies at the base, and which on particular occasions returns only the more strikingly and more glaringly.

In the present supplement what has been done, therefore, is to set out in more positive fashion the idea of philosophy in itself, and that of the Philosophy of Nature especially, as the one necessary aspect of the whole of this science.

The first step to philosophy and the condition without which it cannot even be entered, is the insight that the absolute-ideal is also the absolute-real, and that without this there is only sensible and conditioned, but no absolute and unconditioned, reality. Those upon whom the absolute-ideal has not yet dawned as the absolute-real can be driven to the point of this insight in various ways, but it can be proved only indirectly, not directly, since it is actually the ground and principle of all demonstration.

We shall indicate one of the possible ways to raise a person to this insight. Philosophy is an absolute science; for what can be extracted from the conflicting concepts, as universally agreed, is that, far from borrowing the principles of its knowledge from another science, it also has (among other subjects, at least) knowledge as its object, and so cannot itself in turn be a subordinate science. It follows immediately from this formal definition of philosophy as a science, which, if it exists, cannot be of a conditioned kind, that it can also know its objects, whatever they may be, not in a conditioned but only in an unconditioned and absolute way, and thus also know only the absolute of these objects themselves. Against every possible definition of philosophy, whereby it has as its object any contingency, particularity or conditionality, it could be shown that this contingency or particularity has already been pre-empted by one of the other, supposedly or actually existing, sciences. If, therefore, philosophy, in order to know in an absolute way, can only know of the absolute, and if this absolute stands open to her only through knowing itself, then it is clear that the first idea of philosophy already rests on the tacit presupposition of a possible indifference between absolute knowing and the absolute itself, and consequently on the fact that the absolute-ideal is the absolute-real.

This argument has in no way proved anything as to the reality of this idea, which also, as said, being the ground of all evidence, can only prove itself. Our inference is merely hypothetical: If philosophy exists, then that is its necessary presupposition. An opponent can now deny either the hypothesis or the validity of the argument. Either he will do the first in a scientific manner, and thus will hardly be able to accomplish it otherwise than by himself embarking upon a science of knowledge, that is, upon philosophy. In order to meet him, we must await him in this attempt, but may be convinced in advance that what-

ever he may bring forward for such a purpose will certainly be fundamental principles, which we could contest with adequate reasons, so
that, although we may be unable to persuade him, since he can only
give himself the initial insight, he is also unable to bring forward the
least thing by which he would not expose striking weaknesses to us. Or
again, he will simply assure us in general, without any scientific
grounds at all, that he does not and is not disposed to admit philosophy as a science: This we are by no means to grant, since without
philosophy he cannot know at all that there is no philosophy, and only
his knowledge interests us. This question, therefore, he must allow
others to settle among themselves; he himself forgoes any opinion on
the matter.

The other alternative is that he denies the correctness of the argument. This could happen, according to the above account, only if he
puts forward another conception of philosophy, on the strength of
which a conditioned knowledge would be possible in it. There is nothing to prevent him from calling something of the sort philosophy,
even if it were empirical psychology; but the place of the absolute
science and the inquiry into it will only remain more certain, since it is
self-evident that the misuse of a word indicating something, in which
it is given the meaning of lesser things, cannot abolish the thing itself.
Also, whoever possesses philosophy can be perfectly convinced in advance that whatever conception of philosophy might be brought forward, other than that of the absolute science, he would always and
unfailingly be able to prove that that conception, so far from being
that of philosophy, is not even that of a science at all.

In a word, the insight, that the absolute-ideal is the absolute-real, is
the condition for any higher scientific attitude, not only in philosophy,
but also in geometry and the whole of mathematics. The same indifference of the real and ideal, which the mathematical sciences assume in
a subordinate sense, thus makes philosophy valid in itself, only in the
highest and most universal meaning, once all relation to the sensible
has been removed from her. Upon it rests that authenticity which is
peculiar to the higher sciences. Only on this basis, where nothing but
absolute ideality is demanded for absolute reality, can the geometer
ascribe absolute reality to his construction, which is nevertheless an
ideal one, and assert that what is valid of this construction as form is
also eternally and necessarily valid of the object.

If anybody wishes to remind the philosopher, on the other hand,
that that absolute-ideal is once again only *for him* and only *his thinking,*
as empirical idealism especially can as a rule bring nothing against
Spinoza except only that he erred in not reflecting again upon his own
thought, wherein he would then undoubtedly have realized that his

system, after all, is again just a product of *his* thinking, then we bid such a one, for his part, just to heed the quite simple consideration that indeed this very reflection, by which he makes this thinking *his* thinking, and consequently subjective, is again only *his* reflection, and thus a merely subjective affair, so that here one subjectivity is corrected and removed by another. As he will not be able to deny that, so he must concede that this absolute-ideal is therefore in itself neither a subjective nor an objective, neither his own nor anyone else's thinking, but just absolute thinking.

In the whole of the following exposition we presuppose this acknowledgement of the indifference between the absolute-ideal and the absolute-real, which itself is an absolute, and we must assure everybody that, if he conceives or requires yet another absolute besides that, not only can we not help him to any knowledge of it, but also in our own knowledge of the absolute could not possibly become intelligible to him.

We have to proceed from this idea of the *absolute-ideal;* we define it as *absolute knowing,* the absolute act of cognition.

An absolute knowing is not one in which subjective and objective are united as opposites, but one in which the entire subjective is the entire objective, and *vice versa.* The absolute identity of subjective and objective as the principle of philosophy has been understood in part merely negatively (as mere non-difference) and in part as the mere conjunction of two intrinsic opposites in another, which was here to be the absolute, and partly it is still so understood. The intention was, rather, that subjective and objective, each also considered on its own, should be one, not merely in a union accidental, or at least alien, to them. In general, in this characterization of the highest idea of subjective and objective, it should be not presupposed, but rather indicated, that both, whether opposed or combined, are simply to be conceived from out of that identity alone.

The absolute, as perhaps everybody will automatically admit who has thought it over at all, is necessarily *pure identity;* it is just absoluteness and nothing else, and absoluteness *per se* is equal only to itself; but it does indeed also belong to the idea of that, that this pure identity, independent of subjectivity and objectivity, *as this,* and without ceasing to be so in one or the other, is itself matter and form, subject and object. This follows from the fact that only the absolute is the absolute-ideal, and *vice versa.*

That equal and pure absoluteness, that equal identity in the subjective and objective, was what we have defined in this characterization as the identity, *the equal essence* of subjective and objective. Subjective and objective are, according to this explanation, not one, as opposites are, for with this we should just admit them as such; rather, it is a subjectivity and objectivity only *insofar as* that pure absoluteness, which in itself must be independent of both and can be neither the one nor the other, introduces itself, for itself and through itself, into both as the equal absoluteness.

We have to demonstrate the necessity of this self-differentiation of the undivided absoluteness into subject and object still more precisely.

The absolute is an eternal act of cognition, which is itself matter and form, a producing in which, in eternal fashion, it converts itself in its totality as Idea, as sheer identity, into the real, into the form, and conversely, in equally eternal fashion, resolves itself as form, and to that extent as object, into the essence or subject. Simply in order to make this relationship clear to oneself (for in itself there is no transition here), let the absolute be thought of, to start with, purely as matter, as pure identity, as sheer absoluteness; now since its essence is a producing and it can take the form only out of itself, yet is itself pure identity, so the form too must be *this identity,* and thus essence and form in it must be *one and the same,* namely, the equal pure absoluteness.

At that moment (if we may so call it) at which it is mere matter or essence, the absolute would be pure subjectivity, enclosed and hidden in itself. In that it makes its own essence into form, that whole subjectivity in its absoluteness becomes objectivity, just as in the resumption and transformation of form into essence, the whole objectivity, in its absoluteness, becomes subjectivity.

Here there is no before and no after, no exit of the absolute out of itself or transition to action. *It is itself* this eternal activity, *since it belongs to its Idea* that *immediately through its concept it should also be, that its essence should also be form for it, and the form essence.*

In the absolute act of cognition we have provisionally distinguished two actions, that in which it delivers its subjectivity and infinity entirely into objectivity and finitude, up to the essential unity of the latter with the former, and that in which, in its objectivity or form, it again resolves itself into essence. Since it is not subject, not object, but only the identical essence of both, it cannot, as absolute act of cognition, be here the pure subject or there the pure object, and as subject (where it resolves the form into essence) and as object (where it moulds the essence into form), it is always only the pure absoluteness, the whole identity. Any difference which can take place here is not the absoluteness itself, which remains the same, but only in the fact that in the one act, as essence, it is changed undivided into form, and in the other, as form, is changed undivided into essence, and so fashions itself eternally into unity with itself.

In the absolute itself these two unities are not distinguished. One might be tempted now to define the absolute itself in turn as the unity of these two unities, but to speak precisely, it is not that, since, as the unity of both, it can be recognized and defined only insofar as these are distinguished, which is precisely not the situation here. It is therefore just *the absolute* without further determination. In this absoluteness and in the eternal act, it is utterly one, and yet, in this unity, again immediately a totality of the three unities, namely, that in which the essence is absolutely shaped into form, that in which the form is absolutely shaped into essence, and that in which both these absolutenesses are again one absoluteness.

The absolute produces nothing out of itself except itself, thus again an absolute; each of the three unities is the whole absolute act of cognition, and, as essence or identity, itself becomes form again, just as does the absolute itself. In each of the three unities, seen from its formal side, there is a special feature, for example, that in it the infinite is embodied in the finite, or *vice versa,* but this special character does not remove the absoluteness, nor is it removed by itself, although in the absoluteness where the form is fashioned in complete equality to the essence, and is itself essence, this special character is not distinguished.

What we have designated here as unities are the same as what others have understood under the terms *Ideas* or *monads,* although the true meaning of these concepts has long since been lost. Every idea is a particular, which as such is absolute; absoluteness is always one, just as is the subject-object character of this absoluteness in its own identity; only *the manner,* in which the absoluteness is subject-object in the Idea, makes the difference.

The Ideas are nothing other than syntheses, in which the absolute identity of universal and particular (of essence and form), so far as this identity is itself again universal, is combined with the particular form; and precisely because this particular form is again equated to the absolute form or essence, there can be no individual thing in these Ideas. Only insofar as one of the unities, which again in the absolute itself are as one, conceives itself, its essence, its identity, as mere form, and accordingly as relative difference, does it symbolize itself through individual actual things. The individualized thing is only one moment of the eternal act of transformation of the essence into the form; for this reason the form is distinguished as particular, for example as the embodiment of the infinite into the finite; but that which becomes objective through this form is still only the absolute unity itself. Since, however, all moments and degrees of the absolute embodiment (for instance, of essence into form) lie at once in the absolute form, and since in everything which appears to us as particular the universal or essence is absolutely taken up in the Idea, so nothing in itself has either finitely or truly arisen; it has been expressed, rather, in absolute and eternal fashion, in the unity in which it was conceived.

Things-in-themselves are therefore the Ideas in the eternal act of cognition, and since ideas in the absolute are themselves in turn one Idea, so all things, likewise, are truly and intrinsically one essence, namely that of pure absoluteness in the form of subject-object identification, and even in appearance, where absolute unity becomes objective only through particular form, for example, through individual actual things, all difference between these is still not essential or qualitative, but merely an inessential and quantitative difference, resting on the degree of embodiment of the infinite into the finite.

With respect to the last-mentioned, the following law is to be noted: that insofar as the infinite is embodied into a finite, the latter, as finite, is itself again embodied into the infinite, and that both these unities, with respect to that essence, are again one unity.

The absolute, in the eternal cognitive act, expands itself into the particular, merely so that, in the absolute embodiment of its infinity into the finite itself, it may take back the latter into itself, and in it both are one act. Thus where the one moment of this act, for example, the expansion of the unity into multiplicity, becomes *as such* objective, there the other moment, the resumption of the finite into the infinite, must likewise become objective, just as that which corresponds to the act as it is in itself – where, namely, the one (expansion of the infinite into the finite) is immediately the other also (re-embodiment of the finite into the infinite) – and each in particular become distinguishable.

We see that in this manner just as that eternal knowing permits knowledge of itself in distinguishability, and out of the night of its essence delivers itself into daylight, the three unities immediately emerge from it as particular.

The first, as these differentiate, is Nature, which, as objectification of the infinite in the finite, immediately changes again into the other in the absolute, as the latter changes into it; and the other is the ideal world; and the third becomes distinguished as such where the particular unity of each one, in both of them, in that it becomes absolute for itself, at the same time resolves itself and changes into the other.

But just because of Nature and the ideal world each contains a point of absoluteness, where both opposites flow together, each must again, if it is to be distinguished as the *particular* unity, contain the three unities distinguishably in itself; in this distinguishability and subordination under one unity, we call them *potencies*, so that this general type of appearance necessarily repeats itself also in the particular, and as the same and equivalent in the real and the ideal worlds.

By the foregoing we have led the reader so far that in general he might demand in the first place an intuition of the world in which alone there is philosophy; an intuition, that is, of the absolute world, as also of the scientific form in which it necessarily presents itself. We needed the general idea of philosophy itself in order to present the Philosophy of Nature as the one necessary and integrative aspect of the whole of this science. Philosophy is the science of the absolute, but as the absolute in its eternal activity necessarily grasps two sides in one, one real and the other ideal, so philosophy, seen in its formal aspect, necessarily has to divide itself in accordance with the two sides, although its essence consists just in seeing both sides as one in the absolute act of cognition.

The real side of the eternal act is revealed in Nature; Nature in itself, or eternal Nature, is just Mind born into objectivity, the essence of God introduced into form, save only that *in Him* this introducing immediately grasps the other unity. Phenomenal nature, on the other hand, is the embodiment of essence in form appearing as such or in particularity, and hence is eternal Nature, so far as it takes on itself for a body, and so presents itself through itself as particular form. Nature, so far as it appears as Nature, that is, as this *particular* unity, is accordingly as such already *external* to the absolute, not Nature as the absolute act of cognition itself (*Natura naturans*), but Nature as the mere body or symbol thereof (*Natura naturata*). In the absolute, it exists with the opposed unity, which is that of the ideal world, as one unity, but just for that reason the absolute contains neither Nature as Nature nor ideal world as ideal world, but both are as one world.

If we therefore define philosophy as a whole according to that wherein it surveys and presents everything, namely the absolute act of cognition, of which even Nature is again only one side, the Idea of all ideas, then it is Idealism. Idealism is and remains, therefore, the whole of philosophy, and only under itself does the latter again comprehend realism and idealism, save that the first absolute Idealism is not to be confused with this other, which is of a merely relative kind.

In eternal Nature the absolute becomes, for itself in its absoluteness (which is sheer identity), a particular, a being, but in phenomenal nature only the particular form is known as particular, the absolute veils itself here in what is other than it is in its absoluteness, in a finite, a being, which is its symbol, and as such, like every symbol, takes on a life independent of that which it means. In the ideal world it lays the veil aside, as it were, and appears even as that which it is, as ideal, as act of cognition, but, on the other hand, in such a way that it leaves the other side behind and only contains the one, that of reresolution of the finitude in infinitude, of the particular in the essence.

This aspect, in which the absolute appears in the phenomenal ideal without change into an other, has given occasion for this relative-ideal to be granted a priority over the real, and for a merely relative idealism to be set up as the absolute philosophy itself. The system of the *Wissenschaftslehre* is unmistakably of this kind.

The whole from which the Philosophy of Nature issues is *absolute* Idealism. The Philosophy of Nature does not take precedence over Idealism, nor is it in any way opposed to it so far as it is absolute, but certainly is opposed, so far as it is relative idealism, and accordingly grasps only the one side of the absolute act of cognition, which, without the other, is unthinkable.

In order to fulfill our purpose completely, we still have to mention in particular something of the inner relationships and structure of the Philosophy of Nature as a whole. It has already been recalled that the particular unity, just because it is this, also again comprehends, in itself and for itself, all unities. So too with Nature. These unities, each of which signifies a definite degree of embodiment of the infinite into the finite, are represented in three potencies of Nature-philosophy. The first unity, which in embodying the infinite into the finite is itself again this embodiment, presents itself as a whole through the *universal structure of the world*, individually through the series of bodies. The other unity, of the reverse embodiment of the particular into the universal or essence, expresses itself, though always in subordination to the real unity which is predominant in Nature, in *universal mechanism*, where the universal or essence issues as *light*, the particular as *bodies*, in accordance with all dynamical determinations. Finally, the absolute integration into one, or indifferencing, of both unities, yet still in the real, is expressed by *organism*, which is therefore once more the *in-itself* of the first two unities (though considered, not as synthesis, but as primary), and the perfect mirror-image of the absolute in Nature and for Nature.

But even here, where the embodiment of the infinite into the finite reaches the point of absolute indifferencing, it immediately resolves itself again into its opposite and therewith into the aether of absolute ideality, so that with the perfectly real image of the absolute in the real world, the most perfect organism, the completely *ideal* image, also immediately enters, as reason, although even this again only for the *real* world; and here, in the real world, the two sides of the absolute act of cognition show themselves as archetype and ectype of each other, just as they do in the absolute; reason symbolizing itself in the organism, just as the absolute act of cognition does in eternal Nature; and the organism transfigured into absolute ideality in reason, just as Nature is transfigured in the eternal resumption of the finite into the infinite.

The exposition of the same potencies and relationships for the ideal side, where they return, the same as to essence, although altered as to form, lies here outside our province.

If one considers the Philosophy of Nature on its philosophical side, of which the present work, in its first version, still contained only remote premonitions, confused by the subordinate concepts of a merely relative idealism, then up to the present time it is the most fully worked out endeavour to set forth the theory of Ideas and the identity of Nature with the world of Ideas. In Leibniz this exalted view had at last been revived, but it remained in great part, even with him, and still more so with his successors, confined merely to the most generalized doctrines, moreover quite uncomprehended by them, and not developed scientifically even by him, there being no attempt to apprehend the universe genuinely by means of this view or to make it universally and objectively valid. What had not perhaps for long been so much as suspected, or at best been considered impossible, namely the complete presentation of the intellectual world in the laws and forms of the phenomena, and thus, conversely, the complete apprehension of these laws and forms from the intellectual world, has in part been actually achieved already by the Philosophy of Nature, while in part it is on the way to doing so.

As perhaps the most evident example, we cite the construction that it gives for the universal laws of motion of the heavenly bodies, a construction of which one would perhaps not have believed that the germ of it already lay in Plato's theory of Ideas and the monadology of Leibniz.

Considered from the side of the speculative knowledge of Nature as such, or as speculative physics, there has been nothing like the Philosophy of Nature before, unless one were to count here the mechanical physics of le Sage, which, like all atomistic theories, is a tissue of empirical fictions and arbitrary assumptions devoid of any philosophy. What antiquity provided, of a somewhat more closely related kind, has for the most part been lost. After the blind and mindless type of natural research, which has generally established itself since the corruption of philosophy by Bacon and of physics by Boyle and Newton, with the Philosophy of Nature a higher knowledge of Nature begins; a new instrument for the intuiting and conceiving of Nature is taking shape. Whoever has raised himself to the standpoint of Nature-philosophy, and is in possession of the intuition it calls for and the method it employs, will hardly be able to refrain from admitting that it puts one in a position to solve, with assurance and necessity, precisely those problems which have seemed impenetrable to previous nature research, *although admittedly in an area quite other than that where their solution had been sought.*

What distinguishes the Philosophy of Nature from all that have hitherto been called *theories* of natural phenomena, is that the latter concluded to the grounds from the phenomena, arranged causes according to effects, in order subsequently to derive the latter from the former. Apart from the everlasting circle in which those fruitless endeavours revolve, theories of this sort could still, even on reaching their peak, establish only a possibility that such is the case, but never the necessity. The common pronouncements against theories of this kind, which empiricists constantly denounce, while they can never suppress their inclination toward them, are what even now one hears brought against the Philosophy of Nature. In the Philosophy of Nature, explanations take place as little as they do in mathematics; it proceeds from principles certain in themselves, without any direction prescribed to it, as it were, by the phenomena. Its direction lies in itself, and the more faithful it remains to this, the more certainly do the phenomena step of their own accord into that place in which alone they can be seen as necessary, and this place in the system is the only explanation of them that there is.

Within this necessity, in the universal coherence of the system and in the type which flows from the essence of the absolute and the Ideas themselves for Nature as a whole and in detail, we see comprised the phenomena, not only of universal Nature, about which only hypotheses were previously known, but equally simply and surely the phenomena of the organic world as well, whose relationships have always been counted among the most deeply hidden and forever unknowable. What still remained over for the most pregnant hypotheses, the possibility of accepting or not accepting them, here falls away altogether. For one who has but grasped the coherence as such, and has himself reached the standpoint of the whole, all doubt is likewise removed; he perceives that the phenomena can only be thus, and so must also exist as they are presented in this context: In a word, he possesses the objects through their form.

We conclude with some considerations about the higher relation of the Philosophy of Nature to modern times and to the modern world in general.

Spinoza has lain unrecognized for over a hundred years. The view of his philosophy as a mere theory of objectivity did not allow the true absolute to be perceived in it. The definiteness with which he recognized subject-objectivity as the necessary and eternal character of absoluteness shows the high destiny implicit in his philosophy, whose full development was reserved to a later age. Yet in him there is still a want of any scientifically observable transition from the first definition of substance to the great first principle of his doctrine: quod quidquid ab infinito intellectu percipi potest tanquam substantiae essentiam constituens, id omne ad *unicam tantum substantiam* pertinet, et consequenter, *quod substantia cogitans et substantia extensa una eademque est substantia,* quae jam sub hoc jam sub illo attributo comprehenditur.[1] The scientific knowledge of this identity, whose absence in Spinoza subjected his teaching to the misunderstandings of a former day, was bound to be the beginning of a reawakening of philosophy itself.

Fichte's philosophy was the first to restore validity to the universal form of subject-objectivity, as the one and all of philosophy; but the more it developed, the more it seemed to restrict that very identity, again as a special feature, to the subjective consciousness; yet as absolute and in itself, to make it the *object* of an endless *task,* an absolute *demand,* and in this way after extracting all substance from speculation, to abandon it as just empty froth, while proceeding, on the other hand, like the Kantian theory, to reconnect absoluteness with the deepest subjectivity, through action and faith.[2]

Philosophy has higher demands to fulfil, and is called upon to lead mankind, which, whether in faith or unbelief, has long enough lived unworthily and unsatisfied, at last to vision. The character of the whole modern era is idealistic; its dominant spirit, the return to inwardness. The ideal world presses mightily towards the light, but is still held back by the fact that Nature has withdrawn as a mystery. The

---

[1] [Translation: "that whatsoever can be perceived by the infinite intellect as constituting the essence of substance, belongs altogether only to one substance: consequently, substance thinking and substance extended are one and the same substance, comprehended now through one attribute, now through the other" (*Ethics* [trans. R. H. M. Elwes], II, Prop. VII, Note)].

[2] It is not even necessary to invoke the *Bestimmung des Menschen,* the *Sonnenklaren Berichte,* etc., on behalf of this total rejecion of all speculation from pure knowing and the integration of the latter in its vacuity through faith. In the *Wissenschaftslehre* itself there are passages such as the following: "But for this necessity (the highest unity, as the author calls it, of absolute substance) he (Spinoza) offers me no *further* ground, telling me merely that it is absolutely so; and this he says because he is compelled to assume some absolutely primary, ultimate unity. But if this is what he wants, *he ought to have stopped forthwith at the unity given him in consciousness,* and should not have felt the need to excogitate a higher one still, which nothing obliged him to do" (*Werke,* I, 121; translation, Heath and Lachs, p. 118). Later it is shown that it was a *practical datum* that compelled him *to stop,* namely "the feeling of a necessary subordination and unity of the entire not-self under the practical laws of the self; though this subordination is by no means anything that exists as the *object* of a concept, being rather the *object of an Idea, viz., something that ought to exist, and that we ought to bring about,*" etc. [*Ibid.* Italics and interpolations by Schelling himself.]

very secrets which the ideal harbours cannot truly become objective save in proclaiming the mystery of Nature. The still-unknown deities, which the ideal world is preparing, cannot emerge as such until they can seize possession of Nature. After all *finite* forms have been struck down, and there is nothing more in the wide world to unite mankind but collective intuition, it can only be the contemplation of absolute identity in the fullest objective totality that afresh, and in the final development to religion, unites them forever.

BOOK I

The purest exercise of man's rightful dominion over dead matter, which was bestowed upon him together with reason and freedom, is that he spontaneously operates upon Nature, determines her according to purpose and intention, lets her act before his eyes, and as it were spies on her at work. But that the exercise of this dominion is possible, he owes yet again to Nature, whom he would strive in vain to dominate, if he could not put her in conflict with herself and set her own forces in motion against her.

If the secret of Nature consists in the fact that she maintains opposed forces in equilibrium or in lasting, forever undecided, strife, then the same forces, as soon as one of them acquires a *lasting* predominance, must destroy what they were maintaining in the previous state. Now, to bring this about is the chief device which we have at our disposal, and of which we make use in order to resolve matter into its elements. In so doing we have the advantage that we view the separate forces in freedom, whereas where they work together harmoniously they appear even at the first moment of their operation to be already mutually limited and determined by one another.

We shall therefore begin our discussion of Nature most fruitfully with the primary natural process by which bodies are destroyed and dissolved.

1

Of the Combustion of Bodies

The most commonplace process of this kind is combustion. It is already apparent at first glance that it is hopeless to try to explain it as dissolution from without. It is a transformation which relates to the interior of the substance burned, and such an inner transformation must be *chemically* explained. But no chemical process goes on unless at least attraction occurs between two bodies.

Now in the present case this attraction takes place between the body which is burned and the air surrounding it. This is an undoubted fact. But the question arises, Is this attraction simple or is it twofold? If it is simple, what is the ground of affinity between the body and the oxygen of the air, which that body is supposed to attract to itself? Can one be satisfied with the general assurance that the oxygen of the air has a greater affinity for the body than for the caloric, with which it was hitherto combined?[1] In general the question is, How must we regard combustible bodies? What is required for the oxygen (the vital air) to have affinity towards the body? For if there is no basis for this relationship in the body itself, why does it not pertain to all bodies alike?

The abstract term *affinity* is perfectly proper to *describe* the phenomenon, but it is not adequate to *explain* it. Every verifiable explanation of it, however, would at the same time have to give us clues concerning the nature of what are called basic materials. The new system of chemistry, the work of a whole era, spreads its influence ever more widely over the other branches of natural science, and employed over its *whole* range may very well develop into the universal system of Nature.

If we assume, as everyone agrees, that combustion is possible only through an attraction between the basic material of the body and that of the air, then we shall also have to suppose two possible cases, which can indeed be regarded merely as different expressions of one and the same fact, but which it is nevertheless profitable to distinguish.

[1] Girtanner's *Elements of Antiphlogistical Chemistry* [1792], new edition, p. 35.

59

Either: The basic material of the air fixates itself in the body, the air vanishes, the body is *oxidized* (*oxydé*) and ceases to be combustible. Of these bodies especially the following explanations are valid: Burnt substances are those which have been saturated with oxygen; to burn a substance means nothing else than to *oxidize* it, etc.[2]

Or: The body, as it burns, at the same time volatilizes and itself changes into a variety of air.[3]

The first case will occur, for instance, with such bodies as show at most very little capacity for heat, in which, therefore, the inner cohesion of their basic materials is also harder to overcome than in other bodies. In this class belong the metals. If in the end by the violence of fire they are brought to the point at which they can effect a decomposition of the air, the basic material of the air still passes over much more easily into the body than does the basic material of the body into the air. Of them, therefore, the principle is eminently true that the weight of the air, in which the process occurs, decreases in just that measure whereby the weight of the body increases, and quite naturally so, because here the loss on the part of the air is the gain on the part of the body.

Further, all substances of *this* kind can be *reduced,* that is, restored to their previous state, which, once again, is easily understandable, because in the process of combustion they have lost none of their basic material but have acquired an increase which can very easily be withdrawn from them again. All that is needed for this is *first* to heat them *gradually* and not let the outer air have free access to them, both so that they do not draw the basic material of the air into themselves for a second time; *second,* to associate with them a substance which displays a stronger attraction towards oxygen than they do. We know from the previous experiment that they can lose nothing to the air. The whole process of reduction is, therefore, nothing else than the former process in reverse.

The other case, in which the basic material of the body combines with that of the air, can only occur in such bodies as show very great capacity for heat (the universal means of accelerating all decomposition), like vegetable substances, charcoal, diamond (which, according to Macquer's researches, generates carbonic acid gas), and so forth.

All these substances *are incapable* of reduction; the gain in this instance is on the part of the air, the basic material of the body has

[2] *Ibid.,* pp. 61, 139. Fourcroy, *Chemical Philosophy,* translated by Gehler, Leipzig, 1796, p. 18.
[3] Or: the basic material of the body combines with that of the air, the air loses elasticity thereby, while it gains weight. [First edition].

combined with that of the air, it has increased in weight by precisely so much as the burned substance has lost.

Especially remarkable (in relation to the two types of combustion established above) is the combustion of sulphur and of phosphorus. If one ignites sulphur in vital air under a bell-jar, white fumes are promptly emitted, which gradually extinguish the flame, so that part of the sulphur must necessarily remain unconsumed. Plainly the basic material of the sulphur has united with the air; but the heat is unable to keep them both in a gaseous state, and the sulphur therefore settles on the surface of the bell-jar as acid, which, in comparison with the sulphur burnt, has gained in weight exactly as much as the air has lost.

Still more remarkable is the combustion of phosphorus, because in it three cases are actually possible at once, which with other combustible substances occur only *singly*. If the phosphorus is exposed in atmospheric air for an hour at a high temperature, it deprives the air of a part of its basic material, becomes *acidified*, and changes into a transparent, colourless, brittle mass.[4] So here it behaves just like the metals in calcination.[5]

If the phosphorus is burned with vital air under a bell-jar, it behaves just like sulphur, in that it settles on the inner surface of the bell-jar as dry phosphoric acid in the form of white flakes.[6]

If the phosphorus is *heated for a very long time* in a closed vessel with atmospheric air, one obtains an air which is quite different from all others known (and, specifically, from the inflammable phosphoric air).[7]

It is clear from this that a single substance can go through all the different states of combustion, from calcination up to that in which it becomes air.[8] But the general conclusion, which I think we may draw from the foregoing, is this: To understand the decomposition of a body by fire, we must assume that it contains a basic material which displays an attraction for the oxygen of the air. The presence or absence of this material in the body is the reason for its combustibility or lack of it. This material can be modified in the most diverse ways in different substances. We can therefore also assume that it is everywhere *the same* basic material which makes the bodies combustible, but

---

[4] Girtanner, *op. cit.*, p. 125.

[5] Also metallic calxes, if they are exposed to a more intense flame, glaze to complete transparency.

[6] *Ibid.*, p. 52.

[7] Jäger in Gren's *New Journal of Physics*, vol. II, p. 460.

[8] With metals, however, both cases also in part occur. The same metals which are calcined in ordinary fire are converted to gas in the focus of a burning glass.

that it appears in different bodies under different modifications. All the substances we know have gone through very different states. The basic material they consist of probably went through the hand of Nature more than once and although it has received the most varied modifications, it still cannot belie its origin.

Lavoisier assumes that the basic material of vegetable substances is carbon. This element everywhere betrays its affinity to oxygen very strikingly. How does it come about that it combines so easily with gaseous oxygen, that charcoal is so useful for the reduction of metals, that when ignited several times, it repeatedly absorbs new oxygen from the air, thereby time and again becoming available for combustion, and so generates, until it is completely consumed, a quantity of air which threefold exceeds the weight of the charcoal from which it was produced? Should we not therefore assume that carbon represents an extreme of combustibility, and perhaps the same, in its own sphere, as does oxygen in its? It is therefore very possible, perhaps, to find out how both so-called elements are connected. One would think, in fact, that oxygen, which, according to modern chemistry, plays so great a part in Nature, would not indeed play this part only in atmospheric and vital air. The most recent observations, made by Girtanner, von Humboldt and other acute scientific researchers, of the great influence which it exerts on the growth of plants, on the revival of seemingly quite extinct animal sensibility, etc., must at least awaken the *suspicion* that Nature makes use of this powerfully active element, far more universally and for even more important ends than is commonly assumed. So much seems clear to me, that the oxygen of modern chemistry, if it is what it is given out to be, may well be more than that. Furthermore, the most varied modifications of the same element are nothing impossible, and Nature can endlessly multiply the affinities of the same principle through very many intermediaries.

These remarks may draw attention to the fact that the discoveries of recent chemistry might in the end afford the essentials of a new system of Nature. A relationship so widely operative, as that which is now put beyond doubt, and is no longer (as the presence of phlogiston once was) a mere hypothetically assumed affinity of bodies for a substance all-pervasive in Nature, must necessarily have important consequences for all scientific research, and can even become a leading principle for the investigation into Nature, as soon as this discovery ceases to be the exclusive possession of chemistry alone. Here at least the newer chemistry has before it the example of the old, which pursued phlogiston throughout the whole of Nature, only with this difference, that the former has the advantage over the latter of a real, and not a merely imaginary, principle.

The second question, whether in the combustion of bodies a simple or a double selective attraction takes place, is not easy to answer, expressed as abstractly as it is here. One could ask, Is there, apart from the attraction displayed by the body for the basic material of vital air, a further attraction between the caloric of the air and the basic material of the body itself? No preference for an affirmative answer to this question is evoked by the fact that we are as yet unable to specify the latter alternative more closely, and that as soon as such a determination is attempted, we at once get lost in the wide expanse of imagination and possibility outside the range of real knowledge. The only reliable appearance of combustion is heat and light, and to explain these we need assume no hypothetical element, nor any special basic material in the body. Heat and light, however these two may be related to *each other,* are yet probably both the common portion of all elastic fluids. They are very likely the universal medium through which Nature lets the higher forces work upon dead matter. Insight into the nature of these fluids must, therefore, infallibly open up a vista on the efficacy of Nature at large. That ponderable substances attract each other by numerous affinities, that some of them have the power to decompose the surrounding air, etc., are phenomena which we notice within a very small range. But before all the smaller systems were possible, in which these processes occur, there must have existed the great system in which all these subordinate systems are comprehended. Thus it becomes credible that these fluids are the medium through which, not only bodies cohere with bodies, but worlds with worlds, and that Nature in the large as well as in the small makes use of them to awaken dormant forces and to arouse dead matter from its primordial inertia.

But the mind is not enlarged to such prospects so long as it is still prone to hamper itself with unknown elements, the makeshift of a defective physics. Does not the air, itself the scene of innumerable decompositions and changes, surround our whole earth? Does not light and with it the warmth that gives life to everything come to us from a distant star? Do not life-giving forces penetrate the whole earth? And do we need to conjure up forces, which are everywhere freely operative and freely diffused, as substances in bodies, in order to understand the great works of Nature – to limit our imagination to possibilities, while it is scarcely adequate to encompass the reality?

It is also very easy to perpetuate old opinions, which once served only as means of perplexity, by new interpretations. The old physics thought of phlogiston, not as a compound, but as a simple principle, the clearest proof that it saw itself in no position to explain the phenomenon of combustion. What makes substances combustible? was

the question. That which makes them combustible, was the answer. –
Or if even phlogiston *itself* was supposed to be combustible, the same
question returned more urgently than ever: Does phlogiston then
make things combustible?

Besides, celebrated scientists had long since already been thinking
of phlogiston as a compound principle. Buffon, for example, maintained that phlogiston was nothing simple, but a combination of two
different principles, through whose separation alone the phenomenon of combustion arose. At the stage which chemistry had then
reached, however, it was not so easy for him to define these two
principles, as it has now become with the help of recent chemistry.[9]
Yet Buffon set no great value on his opinion and himself expected,
from observation of the increase in weight of ignited substances
(which he explained by a loss of air), that a great revolution was yet in
store for chemistry.

[9] Buffon's words are these: "The famous phlogistic of the chemists (a creature of
their method, rather than of Nature), is not a simple and identical principle, as they
present it to us; it is a composite, a product of blending, a result of the combination
of the two elements, *air* and *fire,* fixed in the body. So without dwelling on the
obscure and incomplete ideas which consideration of this precarious substance
might furnish us, let us hold fast to that of our four real elements, to which the
chemists, with all their new principles, will always be forced eventually to return."
Histoire naturelle, générale et particuliëre, ed. des Deuxp., vol. VI, p.51.

A New View of the
Combustion Process
(Supplement to Chapter 1)

The ancients worshipped the universal substance under the name of Vesta (Hestia), and this indeed in the sensible image of fire. In this they left us a hint that fire is nothing other than the pure substance breaking through in corporeality, or a third dimension, a view which already gives some light in advance on the nature of the process of combustion, whose main appearance is fire.

The chemical process as such is the totality of the dynamical process in which all forms of the latter meet together and become uniform. The process of combustion is itself in turn the highest and most active phenomenon of the chemical process as such, where we actually see its meaning proclaimed in fire.

Here we have to return to some more general truths, which are the foundations of the construal of all qualitative or dynamical processes.

All qualities have originally been deposited in matter by cohesion, in which we distinguish once more, according to the measures of the first two dimensions, the absolute as determining length and the relative as determining breadth. In the highest context, with respect to the earth, the first of these is that by which she asserts her individuality, the other is that whereby the sun seeks to subordinate her (in axial rotation). Here we already have sufficient reason to designate the first as the north-south polarity, the other as the east-west polarity.

We can now go on to define all cohesion as such as synthesis of identity and difference, of a universal and particular, except that in the first kind the universal is objectified in the particular, which is thus itself posited as universal, whereas in the other case the particular is subsumed under the universal and accordingly is posited as particular. In the respect in question, the first kind of cohesion can also itself be called the universal once more, and the other kind the particular.

Since in absolute cohesion the body makes itself self-dependent through the relative identity of the universal and particular, it thereby shades itself from the sun, which, with respect to the earth and every body, is especially concerned to subordinate them as particulars; the body becomes *opaque*. There is *transparency*, therefore, only [i] *either* where from absolute cohesion [a] either the *pure universal* is produced (which, as Steffens has shown in the *Contributions to the Internal Natural History of the Earth*, is presented in this purity for the earth, in what has been called nitrogen), [b] or else the *pure particular* (which on the evidence of the same author, is similarly presented in carbon, of which the purest manifestation is diamond): [ii] *or* again where, from relative cohesions [a] either the *pure universal* and *particular* is produced (which, according to the arguments in the *Journal of Speculative Physics*, vol. I, no. 2, p. 68, is the case in hydrogen and oxygen), [b] or where the *absolute indifference of both* is produced, not mediated or marred by the intervention of absolute cohesion (which is generally possible only with respect to the factors of this sort of cohesion) – in water therefore, where the whole universal is also the whole particular and the whole particular the whole universal. It is obvious that transparency can also occur, more or less, in different degrees of approximation to those given extremes or to the indifference-point of water. All other transparency which may still seem to occur, apart from the cases mentioned, must in some way or other reduce to one of these, as we shall soon discover more definitely.

Now if oxygen, which is the factor of the particular in relative cohesion, is the universal condition of combustion, then all combustion processess will necessarily have to proceed from an indifferencing either of the universal by the relative particular cohesion itself or of the universal and particular by the absolute – since this relates to the particular of the relative as particular in general, yet again as universal – with the particular of relative cohesion. The most perfect process of combustion will display itself to us where the conflict of universal and particular is perfectly equalized in that attempted process of generation, where the universal and particular of relative cohesion reaches indifference, yielding the hermaphroditic product of water, which, as absolute liquid, is not only the total extinction of the first two dimensions in the third, but also, through the particular is wholly earth and through the universal wholly sun; and just here in this equalization the sun breaks through most completely, except that because of the element of earth which is included therein, it cannot show itself purely as light, but only as fire (light combined with heat).

The universal principle of universal cohesion will keep itself the most independent of this process, but at the point where both principles of the last-named are united into rigidity, a still higher conflict, that of relative and absolute cohesion itself, will take place, the settlement of which, in the highest degree of oxidation of metals, again presents itself as transparency, as it were in a higher potency, where a solid body as such becomes wholly sun and wholly earth.

Because of a misunderstanding of the assertion that oxygen is a cohesion-intensifying principle, whereas it seems as a rule rather to dissolve cohesion through the acids, and also in combustion, we observe that oxygen is the principle of relative cohesion, and that intensification of the latter at any rate coexists with the diminution or dissolution of absolute cohesion, without being the cause; that the solution of bodies by oxidation is therefore merely apparent; that the bodies in dissolution, whether it occurs through acids or, as with diamond, in combustion, through the effects of heat, oxidize in order to withstand total dissolution rather than to be dissolved because they are oxidized.

The further exposition of these principles is to be found in the *Journal of Speculative Physics*, vol. II, no. 2, §112–34.

2

Of Light

The phenomena of heat have been imperfectly explained so long as the phenomena of *light* remain dark for us; both usually exist together and often almost at the same instant; both are so alike, and yet again so different in their way of acting, that it is well worth the effort to fathom their reciprocal relation. Meanwhile, natural science seems as yet to have been more fortunate in investigating the laws according to which this wonderful element moves than in discovering its nature. The recognition of those laws has contributed more than most other sciences to extending the limits of human knowledge, for it has opened up to the human mind the prospect of an infinitude of never-to-be-completed discoveries. But perhaps the fullest enlightenment about the nature of light would widen the horizon of mankind inwardly and for the ideal world no less than the discovery of those laws has enlarged it externally; perhaps it would make much that has seemed inscrutable more intelligible, and much that has seemed great even greater – a gain sufficient to stimulate us to unremitting investigations.

The first question which must occupy us is this: How are light and heat connected? Are they altogether different in nature? Is one, as it were, cause and the other effect? Or do they differ only in degree? Or is one merely the modification of the other, and in that case, could the marvellously rapid, easily mobile element of light be really a modification of heat, a matter (as it seems) which spreads sluggishly and only gradually into much smaller spaces?

They do not appear to be each of a different *nature;* for the striving towards extension and expansion is common to both. But one expands infinitely faster than the other. So might they be different in degree? But the greatest heat is without light, while often far less heat is associated with great flame. These assumptions, therefore, lead to no satisfactory result.

Light *warms.* But whether light is warm *in itself,* according to the mere sensation which we have of it, we can neither affirm nor deny, because we cannot determine what our body contributes to this sensation. But supposing that the mere contact of light were to warm a body, then different bodies, exposed to the same light, would have to exhibit equal heat. But this is not the case.

It is known that light affects black bodies most strongly. From optics, however, everybody knows that bodies look black because they display stronger attraction towards the light, and so also reflect less of it back than others do. Light thus undergoes combination in the body – is more or less attracted – encounters more or less resistance – (or however one wishes to express it), and this more or less determines the degree of heat which it excites in the body. At the highest degree it is capable of exciting, it also becomes *invisible,* and so here light seems to alter its entire manner of operating at the same time as it goes over from the state of visibility to the opposite; although never sensible to the eye, it still does not cease to affect another sense, that of feeling.

M. Pictet enclosed two thermometers, exactly equal and alike except that the bulb of one was blackened, in a cupboard completely impervious to light. When he opened it, both readings were equally high. A short while after they had both been exposed to daylight, the blackened one rose about two- to three-tenths of a degree higher than the other. But in general, light seems to warm in proportion to the resistance it encounters. If one allows a ray to impinge upon a mirror, to be reflected on to a second, from the second to a third, and so on, the ray suffers gradual diminution and sensible heat arises.

M. de Saussure at an early stage did very significant experiments to investigate more precisely the warming effects of sunlight on different bodies, which later M. Pictet repeated with several modifications. He hung a thermometer in the open air, while he brought several others into contact with glass capsules, one enclosed within another. He observed that the first thermometer, exposed to the sun, rose the least, while the others rose more or less in stages, according as they were brought into contact with a capsule standing deeper or higher. One cannot deny that these experiments still allow of different explanations, but the later experiments of M. Pictet establish without any ambiguity the principle that the warming effect of the sun's rays is greater, the more resistance they encounter.

These experiments are closely connected with the generally known observations to which M. de Luc, in particular, has drawn attention. Especially relevant here is the ever-increasing cold on mountains the higher one climbs, of which the most impressive proof is the perpetual snow which covers even the Cordilleras on the equator – and also, the different warmth and cold at the same seasons in similar geographical latitudes, etc. It is found in the descent from high mountains that the warmth of the air always increases directly in proportion to its density, and in inverse proportion to its rarity. We note that overcast summer days without sunshine are much more fatiguing, with their oppressive heat, than the clearest sunny days. From nothing but commonplace observations, made hundreds of times, it might long ago have been concluded *that sunlight shines brighter the less heat it excites,* and *vice versa.*

These facts appear to justify us in asserting that *light and heat are not in themselves different; the latter is merely a modification of the former.* To say that light is a modification of caloric, that for instance it is nothing other than intensified heat, etc., will not do, because in that case the quantity of heat would always have to stand in the same proportion to the quantity of light, which the foregoing observations show to be impossible.

The question arises whether the proposed hypothesis can be reconciled with other phenomena of light quite so easily as it agrees with the findings cited above.

It is customary to suppose two different states of heat, one in which it is completely bound, and for that reason is called latent heat, the other in which it becomes perceptible through an acquired excess and is called sensible heat. I cannot and will not enter *here* upon the correctness of this distinction—nor do I ask what reason and right we may have to regard light and heat as elements, which, like every other, are capable of chemical bonding. It is enough at present to presuppose this distinction and to remark simply that we may assume yet a third state of heat, that in which it escapes its bonds, passes quite freely from one combination to another, and in this passage takes on quite other properties than those it displayed in the two previous states. In this state it would be *light,* and to that extent it seems to make no difference whether, to speak the current language of chemistry, we regard light as free heat, or heat as bound light.[1]

If the explanation of combustion proposed above is correct, then we know that at the same instant in which the vegetable substance disintegrates, and the metal calcines, that is to say, in the same moment at which, according to our assumption, the air is decomposed, heat and light exist *together.* Also it is not without a determinate *degree* of heat that the light first appears, rather the heat as such, be its degree as small as you will, is accompanied by light just as soon as it becomes *free,* as occurs in *combustion,* and, conversely, the greatest heat is without light, so long as no decomposition is produced. Therefore, no light is visible with the dissolution of metals in acids, in spite of the fact that

[1] A proof that precisely that chemistry which assumes a chemical binding of heat, has least need to add to heat-stuff yet another light-stuff.

this process is entirely the same as calcination. The metals deprive the acids of oxygen: The capacity of the latter is thereby reduced, and effervescence and sensible heat ensue; but this does not become free, because it remains combined with the basic material of the acids in order to carry off the residue of the latter in a gaseous state. The whole process is nothing more than a restoration of capacity. The liquid changes into a gas and so binds, in spite of its loss, the same heat as could be bound by a fluid of lesser capacity but greater quantity of basic material.

The opposite happens in the reaction of nitrogen with atmospheric air. In withdrawing the oxygen from the latter, its capacity is *reduced*. Therefore it changes from the gaseous state to that of vapour. But it does not persist in this state, again resumes the gaseous condition, and by so doing binds the heat liberated from the atmospheric air. From this it is clear why in this process also the heat does not become *light*.[2]

With phosphoric phenomena it is quite different. The phosphorus, in virtue of its great affinity for oxygen, extracts this element from the air. Thereby heat is liberated; this heat, one may say, is related to nothing, so it begins to glow; but since the decomposition of the air is very small, only at the point of contact between the body and the air. This is at the same time the clearest proof that light and heat can differ not only in *degree*. For no phosphoric decomposition is accompanied by sensible heat, proving how little heat is liberated thereby; nevertheless, light is the constant phenomenon in these processes. A double decomposition takes place, for instance, if bodies which are more highly combustible are treated with acids. Thus oils mixed with nitric acid ignite. Because they deprive the latter of oxygen, heat is at once liberated, and with that a second reaction begins between them and the surrounding air. The flame is the livelier, the more easily the oils vaporize.

Perhaps one might object that just because heat and light are present *together* in the combustion of bodies, they must also be two elements quite different one from another. But the heat as it is liberated very soon strives to enter again into combination, in whatever way it may be, for that can make no difference at all to us here. In these combinations it maintains preponderance, and in that way becomes sensible heat. Hence, too, the flame which accompanies the burning of vegetable bodies appears much less pure than that which becomes

[2] This could not, however, be asserted with such certainty if special experiments on it, so to speak, had not been performed. The flame of the brightest lamps (the Argand), which burn with the greatest radiance, appears when exposed to the midday sunlight in the form of a dead, yellow, half-transparent fume. Cf. the remarks of Count Rumford in Gren's *New Journal of Physics*, vol. II, no. 1, p. 61.

visible in the combustion of other substances. Out of vegetable matter, in addition to carbonic acid gas and inflammable air, heterogeneous substances are evolved with which the heat enters into combination. One may therefore consider the flame merely as the transition of the light from the state of visibility to that of invisibility. Where flame comes to an end, only smoke is seen, and, instead of saying with Newton that the flame is incandescent smoke,[3] we might just as well say the smoke is the flame which has ceased to glow. The more aqueous and other components the burnt substance (like green wood) contains, the sooner does the flame become smoke, from which it also becomes intelligible why, in a *more rapid* combustion, far more heat is given out than in a slower one.

The main difference between light and heat is that each affects an entirely different sense. Yet it is not so long ago since people ceased to consider light as such to be warm, undoubtedly because it *becomes* heat as soon as it enters into combination with the body. That difference would tell very decisively against the assertion that light and heat are in no way different from each other, but against the assertion that heat is a mere modification of light, it can prove nothing. It is understandable that the *liberated* light (I use always the most accessible terms) should reveal itself to the intellectual organ, while bound light can act only on the lower sense. Light travels with incredible rapidity from its source out into the distance, heat is confined to a determinate sphere; for as such it acts only in conjunction with a matter opposed to it; so for it we possess the sense which receives impressions only through crude contact, while for the other we have the organ which, being capable of a more delicate touch, lies open to the light which comes to us from the farthest distance.

Whatever we take light to be, the time it requires for its propagation disappears into nothing as soon as we deduct the resistance which it meets in its course. This resistance that it encounters prolongs its diffusion to moments of time, and in this resistance it first acquires for us characteristics of matter; its velocity becomes *finite,* a velocity determinable in numbers; like matter it now undergoes attraction and repulsion, and so first becomes a possible object of physics and physical investigation. I consider this observation to be sufficient to decide the question, whether light as such can be treated as material. So long as we find ourselves, as we do here, in the province of merely empirical physics, we shall never be entitled to speak of it otherwise. Physics and chemistry have their own language, which, in a higher science, must be resolved into one quite different. So up to that point we may

[3] "Flamma est fumus candens."

always be permitted to speak of light, of heat, etc., as they must be spoken of in physics.[4] So this question, whether light and heat are *special* kinds of matter, presupposes something which a sound philosophy should not so readily admit, namely, that special kinds of matter may exist at all.

Heat is further said to penetrate bodies, whereas light does not. It would be better to say that the light, on entering into bodies, ceases to be light, and from now on becomes *sensible* heat. Some bodies which, when illuminated for a time, continue to glow in the dark, form a seeming exception.

More important are the *peculiar* effects of light (not pertaining to mere heat), which some adherents of the newer chemistry are accustomed to adduce as proof of the existence of a *light-stuff* different from caloric.[5] These peculiar effects are primarily the following: Vegetation exposed to light becomes coloured by it, changeable, inflammable, sapid, etc. Apart from the fact that plants, as soon as they are exposed to light, are also exposed to the free access of air, that light itself acts upon them only through the medium of the air, and so on, we can still always ask for proof that all these effects are peculiar to light *as such*. Light, one may say, so far as it has influence on plants, ceases to be light and becomes heat. Further, the growth of plants is nothing else but a more complex chemical process—if you prefer, a chemical process of a higher kind. The proof of that is the vital air which plants exhale when exposed to light. All the observations re-

---

[4] "Certainly much will always remain hidden from our eyes about the essential nature of fire, but even if all these ways of representing it are very far removed from the absolute truth, yet they always have a very great relative value for us; they are convenient images, which enable us to conceive the manifold phenomena of Nature in mutual conjunction and facilitate the knowledge of them. Allowing that the cause of heat is no fluid, that it is something unlike anything else in Nature, yet it is not to be denied that the phenomena, as far as we know them, can very suitably be thought of under the image of a fluid entity, and if such a symbol has been fortunately chosen, it can itself serve to lead the mind to new relationships of the unknown entity. What wonder, therefore, if the scientist begins to regard his explanations of natural phenomena as something more than mere metaphorical language. And what then is the reality in our ideas of things outside us in general, and what kind of relation have the former to the latter? Let us, therefore, always study the metaphorical language and exert ourselves to give it greater richness, so that perhaps in the end we may encounter truth, as the instructed deaf-mute finally encounters it, who takes our aural speech for a visual one, and what are essentially sounds for movements of the throat and lips, but, in trying to reproduce these, without knowing it, speaks audibly even to that same sense of which he is altogether deprived." Lichtenberg's *Comments on Erxleben's Theory of Nature*, 6th edition [1791], p. 453.

[5] See, for example, Fourcroy's *Chemical Philosophy*, section 1.

corded by Hales, Bonnet, Ingen-Housz, Senebier and others make it probable that in plants a decomposition of water takes place, that the inflammable component in them remains behind, while the oxygen escapes in gaseous form. That light, therefore, and to that extent heat – both the great agencies of Nature, of which she makes use in every chemical process – promote this generation of oxygen from plants is in itself very intelligible, and since the entire growth of plants depends on the continuance of this process, light (and heat) are to that extent necessary conditions of vegetable life. Should it be so difficult, however, to explain why light far more than heat advances this process? Heat spreads slowly, and therefore penetrates into bodies only gradually, while light takes effect more quickly and energetically, and begins in the interior of the plants the process necessary to their preservation.

It is no more difficult to understand the influence which light exerts upon both the calcination and the reduction of certain metals. Some metals oxidize spontaneously as soon as they are exposed to the atmospheric air. Others are reduced by contact with light, because light causes decomposition in all bodies which are liable to it. So when Fourcroy says:[6] "*It has not been demonstrated that caloric is the same as the light-stuff. The more our physical knowledge increases, the more one finds difference in the effects of both light and heat,*" – it were much to be desired that he had given examples. Nobody has doubted that the action of *light* is quite different from that of *heat*, but nor has anybody asserted that light and heat are identical *states* of the same matter.

If light is the great instrument employed by Nature to bring about decomposition and combination wherever they are necessary for the preservation of vegetable and animal life, it is intelligible that bodies should show an attraction – apparent or real? – for light. Whether light also enters as an element into the chemical process is still very doubtful; but it is beyond doubt that light or heat is *active* in most chemical processes. Even in the process of combustion, since light emerges from its bound state, it is itself just that which initiates and maintains the process. We can only ignite bodies by means of bodies, and usually it is already liberated heat, i.e., light, which begins the process. As soon as the basic material of the air is attracted by that of the body, light appears; from now on the induced process continues on its own, the substance burns, as one says, spontaneously, and the light, which is set free by decomposition of the air, serves only to go on sustaining the decomposition.

Newton has long since put beyond doubt, however, that this attrac-

---

[6] *Ibid.*, p. 11.

tion of bodies for light does not always occur in proportion to their mass. He observed that sulphurous and oily substances refract light altogether without relation to their density, and this single observation was sufficient for him to predict the combustibility of diamond and the presence of an inflammable substance in water. The nisus, therefore, which light exerts for bodies, will stand in relation to their greater or lesser solubility; where there is no solubility, light will hasten to the denser body. According to the above observations, the resistance which light encounters is an incontestable proof that it is *material*. The attractions that it undergoes prove it more incontestably still. If it met no resistance *anywhere*, it would lose itself in the universal repulsive force, and would not be transformed for the senses into matter. In physics it is useful to appeal to analogy. The elasticity of the air is proportionate to the pressure (the resistance) which it undergoes. The air would cease to be elastic as soon as it encountered no resistance, that is, as soon as it expanded endlessly. Following this analogy, light can only be elastic insofar as it encounters *resistance*, from any source whatever, for example, attraction.

If we follow this analogy further, we know that elasticity is possible only between two extreme states, that of infinite *extension* and that of infinite *compression*. Hence it comes about that elasticity in different substances can just as easily be reduced as increased by pressure. A total annihilation of elasticity is impossible, because infinite compression is just as impossible as infinite extension.

If we apply this analogy to light, then light suffers diminution at any rate through *disproportionate* resistance. So in dense bodies, light, as such, meets its death; it becomes *heat*, that is, its elasticity is *decreased*. This is why of two bodies exposed to the same light, the one that offers stronger resistance to the light (which does not happen always precisely in proportion to density) is the more intensely heated. The influence displayed by the quality of bodies on their attraction for light is chiefly apparent from many observations on the origin of colours.

All the light of our atmosphere originates from the sun; but how it is propagated from the sun to us is a question about which there seems as yet to be no certainty. Does the light, say, which streams from the sun, itself reach us, or does it merely produce changes in our atmosphere, by which our planet is illuminated? At least all light, which we can create ourselves, we get only from decomposition of the air.

On these assumptions, the uniformly rapid diffusion of light would become intelligible. If we suppose, with Euler, that light is propagated by merely mechanical vibrations of the aether, we do not understand the regularity of these vibrations, which would always have to propagate in a straight line, whereas according to all other experience, mechanical vibrations of a fluid are spread only by undulations. But if we assume that the light from the sun's aerosphere passes to our atmosphere through empty space, we can let it proceed with a rapidity that is fully proportionate to the brevity of the time in which it is propagated to us.

Or if we must needs assume that the whole space of the heavens is filled with a tenuous elastic fluid, the vehicle of all the forces whereby worlds act upon worlds (is there anywhere a space where everything becomes *light*, as in the Empyrean of the ancients?), then this fluid must become ever more tenuous the farther it is removed from solid bodies. So if the atmosphere of the sun, like our own, were gradually to thin out, light would proceed with ever accelerated velocity, until finally, when it enters our atmosphere, it would gradually propagate itself more and more slowly.

If we assume that light propagates in our atmosphere only through decompositions,[7] we see why light by itself produces no heat. Only where light approaches nearer the earth, where the lower levels of the air become, through the pressure of the whole upper atmosphere, continuously denser and increasingly mixed with heterogeneous components, can sensible heat arise. No wonder that at a considerable height the temperature of the air is everywhere the same. It equally becomes explicable from this that the effect of light must be very gradual with respect to heat, that the heat of the sun only reaches its maximum in the later months of the year, and on individual days only after midday, that the air becomes colder immediately after sunset, and so forth. If besides this we could demonstrate a certain constitution of our atmosphere which made it necessary for it to persist in constant decomposition, then that presupposition would be all the more probable. It would be hard to object that this constant decomposition of the air does not, after all, affect our eye, as do isolated decompositions which probably take place in all meteoric phenomena. Rather one sees how such a uniform, never interrupted, ever repeated modification of the air can produce the phenomenon of *daylight*, that is, of a uniformly diffused brightness, just as, for example a non-uniform generation of light gives the phenomena of morning and evening redness, perhaps too of the northern lights and of other meteors. Because the light is universally and everywhere uniform, it can be especially noticeable at no single point. It even moderates the impression which a single light emission would make on our eye,

---

[7] Here, too, I am again using an expression from chemistry, without even wishing to denote anything chemical by it in this connection.

according to the same law that makes the stars disappear before the brightness of the sun.

I am not overlooking the difficulties of this assumption, which can also hold good only within certain limits. Would the effect on our atmosphere of distant stars, whose rays have reached us only after tens or hundreds of years, be still great enough to produce such a modification on it as we suppose in this explanation?[8] Yet no hypothesis should be confronted with the objection that it assumes effects in Nature that are all too large.[9] Magnitude and distance are here of no account: For what is distant in one respect is near in another, and for everything spatial we have only relative yardsticks. Now if the aether pervading the universe is itself the absolute identity of all things, then in it proximity and distance are completely abolished, since in it all things are one thing and in itself and essentially it is one.

The most general assertion which is possible about light is undoubtedly this, that it is a mere modification of matter—as soon as we ask what light *really* is, not what it appears to be, we must come upon this answer[10]—and *for that reason* at least, the question whether light is a

[8] Or what ought we to marvel at more, the subtlety of light, or the sensitivity of our organ?

[9] [From here to the end of this paragraph the first edition reads thus]: Should we not confess that the system in which we exist is a system of the lowest order, that the magnitude of the next system, to which our sun belongs, already exceeds all efforts of our imagination, that, if our sun itself along with its planets and comets is in onward motion, thousands of years scarcely provide a measure of this movement, and that then perhaps even the light which lightens our darkness, comes to us only from the very frontier of the universe.

[10] A number of philosophical scientists have not found these ideas absurd. As proof I quote here a passage from Buffon, which perhaps may draw attention to the fact that the dispute over the nature of light can be settled only from a higher point of view: "*All matter will become light,* as soon as, all cohesion being destroyed, it finds itself divided into sufficiently small molecules, and as these molecules, being free, would be caused by their mutual attraction to collide with one another; in the moment of shock, the repulsive force will exert itself, the molecules will fly off in every direction with an almost infinite velocity, which nevertheless is only equal to the velocity they acquired at the moment of contact: for as the law of attraction is to increase as the space diminishes, it is evident that at contact the space, always proportional to the square of the distance, will become nil, and that in consequence the velocity acquired in virtue of the attraction, ought at that point to become almost infinite; that velocity would be actually infinite if the contact were immediate, and in consequence the distance between the two bodies absolutely nil; but, as we have often repeated, there is nothing absolute, nothing perfect, in Nature, and likewise nothing absolutely great, nothing absolutely small, nothing entirely null, nothing truly infinite; and everything I have said of the *infinite* smallness of the atoms which constitute light, of their *perfect* elasticity, of the *null* distance in the moment of contact, ought only to be understood within limits. If one could doubt that metaphysical truth, it would be possible to give a demonstration of it, without even

special matter is futile. However, the advantage which physics and the observation of Nature can derive from it is very small or none at all, and it is proper to bring it forward only when a crude physics forgets all too readily what Lichtenberg, for example, has often enough repeated, that what we can say about light, heat, fire and matter is no more and no less than a picture language, which is valid only within its special limits. The task of a philosophical science of Nature largely consists in just this, to determine the admissibility as well as the limitations of such *fictions* in physics, which are absolutely necessary for the continued advance of investigation and observation, and only obstruct our scientific progress when we seek to use them outside their proper limits.

These considerations should teach the pure empiricist to be tolerant of contrary opinions about such matters, and to reject the pretensions of individuals, who seek to make their opinion (which after all is in no case more than opinion) prevail against all others. Allowing, therefore, that we cannot explain the propagation of light, that every hypothesis so far attempted has its peculiar difficulties, etc., that is still no reason for us to refrain from using these hypotheses in the future as we have done hitherto; we might sooner come to think that all these hypotheses may very well be *equally* false and that a common illusion lies behind them all.

In physics, however, which *presupposes*, and must presuppose, this illusion, light can remain as before, a matter which radiates to us from distant worlds, and even if we are no longer in the habit of assuming that the sun is a burning body, we can still always consider it the original source from which light is emitted. So it still remains important for us to investigate what constitution that star must have, in order to deliver uninterrupted light and heat to an entire system of celestial bodies.

If we assume (as we must after the foregoing inquiries) that light plays one of the primary roles in Nature, that it is perhaps the great

digressing from our subject. Everybody knows that light takes about seven and a half minutes to come to us from the sun; supposing then that the sun is thirty-six million leagues away, the light traverses that enormous distance in seven and a half minutes, or what is the same (supposing its motion to be uniform), eighty thousand leagues in one second. That velocity, however prodigious, is nonetheless very far from being infinite, since it is determinable by numbers; it even ceases to appear prodigious when one reflects that Nature seems to move almost as rapidly in large matters as in small; for that one has only to calculate the speed of the movement of comets at their perihelion, where like the planets they move fastest, and one will see that the velocity of those immense masses, although less, can nevertheless be compared closely with that of our atoms of light." [*Histoire naturelle*], vol. VI, pp. 20–2.

means which Nature uses to produce and support life and movement on every single celestial body, then it is to be expected that the body which rules over a whole system of subordinate bodies, and is thus the first and greatest in this system, must also be the primary seat of light and heat among these bodies. Even if light is nothing more to us than a modification of matter as such, which is necessary to sustain a natural system, we easily grasp that the major body of each system must be the major source of light in the subordinate systems.

This supposition is still further confirmed by the conjectures we may venture to make about the first formation of our planetary system. The shape of the earth, prominent at the equator and flattened at the poles, hardly permits doubt that the earth has only gradually evolved from a liquid to a solid state. From this presupposition, at least, Kant has made the gradual formation of the present shape of the earth – in a word – more intelligible, so far as anything of the sort can be, than it has been made by many widespread geological tests and involved hypotheses.[11]

For if, Kant says, the original matter of the earth was initially spread out in the form of a cloud, then when that matter changed from the fluid to the solid state through forces of chemical attraction, a great production of vapours (one may add, also the production of different *kinds of air*) must have gone on in its interior. These, expanded to the highest degree of elasticity by the heat concurrently liberated, and set in still greater motion by mutual intermingling, soon broke through the solid bodies and threw up matter in great masses as mountain ranges. They themselves decomposed and compressed one another until the air, having come into equilibrium with itself, rose of its own accord. Part of it, however, precipitated as water, which, on account of its weight, soon poured into the craters of that universal eruption. Only now did it break its own way through the interior of the earth, and so gradually by its flow formed the regular shape of the mountain ranges (whose angles, at least, largely correspond to it), and by continual floodings, in the course of the centuries, brought about those regular strata of calcareous, vitrified or petrified vegetable and animal bodies in the interior of the mountains. At last, however, it withdrew from ever higher basins finally into the deepest of all, the sea.

This hypothesis of the origin of our earth is all the more important, since by all analogy we are entitled at least to extend it to the forma-

---

[11] See his essay "On the Volcanoes in the Moon" in the *Berlin Monthly,* March 1785. I know very well that the assumption of the original fluid state of the earth is much older than this article; but here we are talking of the application that was made of this supposition.

tion of *our* planetary system. Kant[12] has at any rate rendered it extremely probable that the ostensible volcanic craters on the moon, by analogy to the great basins in which water on earth has collected and which cannot possibly be supposed to be the result of volcanic outbursts, are similarly nothing but consequences of *atmospheric eruptions* by which the great mountain masses, and the basins of rivers and lakes, have been gradually formed on all solid bodies.

If I may add to this hypothesis yet another, the comets, those most puzzling bodies in the system of the world, are to all appearances not *solid* bodies like our earth and the rest of the planets of our solar system. At least, Herschel failed to discover a *nucleus*, even with the strongest possible magnification, in six comets discovered by his sister and five others observed by himself.[13] In this connection, Councillor Lichtenberg[14] recalls a long-standing conjecture that either all comets are only mere clouds which would have to appear denser to us in the middle, or become such clouds in the end. How if this conjecture entitles us to another, namely, that the comets are *celestial bodies in the making*, which, dispersed hitherto in a vaporous state, not yet fully subject to the laws of universal gravitational equilibrium, belong to no system exclusively, and follow an orbit in more than one respect irregular. This presumption enables us to explain what is explicable only with difficulty so soon as we regard comets as solid bodies, namely, that their orbit is no more perfectly elliptical than it is parabolic or hyperbolic, that in their course they take all possible *directions*, whereas planets all take only one, from west to east, etc. I am well aware that one can explain all these phenomena *teleologically*, and Lambert has done so by showing that only through this irregularity in the orbits of the comets does it become possible to have the greatest number of world-bodies in *this* space.[15] But with that nothing is accomplished, for we want a *mathematical* explanation of how the irregularity in the motions of these bodies is possible *according to the laws of universal gravitation*. I know Whiston has already taken the comets for *immature planets*. But he associated quite different notions with that one, for he thought of them as *burning* bodies, which (as our earth formerly was) would first have to be burnt out in order to become planets. This idea admittedly does not have the least probability; but it is also quite different from that proposed above.

---

[12] *Ibid.*

[13] That the comets are not solid bodies is further put beyond doubt by the observations of Herr Olbers, who saw stars of the fifth magnitude through the comet observed in April 1786.

[14] Note to *Erxleben's Theory of Nature*, §644.

[15] *Cosmological Letters on the Order of the World Structure*, 1761.

Supported by these analogies, we can boldly extend the hypothesis of the origin of the earth to the formation of our whole planetary system, and therefore also to that of the sun itself. For the sun, after all, can rank in our system as no more than the first planet. If today we could remove the sun from the centre of its system, then promptly the largest planet would take possession of it; and if again we could remove this also, then it would also have its successor, which would become the sun of the system.

As the solid bodies of our planetary system changed from the vaporous into the solid state, a quantity of heat, which had been necessary to maintain that state, and which we could assume to be as great as we like, must have been set free. That body which was the largest in mass must naturally also have dispersed the largest quantity of heat, and so it becomes intelligible how each central body must necessarily also have become the sun of its own system.[16]

This hypothesis agrees with the latest discoveries in astronomy. After Schröter and others had put atmospheres for the moon, Venus and Jupiter beyond doubt, it was already intrinsically credible that even the other world-bodies, and in particular the sun, were surrounded by an aerosphere. Herschel has given this conjecture a high degree of probability by starting to treat the sun's so-called flares as luminous cloudlike vapours in the sun's atmosphere.[17] At least this much has been established through his efforts, that if the sun is surrounded by an atmosphere, and if in this atmosphere clouds form, which are associated with light-decompositions, the sun must appear to us exactly as it actually does.

Herschel believes that, in fact, these luminous clouds in the sun's atmosphere arise from precipitation and decomposition of the air, and that it is actually this light, produced by decompositions, which shines in the sun, while the other transparent regions of its atmosphere, through which the body of the sun itself can be seen, appear as spots. From this then it follows quite naturally that the sun is no burning, uninhabitable body, but is in general much more like the other world-bodies of its system than we usually imagine.

The hypothesis that the light of the sun is produced by disintegrations in its atmosphere could become still more important as soon as these thoughts are pursued further. By what are these disintegrations caused? And why are they, or do they appear to be, only partial? If once we assume light emissions in the atmosphere of one celestial

[16] Kant, *loc. cit.*

[17] Herschel's discussion is in *Philosophical Transactions,* 1795, vol. I, and in précis in Lichtenberg's *Calendar* for the year 1797.

body, then this can be applied to the atmosphere of the others as well. At least Herschel himself seems to believe that these light emissions are not peculiar to the sun. He invokes the northern lights, which often appear so large and bright as to be probably visible from the moon, and also the light which often overspreads the entire heaven on clear moonless nights. The northern light, one might retort, shines more brightly because (like the red glow of morning and evening) it is a partial light. But now if, through the effect of the sun, the light emission, which in these cases is merely partial, were universal, would not the whole phenomenon of daylight thereby become intelligible?[18]

Herschel also remains insistent that the sun emits light, and so cannot altogether neglect the objection that the sun would have to be gradually exhausted by such abundant light-disintegrations. If the light of the sun is only a phenomenon of its atmosphere, this objection immediately no longer has so much force as if we take the sun to be a glowing or burning body. Meanwhile, in order to meet this objection, he still cannot forgo the hypothesis that perhaps the comets are the vehicle through which the sun's constant loss of light is again replenished. Everything depends on the notions we have of light. Nor can we believe forthwith that in a system where everything coheres together anything would suffer continuous loss without receiving compensation: and one can think of countless sources from which light also streams into the sun. Herschel pays no attention to the remaining objections brought against a dispersion of light-matter from the sun. Only some of these are met by his hypotheses; in any case, taken together they are all curious questions for the empirical scientist, which have to be dealt with, and cannot be dismissed as justly as one would have liked, so long as we are still burdened with crude notions of light.

So every hypothesis about the origin of light, as soon as it is obliged to explain its propagation, remains obstructed by difficulties which it cannot resolve, and the result of an impartial investigation appears in the end to be this, that none of the hypotheses so far advanced has completely hit upon the truth; but this result is so usual, and so common to most of our investigations, that we should not think we have said anything special by this.

[18] Further, the remark would have to be added that light is capable of infinite degrees of elasticity. Without doubt the greater or lesser brightness of light depends on the greater or lesser elasticity of the light particles. Sunlight, however, is the brightest that we know, and between it and the flame which we get from our usual disintegrations of air there can be a host of gradations of brightness – and so of elasticity. [In the first edition "subtlety" is used in this note instead of "elasticity."]

Concerning the Theory of
Light in the Philosophy
of Nature
(Supplement to Chapter 2)

As we shall frequently speak of this subject in the sequel, we shall here give only the main points of the theory of light according to the Philosophy of Nature.

1. As to the connections with heat, these are quite secondary relations, to which no reference is required in defining the nature of light in itself. All heat as such, so far as it is manifested, and we know no other, is an endeavour of the body towards cohesion, by which it restores itself to indifference; for every body is heated only so far as it conducts, but all conductivity is a function of cohesion (*Journal of Speculative Physics*, vol. II, no. 2, §88).

Now, that light can dislodge a body from the state of indifference and thereby set that effort towards cohesion going – not through immediate action, but by means of that wherein it is itself one with the body, the absolute identity, the pre-established harmony, so far as it occurs for this point in Nature – becomes clear from the following.

2. It has already been observed that the constructions of the Philosophy of Nature can only be seen according to their necessity in the context of the whole. We have to supply this here with respect to light. It has already been shown (in the Supplement to the Introduction) that in virtue of the eternal law whereby absoluteness becomes subject and object, the universe, not only as a whole, but also in detail (in Nature, for example, and again even in the individual spheres within Nature), divides into two unities, of which we have designated one as the real, the other as the ideal. The *in-itself* is always the third unity in which the first two are equated, save that it is apprehended, not *qua* third or synthesis, as it is presented in appearance, but *qua* absolute. Thus, the identical essence of Nature is also on the one side necessarily revealed as *real* unity, which happens in *matter*, and on the other as ideal unity, in *light*; the *in-itself* is that of which matter and light are themselves merely two attributes, and whence they emerge as from their common root.

This *in-itself*, this identical *essence* of matter and light, is organism and what appears in experience as third is in itself again the first.

Now we undoubtedly have to determine the nature of light according to the relation of that opposition, since only therein does it exist. Light is the same as what matter is, matter the same as what light is, but the former in the real, the latter in the ideal. The one is the real act of space-filling and to that extent is the occupied space itself. The other, therefore, will not be able to be the space-filling itself, nor the occupied space, but only the *ideal reconstruction* of it according to the three dimensions. On the other hand, if it is universally demonstrated that to every real, for example, the filling of space, the same corresponds in the ideal, then we shall find that this ideally intuited act of production could only occur in light. Light traces out all dimensions, without actually filling the space (this is just the quite peculiar, yet pervasive, relation of light to the construction, that it bears in itself all the characteristics of matter, but only ideally). If light occupied space, then one light would exclude another just as one body excludes others, whereas in the starry heaven, within a certain expanse, *all* visible stars are seen at absolutely every *point* in it, and each of them fills this whole expanse *for itself* without excluding the others, which likewise fill the same expanse at all points.

It is hardly conceivable, indeed, how these simple reflections have not already been sufficient, long since, to drive even the mere empiricists to the higher outlook, as is likewise true of the conclusions which emerge directly from the phenomenon of transparency. Against the argument that because a transparent body is or can be so at all points in the same way, such a body would have to be pierced with straight lines in every direction, and, if the Newtonian conception of light were well founded, would therefore have to be nothing but pores, no other response is forthcoming even from the most meticulous empiricists but that no body is, after all, absolutely transparent. This is entirely correct, except that incomplete transparency is not due to opaque interstices; the (greater or lesser) degree of transparency, possessed by the body as such, is uniform at every point. We might equally mention here the uniform reduction of illumination in precise proportion to distance from the light source, since, if the light was emitted in material rays, the lesser illumination of a surface at a particular distance would presuppose unlighted places, just as the lesser degree of transparency in the case just cited presupposed non-transparent interstices, whereas the weaker illumination of a surface is actually quite uniform: something which Kant has already referred to in a passage in his *Metaphysical Foundations of Natural Science*, although the answer he gives is only superficial and inadequate.

I do not know whether it was these considerations or others, which shortly before the first appearance of the present work, procured some new advocates for the old opinion of the *immateriality* of light. But this expression says absolutely nothing; nor should the doctrine of the Philosophy of Nature be in any way confused with this assertion. Apart from the fact that immateriality is a merely negative determination, and perfectly compatible, moreover, with the aether vibrations of Euler or any other *so-called* dynamic hypothesis of little greater merit, the opinion and presupposition of the immaterialists is that matter, on the contrary, is now really and truly material. This, however, is not in fact the case; for in the sense of those physicists, even matter is not material, and in that sense, in which for them light is immaterial, so also is matter itself. Far higher definitions are required, therefore, to grasp the nature of this entity.

If, after defining light as that which *in a positive way* is the same thing in the ideal as matter is in the real, we now reflect upon this concept itself, it emerges from what has already been said, in the foregoing supplement to the Introduction, that even the ideal is no more a pure ideal than the real is a pure real. Universally and always the real is identity, so far as it is the implanting of the ideal in the real; the ideal is likewise identity, so far as it is the resumption of the real into the ideal. The former is the case in matter, where in its bodily form the soul is revealed in colour, in brightness, in sound; the latter is the case in light, which, therefore, as the finite presented in the infinite, is the absolute schematism of all matter.

Otherwise, insofar as gravity relates to bodies generally as *ground* of existence and receptive principle, whereas light behaves as active principle, we can regard the former as the maternal principle and the natural in Nature, the latter as the generative principle and the divine in Nature.

3. It follows automatically from the foregoing considerations that we no more admit an immediate action of light upon bodies, than of bodies upon light, e.g., by attraction or in refraction, but maintain that all relationship between the two is to be conceived through the third, that *in-itself* in which they are one, and which, entering as it were upon a higher level in the form of gravity, attempts to synthesize them.

This leads right away to the collapse of all arguments for the material nature of light, which have been attemptedly derived in part from the so-called chemical effects of light on bodies, in part from the opposite action of bodies on light. That principle which here still makes but an imperfect emergence from its obscurity is the same which also, on the higher level, moulds soul and body into one and is neither matter nor light.

How much obscurity must remain here in the application to individual cases, into which we cannot enter at this point, the thoughtful reader will estimate for himself.

4. Finally concerning the question likewise touched upon in the preceding chapter about the reason why precisely the central body of every system is also the source of light for that system, we mention in advance only that it is precisely in the centre that the particularity of the matter of this system is reshaped by gravity into the universal, and hence that there, too, light would preeminently have to be revealed, as the living form of the embodiment of the finite into the infinite.

Besides, the outlook of philosophy upon the origin of the celestial bodies as well as their relations to one another is necessarily higher than that empirical way of thinking cited from Kant in the foregoing chapter. The celestial bodies emanate from their centres and are in them in just the same way as ideas proceed out of ideas and are in them, at once dependent and yet self-subsistent. In this very subordination the material universe shows itself as the revealed world of Ideas. Those world-bodies which lie nearest to the centre of all ideas necessarily have more universality in them, those more distant, more particularity; this is the contrast between the self-luminous and the dark bodies, although each one is only relatively self-luminous or dark. The former, in the organic body of the universe, are the higher sensoria of the absolute identity, the latter, the more distant, more external, limbs. There is no doubt that a higher order exists, which apprehends even this difference as indifference, and in which there would lie as a unity, what has separated itself, in this subordinate world, into sun and planets.

Several other remarks pertinent to the theory of the Philosophy of Nature on light will be forthcoming in what follows.

3

Of the Air and the Kinds of Air

Our globe is surrounded by a transparent, elastic fluid, which we call air, in whose absence no process of Nature flourishes, without which animal as well as vegetable life would be totally extinguished–as it seems, the universal vehicle of all life-giving forces, an inexhaustible source, from which both animate and inanimate Nature draw everything necessary to their welfare. But Nature has admitted nothing, in her entire economy, which could exist on its own and independently of the whole interconnection of things, no force which is not limited by an opposing one, and finds its continuance only in this conflict, no product that has not become what it is solely through action and reaction, and does not incessantly give back what it has received, and in a new form again recover what it had given back. This is the great artifice of Nature, by which alone she ensures the perpetual cycle in which she endures, and therewith her own *eternity*. Nothing that is or becomes can be or become unless another concurrently is and becomes, and even the perishing of a natural product is nothing but the payment of a debt it has incurred to the whole of the rest of Nature; hence there is nothing original, nothing absolute, nothing self-subsistent within Nature. The beginning of Nature is everywhere and nowhere, and whether in retrospect or prospect, the investigating mind finds the same endlessness of her phenomena. In order to maintain this perpetual exchange, Nature had everywhere to count upon *contradictories*, had to set up *extremes*, within which alone the endless multiplicity of her phenomena was possible.

Now one of these extremes is the mobile element, the air, through which alone are conveyed, to everything that lives and vegetates, the forces and materials for its survival, and yet which is largely itself maintained in a condition whereby it can support life and vegetation by the constant yield of the animal and vegetable creation.

The atmospheric air changes daily in innumerable ways, and only the persistency of these alterations gives it a certain *universal* character, which can pertain to it only as such and taken as a whole. With every change of season, it would also have to confront a much greater alteration than it actually suffers, if Nature did not restore on the one hand, what she removes on the other, by simultaneous revolutions on the surface and in the interior of the earth, and so constantly prevent a total catastrophe in our atmospheric cycle.

Our air is the result of thousands of developments which occur on and in the earth. While the vegetable kingdom exhales the purest air, the animal kingdom breathes out a kind of air which is unsuitable for the support of life and proportionately lessens the purity of the air. The collectively uniform distribution of substances, which dispenses ever new materials in nicely calculated proportions into the atmospheric cycle, never lets it reach the point where a perfectly pure air would exhaust our vital forces, or a mephitic gas would stifle all seeds of life. Materials which Nature could not entrust to every region of the earth and which are necessary to the constant renewal of the air, she conveys nonetheless to the atmospheric cycle of distant regions by winds and storms. What the atmospheric cycle lends to the plants they restore to it enriched. The raw material they take in is exhaled from them as vital air. When they wither they give back to their great provider what they once derived from her, and while the earth seems to age, the atmospheric cycle rejuvenates itself with the materials it extracts from the general decay. While one side of the earth is robbed of all its beauty, the other displays all the glory of spring. What the atmosphere of the one loses through the expenditure which it must make for the vegetable kingdom, the cycle of the other gains through what it acquires from withering and decaying plants. The great movements, whereby the mass of air which surrounds our globe is kept in equilibrium, begin, therefore, regularly with autumn and spring. Only so is it conceivable how the atmospheric air as a whole retains always the same characteristics, in spite of the innumerable changes within it.

In accordance with these ideas it is easy to assess what has recently been asserted about the constituents of the atmospheric air. It is difficult to understand how two such heterogeneous kinds of air as those of which the atmospheric is supposed to consist can occur in such intimate union as we find them in the atmospheric air. The easiest way to escape from the difficulty is undoubtedly to assume that they occupy the atmospheric cycle not really intermixed but separated from one another. According to Councillor Girtanner, at least,[1] the two types of gas of which the atmospheric air consists are in no exact or intimate mixture. They separate, as he believes, of their own accord,

[1] See *The Foundations of Antiphlogistical Chemistry*, p. 65.

into two layers floating one above the other: the lighter nitrogen floats above, the heavier oxygen sinks below.

This assumption would be very welcome if only one could understand why the lighter nitrogen lies *in layers* between the heavier oxygen, and why it does not rather rise completely above the latter. In that case the lower region of the air would have to be filled with pure vital air and the upper with pure azotic air, which is impossible.

Also one cannot understand, without assuming an intimate combination of both, why sometimes pure azotic air and sometimes pure vital air should not often accumulate in one place. If the azotic vital air were present separately, it would have to be extremely damaging to life; if it is not, then the former would no longer be azotic, the latter no longer pure air.

We therefore seem compelled to assume an intimate mixture of both kinds of air, and have to regard atmospheric air as an actual chemical *product* of the two, of which one can say only this: The air which surrounds us depends on factors such that after their removal it can be vital or azotic air, but is neither so long as these factors persist, because both are what they are only in their purity, and cease when mixed to be what they previously were.

Here, it seems to me, we can unhesitatingly assume a chemical interpenetration. The question is only by what means Nature effects this intimate mixture. I believe that I have found this means in *light,* which, by its whole mode of operation, must keep the air in a constant state of decomposition, and can thus, as in plants, so also in the medium through which it reaches us, cause constant alterations of the mixture. Beyond doubt, experiments would confirm this conjecture.

In *general,* the different kinds of air are distinguished predominantly by the quantitative relations of their constituents. Nature has perhaps achieved the completest equilibrium in the two extremes of vital and azotic air. The relative excess of ponderable parts marks out the mephitic, non-inflammable kinds of air, just as, conversely, the relative preponderance of heat makes mephitic kinds of air inflammable. The former could also be called oxidized, and the latter deoxidized, a nomenclature by which their inner nature and their combustibility and non-combustibility would be indicated together.

To explain the famous synthesis of water from inflammable and vital air, modern chemistry has adopted *hydrogen,* that is, a special water-generating principle, which is supposed to be the basis of all inflammable types of air, but it is questionable whether it deserves those names. The burning of inflammable air with vital air is just the same process as any other combustion. The basic material of the first draws the oxygen of the second to itself; heat is liberated in great quantity, and what is left is no longer able to maintain the heavier air in a gaseous state. It would therefore have to change either into visible vapour or into a liquid, and experience shows that the latter occurs. But surely this process differs only in degree from any other, in which a reduction of capacity occurs. Thus by the same law, nitrogen becomes visible *vapour* through contact with the atmospheric air. Here too a reduction of capacity occurs according to the universal law, that what Nature cannot *keep* in its prior state she *maintains by alteration* of its state, that is, by increasing or diminishing its capacity.

What alone can make the basic material of inflammable air hydrogen is the chemical action which it exerts on the oxygen. Only because, in this passage of the two kinds of air into the liquid state, both their elementary materials become mutually bound by each other, does *water* come into being, i.e., a transparent, odourless and tasteless liquid. By that, this reaction is distinguished from others, for instance, from the disintegration of azotic and vital air by electric sparks. The liquid which is precipitated here has the character of an *acid*, whose basis is the elementary material of the azotic air, namely, nitrogen. The hydrogen thus acts on the oxygen as the means of chemical bonding. This explains why the water derived from this process displays the character of an acid as soon as one of the two kinds of air is not wholly pure, but still contains heterogeneous parts along with its basic materials, or if, as in Priestley's experiments, the appropriate quantitative relation between the hydrogen burned and the related vital air is not observed.

Here, too, a wide field seems to open up for chemical investigation. The appearance of azotic air which is obtained from water-vapours when they are passed through a red-hot earthen tube has not yet been satisfactorily explained. This much is certain from the most convincing experiments, already performed in part before Priestley, that the external (atmospheric) air contributes to this production of azotic air. But *what* it actually provides has not hitherto been made out. What has also been affirmed about it is mere hypothesis. It is indeed *possible* that the azotic air *is merely forced in entirely from the outside* – that, as it were, it is derived merely from the atmospheric air decomposed by the burning charcoal used in the experiment. But the question always continues to arise as to where the water-vapours have come from in this experiment. Whatever may be the result of further investigations on this point, it is permissible, as long as these investigations have not been made, to propose further possibilities for research, which are certainly no more than possibilities at present, but deserve investigation, because they bring into connection many phenomena, which now are still isolated, and could even shed light over a much greater area by their application (to meteorology).

Chemistry will by no means continue to regard the basis of inflammable air simply as hydrogen, or the basis of azotic air merely as azote. Also, meteorology must sooner or later answer the question whether water in relation to our atmospheric cycle is as wholly inactive as it has hitherto been thought good to assume. So much is indeed certain, that pure water-gas, if such exists, could no more be distinguished by inner qualitative characteristics than the water from which it has arisen. But one may ask what would become of water if the inner relationship of its two basic materials were removed. So far we have only one example of that – the inflammable air which arises from the complete chemical *separation* of both. But one can very well think of still other chemical water-processes, which probably Nature does not neglect to use, for all that they are perhaps still unknown to us – an urgent summons to the chemist to investigate the basic material of water, where possible, more closely than has hitherto been done.

The theory of the kinds of air in general has its peculiar difficulties, so long as we remain as uncertain as we still are, to this very hour, about the *formation* of kinds of air, despite many investigations into it. That heat must enter into a *chemical* combination with the basic materials of the air-varieties in order to produce air is indeed almost universally assumed, but is nothing less than established. The main evidence is drawn from water-vapours, which, being destructible by cold and pressure, prove that the heat had only expanded them mechanically. Now since air can be destroyed neither by cold nor pressure, the heat is supposed to constitute a *chemical basic material* of the air, not to be separated from it by any merely mechanical means. That heat is a chemical *means* is beyond doubt. It can therefore *act* chemically without, for that reason, itself becoming a chemical *constituent* of a kind of air. Now if heat, where it generates mere vapours, in fact works merely mechanically as an expanding force, but where it generates air *dissolves* the particles of the air altogether, then in the last case it is acting chemically without on that account itself becoming a chemical element. In the first case it works *mechanically,* in the last *dynamically.* Therefore, in the first case it affects merely the *volume* of the fluid. Vapours are just for this reason also much lighter and far less dense than atmospheric air. Without this great *expansion* they could not persist at all in invisible form, while the air, in spite of its far greater density, remains permanently in this form. In the first case, therefore, the heat obviously acts merely by *separating* the air particles from one another; in the last, however, it acts by *dissolution,* through the fact that it *penetrates* the air-particles. We have naturally to accept a similar penetration of solid bodies by heat in order to explain how a body can be warmed. For if we think of the heat as distributed merely in the pores of the body, then it could very well *expand* the body, but not *warm* it.[2] So in this case we actually must assume *penetration* of the body by the heat, which is not even accompanied by a *dissolution*.

Water provides yet another example of this form of heat action. It is well known that water requires a large quantity of heat merely to become *liquid* (which does not raise its temperature). But water in the fluid state has a smaller volume than in the solid state – a proof that the heat in the water does not expand but *penetrates* its particles. On the other hand, as soon as the heat leaves the water, the fluid parts gradually congeal into more solid ones, in which the heat still acts at least as a *mechanically* expansive force, after it has ceased to act dynamically, or, if you will, chemically. It is known that salt dissolved in water does not crystallize until the water (and with it the heat) evaporates. Likewise, the regular shape of snowflakes and the rays in which ice crystallizes indicate an expansive force active in water, and the expansion of water in freezing is clearly nothing else but the last action – as it were, the last kick – of the departing heat.

[2] Cf. Kant's *Metaphysical Foundations of Natural Science*, p. 99 [Ellington, p.90].

Some Remarks on the History
of the Decomposition of Water
(Supplement to Chapter 3)

It is hard to imagine a more preposterous undertaking than to try to draft a universal theory of Nature from particular experiments; nevertheless, the whole of French chemistry is nothing else but such an attempt: But hardly, too, could the superior value of higher outlooks, directed upon the whole, over such as are based on individual cases, have been so thoroughly vindicated in the end as precisely in the history of this theory, especially of that part of it which touches the nature of water.

In the year 1791 de Luc wrote in a letter to Fourcroy as follows: "If the fundamental principle is conceded (that rain is formed, not merely out of clouds, but out of the air as such, and that, further, this formation is not explicable by a mutual encounter of oxygen and hydrogen), then the inference is unavoidable (that the atmospheric air has *water itself*, as ponderable substance, for its basis). This principle itself must be rejected, therefore; otherwise it is certain that the *twelve ounces* of water, which have been produced in your laboratory within several days, in no way proves the synthesis of water. For this meagre production of water has nothing at all in common with that of *huge downpours* which suddenly form in very dry air, nor with any one phenomenon of rain, which sooner or later will drown the *new physics* unless it can firmly provide against such things."[3]

It is known that Lichtenberg subscribed to quite the same principles; indeed, in the well-known Introduction, in which he stated his view of the new chemistry, he had already perceived, in the famous Amsterdam experiment, what was certainly more palpably recognized after him in the experiment set up with the voltaic pile. In his popular lectures he asks us merely to observe whether the electric matter does not rather decompose, and whether one part of it has not made in-

[3] The whole letter is worthy of attention. See Gren's *Journal of Physics*, vol. VII, no. 1, 1793, p. 134.

flammable air with the *water-vapour* and the other part made dephlogisticated air *with the same* water-vapour (Vide *loc. cit.,* p. xxix.)

In the discussion of the *dynamic process* in the *Journal of Speculative Physics,* vol. I, no. 2, p. 71, the following passage occurs: "It is evident from everything taken together how far one *might* say that negative electricity may be oxygen, namely, *not the ponderable* part of the so-called matter, but what potentiates the matter (in itself mere space-filling) into material, may be negative electricity. The excellent Lichtenberg asserted persistently, and, as it seems, without having any further basis for it than analogy, that the combination of the two kinds of air into water could rather be called a combination of two kinds of electricity. He is quite right. The active principle which actually combines under the crude chemical appearance is just positive and negative electricity, and hence the hermaphroditic water is simply the most original presentation of the two electricities in one whole. For I consider it an incontrovertibly certain proposition that the hydrogen – that is, once again, not *the ponderable part* of the so-called matter, but that which makes it into material – is positive electricity, that the hydrogen has exactly the opposite function to oxygen, namely this: to remove attractive force from the negative-electric body (by deoxidation) and thereby convert it to a positive-electric state. And so, therefore, the two substances, oxygen and hydrogen, would be the permanent and universal representatives of the potentiated attractive and repulsive forces."

Shortly thereafter in Germany J. W. Ritter carried out experiments with the voltaic pile, by which the hope was raised of making this kind of process even empirically observable in the so-called decomposition of water. In this connection the following has emerged:

1. That the great majority of physicists and chemists could not have understood the earlier statements of de Luc and Lichtenberg in the very least.

2. How blind and thoughtless till then were most of the accounts they had given about the facts they had observed. These they had held to be *the theory* of these facts themselves, to be *an actual knowledge of the inner process involved,* since their experiments, for instance, that they obtained in certain cases inflammable air from water, whereas another body was oxidized by means of the same water; or that they had obtained a certain quantity of water by burning the two kinds of air together, certainly remain to them standing unshaken (as, for that matter, de Luc in the above-quoted passage does not deny the fact of the twelve ounces), and these ideas, quite new to them, touched only the *physics* of the whole process, though they nonetheless believed, or let themselves be persuaded, that a total change in *chemistry* itself, *as*

such, was imminent. The empty chemical experimentalism of the French had exerted so oppressive an effect that there was not even the slightest inkling of a higher forum before which these phenomena could be brought. It is hardly to be doubted that anyone who had so much as asked himself, *what is it then that is involved in all so-called dissolution or composition in chemistry, or how does it proceed physically,* would also have seen that this reduction of the decomposition of water to one presentation thereof, and to one substance under different forms, is equally valid in regard to *all decomposition,* and is only an application of the universal formula thereof to the particular case; so that in the sense in which water is simple, so is all matter as such, and conversely, in the (ordinary) sense in which it can be said at all that matter decomposes and is again reconstituted, the same may be said of water as well.

We remark further in passing, with respect to the question touched on in the foregoing chapter, of the manner of combination of nitrogen and oxygen in the atmosphere, that the same can be answered only in a general construction of the relationships of the planets in the solar system, as to which we refer the reader to the presentation contained in the second issue of the first volume of the *New Journal for Speculative Physics* (Tübingen, Cotta), §VIII.

4

Of Electricity[1]

So far we have become acquainted with only one of Nature's forces, light and heat, which could be obstructed in its action only by the opposing stress of dead matter; now an entirely new phenomenon arouses our attention, in which activity seems to arise against activity, force against force. This, however, is also almost the only thing we know with certainty or confidence of the source of that remarkable phenomenon. We believe that we see divided forces existing and at work, and the most exact investigation of which the phenomenon admits has made it almost indubitable. But what essentially the nature and constitution of those two forces may be, whether they are the manifestation of one and the same original force, which is only divided against itself by some third cause, or whether two originally contending forces, which in their normal state some third force holds bound together, are here unfettered – we know not how – and set in mutual conflict, these are questions to which as yet there is still no reliable answer.

Perhaps there is no phenomenon in Nature which has been observed with such precision, in all its relationships, in all the individual variations that it takes, as the phenomenon of which we speak. The swift evanescence of electrical phenomena compelled the scientists to devise artificial means which put them in a position to excite those appearances *as often* as they pleased and as *strongly* or *weakly* as was appropriate to their purpose on each occasion. The inventions of the machine by which the greatest possible electricity is excited, and of the semi-conducting plate by which the weakest is still made detectable, were received with almost equal gratitude. The triumph of their machinery, however, was the block of resin, which, by special contrivances, restrains the electricity longer than any other instrument. As a

[1] Whoever ventures to set up a new hypothesis must not merely adduce the *results*. For the subject itself, and for him, it is more advantageous if he pursues the whole course of his investigations to the point at which no other possibility is left, than just that which he now proposes for investigation.

result the theory of electricity has become almost more an enumeration of the machines and instruments, which have been invented on its behalf, than an explanation of its phenomena. But the more appearances and observations were multiplied with the help of these inventions, the less they fitted into the confines of the hypotheses so far available, and one can actually maintain that, except for the one great first principle of this theory and some propositions subordinate to it, not one single universal principle is to be found in the whole theory of electricity.

After having given up the classification of bodies into electric and non-electric, and replaced it by another, into conductors, non-conductors and semi-conductors, we have still found no law, as yet, whereby bodies are conductors or non-conductors. Bodies which had been relegated to *one* class, further experience soon shifted into both. Changes of quantity, temperature, etc., also make changes in the conductivity of substances. Incandescent glass conducts; dry wood is a semi-conductor; fully desiccated or wholly fresh, it is a conductor. Even the best non-conductors, like glass, can become conductors through frequent use. But far less still do we know where this total difference among substances really comes from, and even now there are numerous other possible ways of presenting it. The reason for it has been sought, now in the greater or lesser attraction, now in the greater or lesser capacity of these substances towards electric matter. Perhaps it would have been better to combine *both*. Are there substances which show neither attraction nor capacity towards the electric matter (we must in any case express ourselves thus, so long as we take the phenomenon as it strikes the senses)? All materials would belong here which are not distinguished by any internal qualities, like glass, the transparency of which already betrays how devoid it is of all inner qualitative characteristics. Do these substances, perhaps, for that very reason, serve best to accumulate electricity, which, attracted by nothing, rests in them as if dormant, until another substance, which shows attraction for it, comes within its effective range?

Are there other substances besides these which strongly attract this electric matter, without having proportionate capacity for it? The maximum which they could take up of it at every single point would be reached at once; the equally strong attraction everywhere would lead the matter away over the whole surface; just as easily as they had taken up the electric matter they would lose it to other substances.

A third class would be those substances which display just as much capacity as attraction towards the electric matter, in which it is therefore just as easily excited as restrained. To this class would belong, perhaps, all substances which are easily melted by heat. These are no more than possibilities, which perhaps only acquire probability or certainty in conjunction with other demonstrated propositions.

Hitherto we have still been in the same uncertainty with respect to the *excitation* of electrical phenomena. Is it the mere *mechanism* of *rubbing,* which sets the electrical matter in the interior of bodies in motion? Or is it heat excited simultaneously by the friction which first acts upon the substance, making it more elastic or even decomposing it? Or – well, I do not want to exhaust in advance all the possibilities which we are bound to hit upon in the course of investigation.

One need hardly do more than read the first and simplest experiments which Aepinus performed with tourmaline[2] to be convinced of how ignorant we still are with respect to these questions. As soon as this mineral is heated it attracts and repels in accordance with the laws of electricity; it unites in itself opposite electricities; heated unevenly it exchanges (so to express myself) its electric poles, and in general seems to be as nearly related to the magnet as to amber.

As yet we can distinguish the different electricities in no other way than by their mutual attraction. At first it was sought to distinguish them according to the substances in which they were excited. But by now we actually know of only one substance that would not be capable of both electricities.[3] Even glass, if it is frosted, or has a rough surface, or (according to Canton's assurance) has been rubbed long enough for it to lose its gleam and transparency, is capable of negative electricity. This much, on the other hand, remains sure, that certain substances rubbed against others always display the same electricity. But of this there are only isolated instances and to this very hour, as far as I know, there is still no definite assertion that would deserve the name of a law whereby different electricities are aroused. This we know, that the electricity of completely similar non-conductors = 0, provided that each is rubbed against the other equally vigorously over the whole surface. But this is a presumption which can rarely be fulfilled; it therefore comes about that this rule seldom applies. But these minor observations can still suffice for certain conclusions.

My first comment is that if we were to assume two *original* electricities opposed to each other, the *laws* according to which now the one and now the other is excited would perhaps not be discovered at all. For in order to think of both electrical matters as at rest, we should

---

[2] Aepinus's two tracts, *On the Similarity of Electrical and Magnetic Force* and *Of the Properties of Tourmaline.* Translated into German, Gräz, 1771. In the former work there is also the report of a sulphur-electrophore of which the author had already made use.

[3] See the table in Cavallo, *On Electricity.* German translation, p. 19.

have to let them bind each other reciprocally. In that case both would have to be excitable in every body. Now every substance that we know today is in fact capable of both electricities; but by what means do we get these *distinct* electricities? That, for example, the rubbed body has a smooth or a rough surface can have no influence on the differing excitability of *heterogeneous* electricities, that is, such as are distinguished from each other, not by quantity, by *more* or by *less,* but by their inner *quality.* At most, this surface has influence on the mere mechanism of the rubbing, which in this case occurs with greater friction. But that at most brings about a difference in the *ease* of excitation. And does this greater or lesser facility of excitation make a difference between the electricities themselves? I shall just give some examples. Why is the electricity of the same body often *different,* depending on whether I have rubbed it *more vigorously* or *more gently?* Why does a different degree of dryness bring forth different *electricities?* Moist bodies are conductors, that is, they evince strong attraction towards electricity; but they conduct *both* electricities *equally strongly;* so here, it seems, we are left with nothing else which might explain the difference of the electricity aroused in moist and in dry bodies, save the greater *facility* with which it is aroused in the *latter.* Thus here also it is again the difference in the ease of excitation which seems to make the difference in the electricities. The question, however, arises, what then makes the difference in the ease of excitation, and with this question we shall, perhaps, come nearer to the fact of the matter.

In bodies in their usual state, electricity is at rest. This inactivity has been explained in various ways. The electrical matter, says Franklin, is then equally distributed everywhere and so in equilibrium with itself. According to this hypothesis, all electrical phenomena are initiated only when two bodies, rubbed together, acquire more or less electricity than they have under normal conditions. The only active one in this case is the *positive* electricity, that is, the electrical matter accumulated in one body. But there are phenomena in which negative electricity also seems to be not inactive. This is the basis of Symmer's hypothesis of two *positive* opposed electrical matters. But the observations, to which this theory appeals, do not necessarily presuppose these electricities to be *originally* opposed to each other. They could very well be set at variance only by the means which we employ to excite them, and yet both appear *positive,* that is, *active.*

Such a hypothesis would combine the advantages of Franklin's and Symmer's, while avoiding the difficulties of both. Also, the system of Nature becomes obviously simpler if we assume that the cause of electrical phenomena – the force, the activity, or whatever we may call it—which seems thrown into conflict in electrical phenomena, is *one* originally quiescent force, which in its unity with itself works perhaps merely mechanically, and first acquires a higher efficacy only when Nature divides it within itself for special purposes. If that which causes electrical phenomena is originally *one* force or one matter (for both at present are only hypothetically valid), then it is intelligible why opposite electricities fly towards each other—why divided forces strive to reunite. It is obvious that both are actual only in their *conflict*, that only the mutual effort towards unification gives to each a separate existence of its own.

If this hypothesis is true, then one can understand the opposition of the two only by presupposing a *third* by which they have been set in conflict and which prevents their unification. Now this third could be sought nowhere else but in the bodies themselves. What difference then do bodies display which exhibit different electricities when they are rubbed together?

What may strike us at first sight is the different *elasticity* of these bodies. Since the phenomenon of opposed electricities might be explained by an *unequal excitation* of one and the same force, it would be understandable why the electricity in the less elastic body should be more weakly excited (negative), and more strongly (positive) in the more elastic one. The analogy can actually be pushed very far. It is known that friction as such increases or decreases elasticity, depending on whether it occurs proportionately or disproportionately. Everything which increases or decreases elasticity seems also to promote or prevent the excitation of electricity. A substance excessively expanded by heat loses its elasticity. Thus incandescent glass becomes a conductor. A body loses elasticity if it becomes moist. The same results with the electricity. It is more weakly excited if the body is moist, and a different degree of dryness also produces different electricities. Polished and opaquely ground, pure and impure glass differ, so it seems, merely by greater or lesser elasticity, and yet each gives different electricities. And one only needs to have heard, say, of Du Fay's resinous and vitreous electricity to make the inference: the brittle glass is more elastic than the resin, therefore, etc.

One might almost marvel that no scientist has yet arrived at the idea that the electric matter might possibly be the fluid, which some physicists take to circulate in the bodies, in order to explain their elasticity! This would admittedly be to explain an uncertainty by something more uncertain still, but it would by no means be the first case of this sort.

This entire line of thought is therefore provisionally of service only in drawing attention generally to the fact that, by investigating the varying relation of bodies to electricity, or of electricity to bodies, we may perhaps be able, gradually, to reach firm conclusions about the nature of these phenomena. This is at the same time the surest means of guarding against a *lazy Philosophy of Nature,* which believes it has explained everything if it postulates the causes of phenomena as basic materials in the bodies, from which they then emerge (*tamquam Deus ex machina*) only when needed to explain some phenomenon in the shortest and most convenient way.

We do better, therefore, to consider the varying relation of electricity to different bodies rather more closely than has hitherto been done. Every discovery we make about the difference of the two electricities, is at the same time a discovery about electricity as such. The question is therefore this: When two bodies are rubbed together, by what characteristic is that which becomes positively electrified distinguished from the other, which becomes negatively electrified, or *vice versa?*

Without doubt, the goal will most quickly be reached if we choose *extremes* among substances, for example, glass and sulphur, glass and metal, resin and metal, and so on.

Thus, glass and sulphur rubbed together give – the former positive, the latter negative – electricity. By what qualities are these two substances distinguished? For very many external qualitative relations, glass, so it seems, is inert.[4] Light makes its way through it unhindered, and the refraction that it undergoes in glass is regulated merely in proportion to the *density*. Water-vapour passed through incandescent glass tubes does not change its nature because the glass is incapable of attracting any of its basic materials, or of causing any decomposition of the water. Glass is only smeltable in fire, not combustible. Sulphur, on the other hand, is a substance which betrays by colour, odour and taste, that it possesses intrinsic qualities. Still more does it distinguish itself by its inflammability, by the strong attraction it displays towards the oxygen of vital air. Likewise glass and sealing-wax, glass and resin, etc.

But if we compare combustible with combustible substances, say hair with sealing-wax, wood with sulphur, and so on, what transpires? Hair and sealing-wax rubbed together become, the former positively, the latter negatively, electrified. Wood with sulphur show, the former positive, the latter negative, electricity. How do these substances differ – especially with respect to their inflammability – a relationship to which our attention has already been drawn by the first experience. Answer: Both are combustible; both show attraction for oxygen – but those

---

[4] Completely denuded of all inner qualities. [First edition.]

which become negatively electrified are more inflammable and display more attraction towards oxygen. Expressed in accordance with Franklin's theory, the greater or lesser electricity stands in inverse relation to the greater or lesser of the combustible matter in the substance (as I put it for the sake of brevity).

If we compare with the *metals* all the substances hitherto compared with *one another*, then sealing-wax and sulphur – the same substances which previously became negative with others – with metals become positively electrified. If we compare glass with metal, then here too glass still displays positive electricity and metal, negative. Metals, however, are distinguished by nothing so much as their affinity for oxygen, which is great enough to make them capable of calcination (compare Chapter 1 on this point).

So this is the conclusion we are entitled to draw: *That which makes substances negatively electric is at the same time that which makes them combustible*, or, in other words: *Of two substances, that which has the greatest affinity for oxygen always becomes negatively electrified.*[5] Therefore (this conclusion follows immediately from the foregoing, that is, if we assume in general an electrical *matter*, and do not seek even more arbitrarily to make this matter an absolute, different from all others known): *The basis of negative electrical matter is either oxygen itself, or some other basic substance wholly homogeneous with it.*[6]

Looking now at the way in which electricity is excited, there is nothing present besides the two rubbed bodies except the surrounding air. No oxygen can come out of the bodies – so does it come out of the air? But oxygen is obtained from the air only through decomposition. *Is*

---

[5] I do not deny that there are apparent exceptions, for example, as soon as one rubs conductors with non-conductors, because one and the same law can, of course, be differently modified according as two bodies of the same class or of different classes are set in conflict. In general, however, the concept of *combustibility*, of degrees of affinity to oxygen, still admits of great ambiguity, so long as it is not determined how the former and the latter are assessed.

[This note appears in the first edition thus: "I do not deny that there are apparent exceptions, as soon as one rubs conductors with non-conductors. Metal, for instance, has obviously greater affinity for oxygen than silk ribbon, which nevertheless rubbed with it displays *negative* electricity. But in this case the metal shows *no* electricity *at all*, a proof that it has served here merely as *conductor*, which has more easily conducted the positive electrical matter than the negative, and therefore has transferred the latter to the non-conducting substance."]

[6] For this reason it becomes a very remarkable observation that – other things being equal – the *colour* of the body determines the difference of the electricities. According to the experiments of Symmer (in *Philosophical Transactions* [1759], Vol. LI, Pt. 1. No. 36) black and white ribbons, for example, rubbed against each other become, the former negative, the latter positive. To find this explicable one must remember the connection between the colour of the body and its relation to oxygen.

the air therefore also decomposed, say, in electrification? But then we should
have to have caused the phenomenon of combustion by it. So how do
electrification and combustion differ? The latter never results without
chemical decomposition of the air. Moreover this cannot occur in electrification. Besides, electricity, at least as a rule, is excited by mere
friction, that is, by a merely *mechanical* means.

Therefore: *As a chemical decomposition of the air causes the phenomenon
of combustion, so a mechnical disintegration of it* (by which we here understand, in general, any which is simply non-chemical) *causes the phenomenon of electricity –* Or: what combusion is from a *chemical* point of view,
electrification is from a *mechanical* point of view. It is well known that
friction excites not only electricity but always heat as well, and in
certain cases even fire. The savage seldom makes his fire otherwise,
and in the language of savage peoples in the past and occasionally
even now (as in Arabic) there are still words by which they designate
the two rubbing-sticks. But the stronger or weaker friction seems to
make all the difference – as to whether heat and electricity – or also
fire – is produced. If the friction causes a *total,* and *to that extent chemical,* disintegration of the air, fire must ensue; a *lesser,* and to that
extent merely *mechanical,* decomposition produces *heat,* and, if both
bodies are non-conductors or insulated, and, *which is the main thing,*
have a *different* relation to *oxygen –* (for the rubbing of like bodies with
like yields o) – *electricity.* Thus I do not deny that a chemical disintegration of the air can be occasioned even by mere friction. In being
rubbed the body can be converted, in whatever way it may be, to a
state in which it attracts oxygen more strongly, and thereby fire can
result. But I do deny that this occurs with electricity; indeed there are
cases in which rubbing could obviously have caused heat merely by
mechanical decomposition of the air.

I could conclude here and leave the further application to others.
Nor do I claim to have covered everything by the following explanations. It is still possible that a number of other factors (perhaps azotic
air) contribute to the electrical phenomena. That must be decided by
experiments, whose performance I must leave to others more fortunate. The following, therefore, makes claim to no other than hypothetical validity. For it rests on the assumption that electrical phenomena owe their origin to vital air *alone,* which I am in no position to
prove (as distinct from merely suggesting its *possibility*).

So what, then, is the nature of that mechanical decomposition of vital
air, whereby, on this assumption, electrical phenomena arise? It follows
from the above that the decomposition cannot be *total,* that is, cannot be
preceded by any complete separation of the heat and the ponderable
matter. So if two dissimilar substances are rubbed together, the air,

which, trapped between the two bodies, is exposed to the full pressure
of the rubbing, deposits the greater part of its ponderable basic material, which is never fully detached, however, from heat, on whichever of
the two bodies displays the greater attraction for oxygen. The rest of
the air, made more mobile – more elastic – by this loss, accumulates as
positive electricity on the other body, until such time as it leaves the
latter, attracted more strongly by a third. Thus, if the machine is a glass
cylinder, the air will largely deposit its oxygen on the rubbing fabric.
Hence the advantage of amalgam, especially quicksilver amalgam, with
which the former is overlaid. The rest of the displaced air, however,
clings to the glass cylinder and rests half-attracted until another body
comes into its vicinity and conducts it off. Where the rubbing fabric
touches the cylinder, or where the latter connects with the first conductor, we see *light,* a clear proof that here a decomposition of air has taken
place. If the machine consists of a cylinder of resin, exactly the opposite
process will take place. (It is questionable what sort of rubbing material
is most suitable in this case.)

What seems to have great influence on the phenomena of electrical
matter is the pressure of the surrounding air which it has to undergo.
Too weak to decompose the air, and yet attracted by it, it lingers much
longer on the solid body on which it has accumulated. If it leaps from
one body to another, then it encounters even here the same resistance
of the air, which it nevertheless overcomes. For that very reason, it
traverses a space in which the air has been rarified with astonishing
rapidity, and instantly decomposes all the air enclosed within it. If an
electric brush discharge is introduced into a glass tube with rarefied
air, the whole space is instantly filled with light; a spark that traverses
it gives the effect of lightning. If the same glass tube is rubbed on the
outside, the positive electricity excited penetrates from without and
lights up the entire space.

That electricity can be excited under the bell-jar of a vacuum-
pump,[7] proves nothing against the hypothesis assumed, partly because we are unable to produce an *airless* space, and partly because the
experiments performed on it, according to the conceptions of electricity then prevailing, were probably not conducted with the care that
would be needed for them to prove anything against the hypothesis.[8]

---

[7] Erxleben's *Theory of Nature,* p. 487.

[8] According to M. Pictet's findings, much more heat is actually excited by equal
friction in rarefied than in normal air. (*Experimentation with Fire,* German trans.
Tübingen, 1790, pp. 184ff.) It should not be forgotten here that if indifference of
the bodies involved in the process is the prime condition for the arousal of heat by
friction, the rarefied air, as itself different and as means of differencing, prevents
the above-mentioned excitation far less than denser air. On the other hand, the

An experiment conducted in pure vital air would surely be far more conclusive.

The resistance of the air probably also has great influence on electrical attraction and repulsion. (That it also occurs in rarefied air proves nothing to the contrary.) The electrical matter would escape with far greater velocity, if it were able to overcome the resistance of the air. It therefore strives to make *way* through the air, and is naturally drawn to where it finds the least resistance. But it finds far less resistance where it meets with kindred electricity than where it has to overcome the whole reciprocal connectedness of the air particles. It is equally conceivable, however, that *similar* electricities offer more resistance to each other than the air can exert against them, and that they repel each other *on that account.* Dissimilar electricities, however, are also *unequally elastic,* so that they can interchange their elasticities, and for that reason attract each other. All opposing electricity has not vanished, but this striving and counterstriving between the two had momentarily extended their separate existence.

From that also there now follows the great law of *distribution* and of the *electrical sphere of action* which alone explains almost all the phenomena of electricity. Positive electricity causes a separation among the adjacent air particles and, owing to its nisus towards combination, attracts the ponderable parts of the air; negative electricity does likewise in that it attracts the elastic particles to itself. Hence, if a non-electrified body comes into the atmosphere of a positively electric one, negative and positive electricity always arise at once; negative on the side turned towards the positive, positive on the opposite side, and *vice versa;* and this distribution is propagated ever the more widely, the stronger the original electricity is, and the larger, therefore, is its sphere of action as well. Hence the electrical zones which Aepinus especially has noticed.

So no electricity of one kind exists without the other; for each is only what it is in contrast to the other; neither is generated unless the other is generated with it.[9] On that alone rests the whole mechanism of the Leyden jar, the electrophore and the condenser.

condition for excitement of electricity is the opposite of that just given, with which other observations of that learned gentleman closely agree, e.g., p. 189, that friction in rarefied air produces no sparks, but only a phosphorescent gleam at the points of contact of the two bodies, similar to that seen when two hard stones are struck together in the dark. M. Pictet's apparatus can very easily be used to test the hypothesis proposed above.

[9] In the phenomena of division there can at least be doubt that all electricity comes out of the air, since these phenomena tend to appear most frequently and strikingly in *conducting* substances, which thus also *themselves* become electrified with the greatest difficulty.

Another hallmark which distinguishes negative and positive electricity is the different light of each, the glowing point, the constant phenomenon of the first, and the radiating pencil, the phenomenon of the second. Yet the latter appears only if a sharp point is held opposite the electrified body. It is well known that there is as yet no agreement about the electrical conductivity of the points. M. de Luc (in his *Ideas on Meteorology*) has shown that the electric matter goes round a circular conductor in a circle. Hence the round shape of the conductor from which we try to draw a spark opposes great obstacles to its arousal. So if its electricity is withdrawn from such a conductor by a blunt object, it breaks out violently and in the form of a spark. But if a sharp point is placed against it, or a projection raised on its surface, the circuit of the electrical matter is more easily interrupted, it flows almost noiselessly with a gentle hiss out of the raised projection or to the point held against it, presuming that the body is positively electrified; for, if it is negative, the point appears, in its turn, at the opposite tip of the conical ray. This difference of the electric light is very well explained by our supposition. For it is intelligible that the freer electricity (the positive) discharges more easily (in rays), while the opposite, whose ponderable parts are far more strongly attracted by the body, is extracted from it only *with difficulty,* and appears *always* as a *point,* just as the positive only discharges in rays if a sharp point is applied to it, i.e., if it is conducted off very *easily.* The *figures of Lichtenberg* would appear to rest on the same law, since when they have arisen from positive electricity, they show rays emanating in straight lines, but are blunt and rounded in the opposite case.

There can now be no further question as to the differing relation of bodies to electricity. A body which displays little or no attraction for the basic material of vital air is the most suitable for the accumulation of positive electricity. Yet a body of which the opposite holds can also become positively electric, provided that the other body with which it is rubbed has *still greater* affinity for oxygen.

Since the electric matter is nothing else but a decomposed vital air, all bodies which display attraction for heat and oxygen will display attraction for it.[10]

But among the bodies which attract electric matter, a second difference can occur in regard to capacity. Those which show great attraction, indeed, but little capacity for electric matter, will conduct it; in the rest the opposite will occur. Hence the difference between *con-*

---

[10] Cf. *Mémoire sur l'analogie, qui se trouve entre la production et les effets de l'électricité et de la chaleur de même qu'entre la propriété des corps, de conduire le fluide électrique et de recevoir la chaleur,* by M. Achard (*Rozier* vol. XXII, April, 1785).

ductors, semi-conductors and non-conductors, of which we have already
spoken above, is due to the combined relations of attraction and capacity which the bodies display for electricity.

The origin of electrical phenomena now makes it intelligible how
and why electricity is one of the strongest means of decomposition,
which Nature employs as often perhaps in the large as in the small.
Electric matter forsakes one combination only to enter into another.
Free, but unused to freedom, it strives to separate what opposing
force holds combined, and commonly perishes in the attempt. More
exact observations have shown that, with respect to the path it takes,
electricity follows the same laws as light, that among different bodies it
seeks out that which either conducts it fastest, or is *the most decompos-
able,* and that only where everything is equal in this respect does it
hasten to the *denser* substance. From this we may understand the
destruction it causes in the interior of bodies, where it separates with
violence what was formerly combined, or combines what was formerly
averse. Intelligible too is its violent effect on the animal body, whose
innermost parts it penetrates, rushing irresistibly to the muscles, the
seat of animal contractility, everywhere to combine what in the economy of a living body ought eternally to be separate. Intelligible, likewise, its great efficacy in reviving extinct vitality in the whole body, or
in individual members thereof, because, momentarily at least, it again
separates that with whose separation life begins—a phenomenon to
which our investigations will later return, and whose explanation will
be found in the hypothesis here proposed.

It is no less intelligible that the electric spark calcines and restores
metals,[11] while other metals, which are incapable of calcination and
merely sublimate in the heat of the burning-focus, it converts into
vapour—the latter, be it noted, *without diminution of the vital air* in
which it occurred, proving that here the electricity alone was able to
do what could otherwise be expected only from a disintegration of the
vital air. No wonder that even in mephitic kinds of air (so van Marum
tells us, in nitrogen, inflammable air and carbonic acid gas) the result
is the same; proving that electrical matter yields the basic material
required for the calcination of metals, no less than vital air is otherwise
accustomed to do.

Priestley found that atmospheric air is at once *diminished* by the
spark. Since the litmus tincture, with which the bell-jar is coated (on
the surface, at least), changes colour, it is plain that a decomposition is
here occurring of both types of air, the vital and the azotic, and that

---

[11] Question: Is no difference to be seen here between positive and negative
electricity?

nitric acid is deposited from atmospheric air, exactly as it was (in Cavendish's experiment) from an artificial mixture of azotic and pure vital air. The electric spark extracted from lime water precipitates the lime. The Dutch physicists have succeeded in decomposing water by means of the electric spark.[12]

It is evident, however, in at least some of these experiments (for example, in the calcination of metals in mephitic types of air by the electric spark) that the electricity did not act merely *mechanically,* and hence it is credible that in all these experiments it was itself contributing *chemically.* I do not know whether, when the effects of both electricity and vital air are so completely similar, a still more convincing proof of their identity can be required. It is understandable that the decomposing-power of electricity must be doubly strong, since it is at the same time *force* and *medium,* because it is equally closely related, on the one hand, to fire and, on the other, to the basic material of the air which must contribute to all decompositions.

If electricity is so powerful a means of decomposition, it cannot remain unused even on the large scale. At the moment when Nature is most actively at work, the oft-repeated drama of the thunderstorm begins. An electric fluid undoubtedly penetrates our very earth, as soon as she has cast off the fetters of winter. Hence those stirrings of the vital force, which with the first rays of the spring sun, seem to penetrate all that lives and vegetates; hence the rapid universal germination in the realm of the organic, and the new life which seems, as with one breath, to rejuvenate everything in Nature. The more strongly the electrical matter accumulates in the free space of the heavens, the more palpable become these movements in the interior of the earth, and at this moment it actually seems that not just the laws of gravity alone, but living electric forces, are drawing us towards the sun. Years of thunderstorms are not infrequently years of great earthquakes, in any case they are the most fruitful. Mutually distant volcanoes not infrequently erupt at the same time, and the water on the surface and in the interior of the earth is perhaps the swiftest vehicle of electric currents. The vibration produced by the great electrical explosions seems to work not merely mechanically.[13] Undoubtedly it causes beneficial chemical revolutions, not only in the vegetable kingdom, at least, but also in the interior of the earth.

After all the investigations so far made, the origin of atmospheric

---

[12] Perhaps it is easier to explain by the proposed hypothesis what is otherwise not so easily explicable (cf. Gren's *Journal,* vol. III, no. 1, p. 14), namely, why in the decomposition of water by electric sparks, inflammable air is generated *without vital air.*

[13] Quo bruta tellus . . . concutitur. Horat.

electricity still remains a riddle. That it is also excited in the upper atmosphere according to the same law by which we are able to excite it, is surely beyond doubt. But the question is by what means Nature causes such a large-scale mechanical decomposition of the air. That there *can* be very many of these means is, after all, believable. But the question is which of them Nature *actually* uses, according to the observations which, from our standpoint, we are able to make.

It is certain that where vapours and mists are engendered electricity is also produced. Where we fail to notice it, then either it is too weak or the deficiency of our instruments is to blame. Cavallo found that if water is poured on to glowing coals in an insulated metal container, this container shows signs of negative electricity; M. de Saussure found that not infrequently positive electricity is produced. Sr. Volta, relying on similar findings, assumed that in the atmosphere the opposite process occurs; when vapour again becomes water, electricity is liberated, etc. M. de Luc[14] raises the objection against him that this would then be *generally* valid, and that whenever vapour condensed to water, electricity would have to appear. Volta could allow this objection, for in fact there is seldom rain without electricity; that at times it does not register on our electroscopes proves nothing to the contrary.

These remarks are sufficient, perhaps, to yield some conclusions about the generation of electricity on a large scale. That where vapours and mists arise or are condensed, a disintegration of the air occurs, is intelligible, because in the first case an expenditure of heat is necessary, and in the other heat is liberated. But it is equally evident that this decomposition is not a *total* chemical decomposition. Hence this breakdown of the air by vapour is, approximately at least, the same as we are accustomed to excite by friction, which is to say, a merely partial, and to that extent mechanical, decomposition. This decomposition also undoubtedly goes on far more often than we imagine. Lightning breaks out of the smoke plumes of Vesuvius, and we should be aware of something similar in all smoke if the excited electricity were not too weak. It can generate in every vapour, except that it cannot have an effect like that of the electricity engendered by large clouds extending over broad stretches of land. An electric storm, indeed, never arises without clouds, at least whenever thunder is heard clouds form, and it often happens that storm and clouds are present at the same moment. So where vapours condense as clouds, electricity can be generated, not only in the region of air from which they condense, but also in the lower levels to which they sink, because in both a

[14] *Idées sur la Météorologie.* vol. II, §644.

decomposition of the air goes on, whereby the generation of opposite electricities in the atmosphere is likewise explicable.

Meanwhile, we need by no means limit ourselves to this single possibility. Electricity can be produced wherever no *total* decomposition of the air (as with fire) takes place, and the attention of the scientist, once alerted, will soon be able, with the help of the newly invented instruments, to discover many other examples beyond those already known, in confirmation of this principle.

The most beneficial effect of the great electrical explosions on our atmosphere is undoubtedly the decomposition which they cause in it. The air of the lowest levels of the atmosphere is full of a host of alien ponderable components, which gradually drive the purer air upwards. Thence, in large measure at least, comes the ominousness which precedes every thunderstorm, and the sultry state into which everything then seems to fall. Perhaps even the more abundant production of vital air in summer has a great influence on the creation of thunderstorms. The result of such a storm is that the heterogeneous parts are precipitated out of the air, and that the two kinds of air of which the atmosphere consists are more intimately mixed. The refreshing coolness after the storm is partly due to the attenuated air, on which light can no longer act as it does upon the denser, and partly also to the expenditure of heat which is at once incurred for the copious downpour of rain, so that often the full effect of a thunderstorm on our atmospheric cycle is only completed by a long-lasting fall of rain.

The hypothesis so far put forward about the cause of electrical phenomena cannot be called entirely new. One already finds traces of it in earlier scientists, whose language need only be translated into that of contemporary chemistry and physics in order to uncover the germ of this hypothesis in their thought. Thus Dr Priestley claimed to have discovered, by electrical experiments which he conducted with various kinds of air, that the electric spark causes a phlogistical process in them. In accordance with his system, he therefore conjectured that electricity is either phlogiston itself or at least contains phlogiston. And he thought to vindicate his hypothesis still further by the observation that what is common to all conducting substances, even water (which Priestley nevertheless excepts), is phlogiston. But that they owe their conducting property only to phlogiston, he concluded from the fact that with phlogiston they retain that property, and otherwise lose it.[15] That Priestley undertook to explain electricity—a phenomenon

---

[15] *Observations on Different Kinds of Air*, vol. II, Sects. 12, 13. Cavallo, *op. cit.*, chaps. II, III.

whose causes were unknown – by an even more unknown and precarious principle, namely, phlogiston, was certainly not the main reason why his hypothesis – admittedly repeated here and there, but only seldom openly adopted or even defended – no longer found approval. Priestley's remark, that the common constituent of all conducting substances is phlogiston, retains its value in any case, for the *fact* is correct, only the *explanation* is false. But where this hypothesis fails is that, even with the surest conviction that electrical matter is either phlogiston itself or a constituent of it, we are still very far from explaining the electrical phenomena.

It is an unnecessary labour which many have given themselves to prove how altogether differently fire and electricity act. Everybody knows that, who has once seen or heard anything of either of them. But our mind strives towards *unity* in the system of its knowledge. It does not tolerate a special principle being thrust upon it for every single phenomenon, and it believes that it sees *Nature* only where it discovers the greatest simplicity of laws amid the greatest variety of phenomena, and the most stringent parsimony of means in the highest prodigality of effects. Therefore every idea – even hitherto rough and unelaborated – deserves attention so long as it tends towards simplification of principles, and if it serves no other purpose, yet it serves at least as a stimulus to inquiring for oneself, and to tracing out the hidden course of Nature.

Nor should it be supposed that this idea has never been further pursued or elaborated than it was by Priestley. Henly (the same to whom we owe the well-known electrometer) assumed, as the result of various experiments he had performed, that electric matter is neither phlogiston nor fire itself, but yet a different modification of both – all those phenomena are nothing but different states through which the same principle runs, and in which it displays ever new and different appearances. He based himself primarily on the following observations: that substances which contain the same quantity of phlogiston, like metal, when rubbed together, display little or no electricity; that *a certain degree* of friction produces electricity, but a more vigorous rubbing, *fire and no electricity;* that bodies which contain a greater amount of phlogiston, when rubbed against others which contain less of it, become negatively electrified, because (as he explains it according to his assumption – falsely, of course) they let their surplus of electrical matter pass over to the other body. Thus he says, for example, that vegetable substances, especially aromatic herbs, when rubbed on a cloth become negative, and animal substances positive, because the former contain far more phlogiston than the latter, and so *give up* electrical matter to other substances, while the latter absorb it. Now from these observations Henly concluded that phlogiston, electricity and fire are merely different states of the same element, the first being its *quiescent* state, the second the *first* degree of its efficacy, and the last the state of its *vigorous motion*.[16]

I shall not now pursue the history of these hypotheses (besides, anybody can inform himself on the subject from such works as Gehler's *Dictionary* and others). I shall have reached my goal if the reader, on the one hand, perceives in these examples the general effort to simplify the principles of Nature and, on the other, takes note of the fact that, since the new discoveries about the nature of fire, light and heat have gradually become ever more certain and assured, we also have a better right, with our more reliable principles, to undertake afresh the same endeavour that was previously ventured upon with more imperfect principles.

The appearance of light in the electrical experiments was actually a directive from Nature to seek out a unity of principles between the two phenomena. Thus the hypothesis about electricity which M. de Luc has put forward in his *Ideas on Meteorology* is fully analogous to his hypothesis about light. Here again he distinguishes the *fluidum deferens* (*fluide déferent*) of electricity (light) from the electrical matter, and, if I am not mistaken, he takes the former for the cause of *positive*, and the latter for that of *negative* electricity. Moreover, the specific odour pervading a room in which electrification occurs, the acid-astringent taste that is sensed when one puts an electrode on the tongue, could long since have made it apparent that decompositions occur with electricity, or that the electrical matter stands, or has stood, in combination with a ponderable basic material before it was excited. Perhaps Herr Kratzenstein was induced by this to declare that electrical matter consists of phlogiston and an acid. Councillor Lichtenberg, to whom I am indebted for this reference, not long ago *proposed* to make electrical matter consist of oxygen, hydrogen and caloric.[17] Earlier La Metherie had already alleged that electrical matter is nothing other than a kind of inflammable air. Also M. de Saussure seemed inclined to regard the electric fluid as the result of a combination of the element of fire with some other, as yet unknown, principle. This, he says, would be a fluid similar to inflammable air, but far subtler.[18] With this hypothesis our own is so far, at least, in agreement, that it permits positive electricity to arise from vital air by a *deposition of oxygen* on one of the substances.

[16] Cf. Cavallo, *op. cit.,* chap. II.
[17] Preface to the 6th edition of Erxleben's *Theory of Nature,* p. xxxi.
[18] *Voyages dans les Alpes,* vol. III, §222.

Still more remarkable in this connection are the experiments performed by van Marum to show that caloric is present in the electric fluid.[19] It is thereby established that if a thermometer bulb is held in an electric current, the mercury rises, and that the reason for this cannot lie in a decomposition of the atmospheric air; that moreover non-elastic fluids (like water, alcohol, ammonia, etc.) are converted by electricity into elastic, gaseous, ones. The result of these experiments, which is in full agreement with the proposed hypothesis, is important: "It is very evident (so van Marum concludes the description of his experiments),[20] that electric fluid is not caloric itself; for if, where we see it pass from one body to the other as a spark, it were merely caloric liberated by friction, then it would have to heat the bodies through which it goes. But since the experiments described demonstrate that bodies are not heated in the least, even though the quantity of electrical fluid they take up is very considerable in proportion to their mass, it is clear that the electric fluid, which we see going in the form of a spark from one body to the other, is not caloric *alone*. These experiments therefore permit us to assume that the caloric which occurs in the electric fluid is even there combined with another substance which prevents it, in some electrical phenomena, from acting freely, and that consequently the electric fluid heats the bodies only when the caloric is separated from the substance with which it is combined, and is thereby put into free operation.

"If these consequences deduced from the foregoing experiments are well founded, as in fact they seem to me to be, then they prove straightaway that the electric fluid is not simple and not totally different from all other fluids, as many persons have imagined, but *that it is a compound fluid in which caloric is combined with another still unknown substance.*"

So if authorities can be credited, it is clear that the proposed explanation has on its side the hypotheses as well as the experiments of distinguished scientists, and there is no doubt that experiments set up with a view to testing it would soon confirm it just as much as it has already *been confirmed* by the above-mentioned experiments of van Marum (especially the calcination of metals in mephitic types of air by means of the electric spark).

[19] Gren's *New Journal of Physics*, vol. III, No. 1, pp. 1ff.
[20] Pp. 16–17.

On the Construction of
Electricity in the Philosophy
of Nature
(Supplement to Chapter 4)

The following points are undoubtedly those which a theory or construction of electricity has to consider: the nature of electricity itself, the manner of exciting this form of action, the basis of positive and negative electricity and its relation to the quality of bodies, the mode of conduction and the difference between conductors and non-conductors. The advantageous phenomena, like all effects of electricity, emerge automatically from these points, if they are brought to light beforehand. And here too the construction of electricity in the Philosophy of Nature will be briefly set out in accordance with them.

Since the form of bifurcation into subject and object prevails endlessly in the universe, even matter, although reality here seems to lose itself, as at the extreme limits, in pure objectivity and corporeality, can still not be considered inanimate. Animation is bestowed on it by the first act of embodiment of the infinite into the finite, of which it is the outermost moment. Besides being, as finite, in the infinite and subordinate to the universal identity, it also has thereby (in gravity) the ability to be *in itself equal to itself,* and to maintain itself in this identity. From these fundamental principles, absolutely all dynamic phenomena are to be conceived, entirely without any assumption of special, subtle, and indeed quite imponderable, matters, which are not only in themselves merely hypothetical, but also utterly inadequate to the construction of these phenomena.

We can now lay it down as a universal principle, that every body, where there is no change in relations to another outside it, would constantly persist in the same state of identity with itself, whereas every change of those relations posits in it an endeavour, regardless of this change, to maintain its equality with itself. In general this change will be a change of spatial relations, and thus of nearness or distance, and every approach or separation of one body to or from another will necessarily have to posit dynamic changes in both. Convergence to the point where the respective boundaries merge is contact: so these changes will pre-eminently *occur in the contact of any two bodies that are spatially distinct* (located outside each other).

Here, however, two cases can occur. It is either two qualitatively indifferent (similar) bodies that are touching, or two different bodies, whose qualities are distinct.

We must now observe that that by which a body is one with itself is also, at the same time, necessarily that whereby it can be one with another, presuming that the latter could bring it to completion; for since each is striving, for its own part, to be a whole, a totality, and is posited as a not-whole merely by the contact of another, it strives, along with the latter, to present a totality in the contact therewith. But for this it is requisite that the two are actually related to each other as the two different sides of one unity, so that in each of them there lies a determinate or determinable feature, which does not lie in the other, for only to that extent can the one become a means of completion to the other.

Now that cannot be the case where indifferent, qualitatively similar bodies are in contact. So in this case the reciprocal efforts of each to penetrate into the individuality of the other can only have the result that each withdraws all the more into itself, and strives all the more to maintain identity with itself. Now we must mention here that this relative equality with self is expressed in the body by the rigidity, the cohesion which, as can be seen without proof, is simply the body's being-in-itself, the individualizing principle, the act of separation from the totality of bodies. We shall therefore be able to state the postulated law as follows: *Contact of indifferent bodies posits in each of them, on its own account, the endeavour to cohere in itself, without integration by the other.* But now the form of cohesion, so far as it is active, is in general *magnetism*, a proposition which we here wish provisionally to establish on the mere fact that precisely with the maximum of active cohesion, the maximum of magnetism also occurs, and *vice versa*. But magnetism is not without a differentiating of the body in opposite directions, so that identity (the universal) becomes preponderant on the one side, and difference (the particular) on the other (expressed in the magnet by the two poles), where there is otherwise perfect equalization of both in the whole. This indifferencing in differencing occurs, moreover, *ad infinitum* and in the same form in the individual part as in the whole of the body. To apply this now to the case in hand, in the contact of homogeneous substances, although each strives to be a totality for itself, yet because each, in being this, must at the same time be in equilibrium with the other, so either will determine the other as far as is necessary for them to be simultaneously in mutual equilibrium, without prejudice to the internal unity of each; both, that is to say, besides positing reciprocally active cohesion *in themselves,* will also posit it *between them* (though which pole each of the two assumes for this cohesion with the other depends on determining grounds which we cannot pursue further here).

This state of cohesion between indifferent bodies is what we are accustomed to call adhesion, since this kind of connection normally takes place in relation to the quantitative similarity of the two bodies, and the most homogeneous cling together the most strongly.

If we now replace contact with friction, which is only successive, repeated touching, in which the contact itself and the point of contact are constantly changed, then, because no permanent state of equilibrium can arise between the two in this contact, the active cohesion, which each posits in itself, will be raised that much higher; as in every transition of a body from the state of lesser into higher cohesion, sensible heat will arise, which will increase the more, since the process of conduction, by which the body cools (and which is again a process of cohesion, into which it enters with other bodies), is disturbed by the constant alteration of the point of contact, so that in the course of the process the point is necessarily reached where the maximum of active cohesion is relaxed by the transition to relative cohesion, and the body goes over into the process of combustion (as was shown in the Supplement to Chapter 1). In this way we construct the origin of *heat* through friction, together with its law, namely, that it is actually *indifferent* bodies which mutually engender the greatest heat.

We had to pursue the consequences of the first of the two supposed cases to begin with, in order to obtain those of the second the more purely. If we limit ourselves to the most general statement with respect to the first case, we can express ourselves thus: Indifferent bodies in contact *magnetize* each other.

The result will be different in the other supposed case, *in which two different bodies touch each other.*

For since each is so related to the other as to be able to complete it, they will endeavour to present together a totality, a closed world; and since, as has been shown, this is possible as such, and so here too in turn, no otherwise than under the form of cohesion, and in such a way that there occurs in the one the opposite determination to that which occurs in the other, *the two will reciprocally posit cohesion-changes in each other, such that in proportion as the one is enhanced in its cohesion* (the factor of the particular becomes preponderant in it), *the other diminishes in that respect* (the factor of the universal becomes preponderant in it).

Now, that these reciprocal changes of cohesion can be manifested *as such* only in the moment of contact or in that of its cessation is self-evidently clear, since both bodies in the state of quiescent contact constitute, as said, a closed world, and neither has to strain outwardly in order to restore its condition through another, and to enter into a similar process with that. The difference, however, may further occur, that the bodies in contact are, or are not, able to spread the change of cohesion posited in them over their entire surface (in whatever way this may happen); in the latter case, this change will be confined merely to the point of contact, and in order to spread it over the whole, successive contacts of the two at all points, that is, friction, will be required. It is further self-evident that if, in the first case – the contact of *indifferent* bodies – active and thus absolute cohesion was posited within and between them, which, as we know, is a function of length, then in the case of contact between *different* bodies, *relative* cohesion would have to be posited, which, as we also know, is a pure function of *breadth*. So it follows that if the form of the mode of action in the first case is pure length, that of the mode of action in the second will be breadth.

But we also need to subjoin nothing further in order to show that the mode of action of the bodies, under the conditions of the second of the supposed cases, is *electricity*, since both they (the conditions) and also the determinations of the latter (the mode of action) uniquely coincide with electricity. Since numerous examples will be extensively referred to in the sequel, we cite in this connection only the confinement of electricity to the surface of bodies, and what is more, its determinability, for instance, in regard to the quantitative distribution between different bodies through the uniformity and similarity of the surfaces.

We can now, in a few words, discuss each of the points defined above.

1. *The nature of electricity itself.* It is clear that it is the dynamic or identity-nisus of two different bodies entering into relative cohesion with each other. The reduction of all electricity and electrical phenomena to the principle of *cohesion* is a result quite peculiar to the Philosophy of Nature. For even Volta, who deserved such unique credit for establishing the principle of the contact of *different* bodies, himself had to leave unanswered the final question of *how* these bodies can reciprocally excite electricity in each other, and indeed could not answer it so long as he, too, continued to seek the basis of electrical phenomena in the streamings of a fluid. What has supported this opinion, apart from certain effects of electricity, of which we shall speak later, is undoubtedly the similar opinion in regard to light, which, as the accompanying phenomenon of electricity, actually had to be counted among the components of electrical matter, according to the empirical way of reasoning. We have also to take this into account, or rather we have done so

already in what was discussed above (Supplement to Chapter 1). In magnetism identity is taken up into difference, and here light cannot appear. The phenomenon of light is that of the resumption of difference into identity (*loc. cit.*); and it occurs, precisely, in electricity, which differs from magnetism in that here a difference becomes identity, whereas in magnetism identity becomes difference.

From this we see at once that in another connection magnetism and electricity are again one, that is, one and the same dynamic activity, which *affects* bodies, there under the form of the *first dimension* only, here under that of the *second*.

2. *The mode of excitation of electricity.* We see from the foregoing that it has its basis only in the respective changes of cohesion which different bodies posit in each other, solely through contact, and without any intervention of another agency. On the general view of it, the overall excitation-mode of electricity, as *breadth-polarity*, in the relationship of the earth to the sun already touched upon above (see the Supplement to Chapter 1), can no longer appear in doubt.

3. *The ground of positive electricity and its relation to the quality of bodies.* In the contact of two indifferent bodies the indifference-point of the magnet is restored, albeit only in difference. The two bodies relate to one another in the state of contiguity, as do the two sides of the magnet; and as surely as these bodies (like the earth and solar system in the large) must on one side be in a state of reduced cohesion, and on the other, in a state of heightened cohesion, so surely also, of two bodies that reciprocally electrify each other, the one that is expanding (a situation evinced in the erupting fire-plume) will be in a state of *positive* electricity, and the one that is contracting (also indicated by the appearance of the light-point) will be in a state of *negative* electricity.

We can accordingly state the general law of the electrical relation of bodies thus: *That one of the two which enhances its cohesion in opposition to the other will have to appear negatively electric, and that one which diminishes its cohesion, positively electric.* It is evident from this how the electricity of every body is determined, not only by its own quality, but equally by that of the other. As is shown in the foregoing chapter, though very incompletely, the bearing which the electric relationship of bodies has upon that of their oxidizability is intelligible, since this too is determined by cohesion-relationships (Supplement to Chapter 1). One only has to look through the tables on this subject compiled by the physicists, to be convinced of the thoroughgoing validity of this law. Glass becomes positively electric inasmuch as an easily oxidizable substance is applied to it as the frictional agent; it is known that in the process of electrification, quicksilver-amalgam is simultaneously oxidized, that is, enhanced in its relative cohesion. In galvanic experiments, the $+E$ is consistently on the side of the body of lesser cohesion, for example, zinc in opposition to gold, silver or copper. But even the metals which remain most constantly negative, such as platinum, can become positive when heated with others that are otherwise positive, and even with an otherwise homogeneous, unheated piece of the same metal. (See Cavallo's treatise, latest edition, in the second Part.) We see from this the great influence of surfaces, of roughness (so that ground glass, for example, becomes negatively electric in the same degree to which other glass becomes positive), of colours, etc. Now to whatever extent the capacity for relative enhancement or diminution of cohesion also determines all chemical and other qualities of substances, we can easily pursue further from this the consequences of the one relationship, which remains ever the same, though always returning in different forms.

4. *The mechanism of conduction and the difference between conductors and non-conductors.* Here I primarily insist upon the principle that the mechanism of conduction rests entirely on the same grounds as that of the first excitation. For in that a body is electrified by contact with another at one point, it is *ipso facto* in difference with the adjacent point, and thus the condition of the electrical process has been given, and indeed, since the first point has the necessary nisus to reconstitute itself to identity, it will either enhance or diminish its cohesion at the expense of the other, thereby making it negatively or positively electric, and appear to have conveyed its own electricity to it. But the same also takes place between two different bodies, so that we by no means admit a true and genuine communication of electricity, by transfusion, as it were, but only a propagation by constantly ongoing excitation.

Now concerning the difference between conductors and non-conductors, it will be admitted that the physicists have hitherto been completely in the dark about this relationship and could give not the least information about the ground of this difference.

In accordance with the principle that all conduction occurs in the form of cohesion and magnetism, all those bodies are of necessity *intrinsically* incapable of conduction which fall at the limits of the general cohesion-series, and so lie closest to either the contracted or expanded pole, because they contain the one factor of cohesion in great excess, and thus can establish cohesion only *in conjunction with other bodies*. In contact with an electrified body they do indeed conduct, in the sense that every other conducts, that is, they enter into a cohesion-process with it, but they do not conduct beyond the point of contact, because they are not *intrinsic* conductors. One may easily discover for oneself that all possible insulators fall into one or other of these two classes of bodies, as, for example, the metallic glasses, the earths, etc., fall into the category of substances with excessive, merely relative cohesion, and others, like sulphur, etc., already fall on the side of excessive expansion. So the seat of absolute conductivity will be purely in the sphere of predominantly active cohesion, that of the metals, though for reasons which it would here take us too far afield to pursue, it is not actually bodies of the highest degree of cohesion which have the most perfect conductivity. Water, as indifference-point of relative cohesion, corresponds to the indifference-point of active cohesion. Since being outwardly quite inert, it takes on every determination from outside, and is *equally one* in itself, it enters into every conduction-process as a single factor and transmits the change of cohesion through itself, that is, it does not insulate, without on that account being intrinsically more than a merely relative conductor. It is known, however, that in a state of ebullition, or equally by addition of more coherent liquids, such as mineral acids, its conductivity is considerably increased.

5. *Accompanying phenomena and effects of electricity.* The former can doubtless be grasped automatically from the foregoing, e.g., the phenomena of attraction and repulsion. We have already spoken in (1) of the phenomena of light. Yet it is still worth remarking, in connection with what was there said, that electricity can be rendered luminous to the degree in which the bodily content of the conducting medium or electrified substance is diminished, and thus the surface relatively increased. Hence the electrical phenomena of rarefied air.

The effects of electricity, so far as they are the dissolution of cohesion, melting or even the change of absolute into relative cohesion through oxidation, need no further elucidation. Of the effects of electrical polarity in the voltaic pile, it should be remembered that here too the electricity displays itself as breadth-polarity in the presentation of both its chemical forms, oxygen and hydrogen (Supplement to Chapters 1 and 3); and indeed one must either have completely failed to understand the course of this potentiation of water, or must have succumbed to a deplorable passion for originality, in wanting to call the +E oxygen-electricity and the −E hydrogen-electricity, because it is the determination proceeding from the positively electric pole which presents the water as oxygen, and that from the negative pole which presents it as hydrogen. In the system of the voltaic pile, each pole always and necessarily posits its opposite; thus the plus of the zinc-pole posits the minus or *negative* form of water, just as the minus of the opposite pole posits the plus or *positive* form of it. The former nomenclature would have been just as much selected on crude appearances, as if one were to want to call the north pole of a magnet the south pole, because it excites the south pole in the iron, and *vice versa.* In any case, the appearance of hydrogen as the chemical representative of +E, and of oxygen as similar representative of −E, is uniquely consistent with all other relationships.

As to the effects of electricity on organization, especially on the animal organism, it is sufficient to remark that nerve and muscle are generally in the relation of + and −E, just as water, conversely, is articulated in muscle and nerve, albeit in a way unknown to us; that the nerve is naturally striving to increase its cohesion at the expense of muscle, just as the latter destroys by contraction every tendency to a lessening of cohesion. In the organism itself, therefore, external electricity already finds the most perfect electrical relationships, though developed here to a higher power.

5

Of the Magnet

So far we have succeeded in showing that we need no unknown forces hidden in the particular substance, as such, for the explanation of physical phenomena; rather that Nature would have known how to maintain the multiplicity of these phenomena by the simplest means, namely, by surrounding solid bodies with a fluid medium, which she determined, not only to be the general repository of the basic material which seems to be the midpoint of all partial attractions, but also at the same time the vehicle of higher forces, which alone are able to bring about all those phenomena accompanying the exchange of relationships among the basic materials of bodies.

Now, there is still one phenomenon left, which threatens us with having to forsake the principle which we have hitherto followed, and in the end to accept, at least in individual bodies, something which we have steadfastly refused to admit in bodies generally – an inner fundamental force, not universally active, peculiar to the individual body *as such*. The cause of *magnetic phenomena*, one may say, is in no way given to the senses. So here our physical explanations seem to be at an end. It works originally in a body without being excited; this body need not be insulated in order to retain its power; it loses none, or very little, of it by communication – obvious proofs of a force which seems to attach to the primary basic parts in the interior of the body. Only forces which permeate bodies, like heat and electricity, not such as merely reach its surface, like water among others (which are hazardous to electricity), are able to weaken this force – a proof, once again, that our former principle seems *here* at least, to forsake us utterly. But one has to bear in mind that, to all appearances, magnetism (as I here call, for short, the properties of the magnet as such) is nothing *original*, that not only can it be *excited* artificially, it is even possible to *produce magnets* by art.

This remark alone already gives hope that we have no reason to despair of a physical explanation of magnetic phenomena, and must sooner or later succeed in discovering the real (and not merely the imagined) cause of it.

This remark also puts it beyond doubt that a force is at any rate active in the magnet which can certainly be called an *inner* force, not as if it were such originally and by its nature, but because it is precisely in *this* connection alone that it is able to produce *these* phenomena; that this force, moreover, is indeed the magnet's *own*, but is not *peculiar* to it, and hence originally may well be no special, *purely magnetic* force (in the essential meaning of that term); and finally, that this force is *accidental* to the magnet and cannot be regarded as a force necessary to it, that is, a force belonging to its very essence.

Indeed we do not know how the magnet is formed in the interior of the earth; but this much we know, that it is no more an *original* natural product than metals generally, that it had to go through several stages of formation before it became a magnet, and that probably in its formation the great active and formative forces of Nature, fire and heat, were not idle. We know that the magnet (an iron ore) is found in all rich iron mines; that iron itself is subject to continuous changes in the interior of the earth; that in the course of centuries iron is produced, where previously none was to be found; and that iron mines disappear where formerly they were frequently met with – observations which make everybody aware that the cause of magnetic properties is doubtless to be sought in the original formation of the iron and the magnet – that the magnet may well be nothing else but an *imperfect iron* which was *non-uniformly* generated in the interior of the earth, in which perhaps certain basic materials – or forces – which *are dormant in iron* have not come to rest, etc.

More than by anything else, this view of the magnet is confirmed by the artificial method of giving iron itself magnetic properties.

I am not here referring to the magnetic excitation which occurs through stroking with a magnet. This is important in other respects, because it demonstrates the great similarity of magnetic and electrical phenomena. If I draw one pole of a magnet over half an iron bar, the opposite force is here excited; from now on, the magnet and bar have cognate poles. If I reverse these poles by stroking the same side with the other pole of the magnet, or the opposite side with the same pole, nothing results. But if I stroke the other half of the bar with the opposite pole, these become cognate and the iron has poles like the magnet. It is still more remarkable in *this* respect, that the phenomena of *division* occur in the magnet exactly as they do in electricity.[1] Indeed

---

[1] Lichtenberg in Erxleben, p. 551.

all magnetic effects can be reduced to *division*. No wonder that the magnet loses as little of its force thereby as the electric body. Electricity, however, can also be excited by *communication,* which, owing to its *limits,* is impossible for magnetic force. Almost all the differences between electric and magnetic phenomena are explicable from the fact that the magnetic force is by its nature *confined.*[2] Aepinus[3] has already quite rightly remarked, therefore, that one can certainly match every magnetic phenomenon with an electrical one, but cannot, conversely, match every electrical phenomenon with a magnetic one – a proof that both are fully alike in their *laws* and differ only in their *limitations.* Yet it does not follow from this that the *causes* of both phenomena are one and the same, but rather that both belong to *one kind* of cause.

What is more nearly and immediately to my purpose is that iron can be magnetized without the help of a magnet. The following experiments are relevant here.

Iron and steel become magnetic if, when heated to incandescence, they are rapidly cooled in cold water. The same results if a red-hot iron rod is set up perpendicular and so cooled. In both cases the cooling is *non-uniform.* Not only is the *surface* cooled more quickly than the interior, but in both cases also one *end* is cooled more quickly than the other. What conjectures might be founded on this observation, my readers may judge for themselves.

Further, iron (and also sulphurous iron ore)[4] becomes magnetized when struck by lightning, or concussed by a strong electric spark (the most violent means of disintegration in Nature) – a fact also confirmed by Franklin.

Indeed, a strong, merely mechanical, shock to the iron also has the same effect, but the question still remains: Has the shock acted immediately here, or has a *decomposition* first been *mediately* effected by it, which is now the true cause of the magnetism excited in the iron?

Conversely, the magnetism of the magnet can be destroyed by just the same means whereby it is excited in iron.

Experiments with the magnetometer have shown in an arresting manner that even mere heat weakens the magnetic force.[5] It is altogether destroyed if the magnet is made red hot and then *gradually* and *uniformly* cooled. Even mere exposure to the open air, so that the magnet rusts (attracts oxygen to itself), robs it of its force.

---

[2] Cf. the same author, p. 554.

[3] See the two works already cited above [chap. 4], of which one deals with *the similarity of electrical and magnetic matters.*

[4] See a letter from Beccaria in *Rozier,* vol. IX, May 1777.

[5] Prévost, *Of the Cause of Magnetic Force,* German trans. by Bourguet, with preface by Gren, p. 165.

Electric shocks can totally deprive the magnet of its magnetic force. Even if doubt has been cast by van Marum's experiments on whether, in fact (as Knight maintains, also with the support of experiments, in the *Philosophical Transactions*), the magnetic poles can be reversed by the effect of electricity, there nevertheless remain always the reports which he cites from seafarers, who saw the compass suddenly reverse its poles when struck by lightning.

A merely mechanical – but sharp – shock robs the magnet of its force just as well as an electric one, and so the following proposition may well rank as a general law: *What magnetizes iron demagnetizes the magnet itself.*

These findings show that one has no right to assume a *special* magnetic force – or even one, or two, *magnetic matters*. The assumption of the last is admissible so long as it is treated merely as a *(scientific) fiction*, on which to base *experiments* and *observations (as regulative)*, but not *explanations* and *hypotheses* (as *principle*). For if we speak of a magnetic matter, we have in fact said nothing more by this than what we knew anyway, namely, that there has to be *something* which makes the magnet magnetic. But if we go further, we necessarily arrive either at *Cartesian* vortices, or at Euler's magnetic canals and valves, and the like. Aepinus did it quite otherwise (a scientist whose experiments and hypotheses both bear the mark of the simplicity which everywhere characterizes the resourceful mind), in that he first made a *hypothetical* application of Franklin's theory of electrical phenomena to the magnetic, and, in accordance with this hypothesis, did not explain, but rather *observed and experimented*.

When Haüy, for example, to whom M. Prévost appeals,[6] says, "It is very probable that, when once the nature of these phenomena becomes better known, we shall discover that they depend upon the simultaneous effects of *two fluids, which are so constituted that the basic masses of each possess the property of mutally repelling one another and at the same time attracting the basic masses of the other,*" I ask, what then, would we actually have gained by these *more detailed disclosures* about the nature of magnetic phenomena? Obviously nothing except the word *fluids*. For *to assume* that these are internally *self-repelling* and attractive *to one another* is not to explain the phenomena at all, but merely to *push* the question *back*. Instead of having to investigate, as before, why like magnetic poles repel and unlike attract each other, we now ask why this happens with the supposed fluids – and by this *alteration* of the question it has obviously not become any easier to answer. Such futile explanations of *Nature* are thus nothing else but self-deceptions, since

[6] *Op cit.*, Preface, p. x.

it is believed that by changing the *designations* of the fact we have come closer to the fact itself, and are thereby taking payment in words instead of realities.

M. Prévost perceived that on such assumptions we really do not get anywhere in science. He therefore undertook in his work to prove what M. Haüy had only felt, namely that those assumptions never clarify *anything* about the *origin* of these phenomena, that is, about the *main issue* – and that more difficult investigations would have to be undertaken in order to be able to rest content with explanations of this kind.

In the hands of M. Prévost, therefore, the assumption of two elementary fluids, which he treats as the cause of the magnetic phenomena, certainly acquires a quite different shape from that which it had in most of his predecessors. By basing it on the principles of M. le Sage's mechanical physics, he gives his hypothesis not only general support, but also what is more, a *real* content and significance. As we know, the older physics was in general very liberal with elastic matters, which, in order that they might be ready to hand in every phenomenon, were taken to be spread about everywhere. This fiction, through the new discoveries about the nature and constitution of the air, has ceased to be merely a *fiction*. M. Prévost employs it likewise. But in his system it has actual *coherence* and *necessity*, because these elementary fluids are actually *necessary* in the mechanical physics which he defends. To refute his hypothesis, therefore, one has to destroy the system itself and the context in which he asserts it. In this system, after all, there is also no *lack of explanation* as to why the fundamental particles (*les molecules*) of the two elementary fluids *reciprocally* attract one another, and this because the fundamental particles of *heterogeneous* fluids strive to unite with greater force than do those of *homogeneous* ones. As soon as we assume (with M. Prévost) that this reciprocal attraction is mechanically explicable, and as soon as we try at least to explain it in that fashion, the assertion ceases to be arbitrary, and we find ourselves on firm ground, so long at least as the system is not refuted. So until we can subject this system to our inquiry, we must also leave untouched M. Prévost's hypothesis of the origin of magnetic forces.

M. Prévost ascribes to iron a *selective attraction* towards the combined magnetic fluid. Since even selective attractions receive a mechanical explanation in the mechanical physics, we must also await its disclosures about this particular kind of magnetic selective attraction.

Until this is forthcoming, or so long as we are not yet convinced that in *this* way it is possible for a *speculative* physics (for I shall prove that the mechanical physics is nothing else but that) to be a natural science at all, the above-stated proposition (that what magnetizes iron demagnetizes the magnet itself, and conversely) at least provides a guiding principle for research into the reason for this selective attraction, in the usual and hitherto still the only reliable way. The attention of the scientist will be primarily directed to observing under what changes of the iron its relation to the magnet is also changed. A major change of this kind is the calcination of the iron, whereby it ceases to be attracted by the magnet as strongly as it was before. That a *partition* takes place, perhaps, in the iron itself, as it does in the magnet, might be inferred from the fact that other metallic bodies, for example, according to Bergman, the *purest* regulus of nickel, are themselves attracted by it. Discoveries of new metallic or metallurgic substances, which either themselves display magnetic properties,[7] or are attracted by the magnet, will surely yield many other disclosures on the subject.

The pointing of the magnet towards the pole, and its deviations from this direction, make it clear that the cause of magnetic phenomena must be related to the first active causes in Nature, or that the unknown to which it is related, and which perhaps contains the reason for all its individual affinities (to iron, for example), must be spread over the whole earth. There is almost no phenomenon of Nature that will not have had influence upon the direction of the magnetic needle. It shows a *daily* aberration which is probably attributable to mere alterations of the air. Earthquakes and volcanic eruptions affect it. Both the northern lights, as well as the zodiacal light, have influence upon it, and a new investigation, undertaken now from a broader viewpoint, of its present as well as its past deviations, could easily be the way to fathom at last the cause of all magnetic phenomena.

[7] Such discoveries as those recently reported by Herr von Humboldt in the *Allgemeine Literarische Zeitung* must therefore be extremely gratifying to the natural scientist. [See the Information Sheet of the *ALZ* of 1797, no. 38.]

The Doctrine of the Philosophy
of Nature on Magnetism
(Supplement to Chapter 5)

Since very many points in the theory of magnetism have been touched on, in passing, in the Supplement to the previous Chapter, we shall confine ourselves here to setting out the most significant of them, which are as follows:

1. Magnetism is the general act of animation, the implanting of unity into multiplicity, of the concept into difference. The same embodiment of the subjective into the objective, which, viewed in the ideal as potency, is self-consciousness, appears here expressed in being, although even this being, considered in itself, is again a relative unity of thinking and being. The general form of relative embodiment of unity into multiplicity is the *line, pure length;* magnetism is therefore *determinant of pure length,* and since this is manifested in body by absolute cohesion, of *absolute cohesion.*

Through magnetism every body is totality in regard to itself, and its two poles are the necessary appearance-modes of the two unities of particular and universal, so far as they appear at the deepest level of being, as at once differenced and indifferenced. By virtue of gravity the body is in unity with all others; through magnetism it picks itself out and gathers itself together as a particular unity: Magnetism is therefore the universal form of individual being-in-itself.

2. From this point of view it is self-evident that magnetism is a *universal* determination and category of matter, that it therefore must be, not exclusively peculiar to a single body, but common to all self-individualizing and self-individualized bodies. This is one of the first lessons of nature-philosophy, which in the *Outline of the System* of this science (p. 301) is expressed as follows: "Magnetism is as universal in Nature generally as sensibility is in organic Nature, where it belongs even to plants. Only for *appearance* is it (magnetism) abolished in particular substances; in the so-called non-magnetic substances, what in magnetic substances is still distinguished as magnetism is immediately lost upon contact, as electricity; just as in plants, what in the animal is still distinguished as sensation is lost immediately in contractions.

Thus in order to recognize the magnetism of so-called non-magnetic substances, only the means are lacking," and so on.

Even these means have now been found; Coulomb is the first to have broken through these limitations even for appearance. It is amusing enough that there have been people who brought against this universal view of magnetism, and the construction of it as a necessary category of matter,[8] the objection that on such a view, all rigid bodies as such would have to be magnetic, which *experience*, however, contradicts. The same experience, thanks to Coulomb, now tells against the claim that *not* all rigid bodies are magnetic.

According to his assurances, none of the bodies so far investigated has escaped the influence of large magnetic rods, though the effect in some bodies is so small that until now it has eluded the notice of physicists. Coulomb gave each of the bodies tested the shape of a little cylindrical rod, and in this state he hung them up horizontally on a thread of raw silk, and brought them between the two opposite poles of two steel magnets. With rodlets 7–8 millimetres long and ¾ millimetre thick, the effect in non-metallic bodies (for in metallic ones it was further reduced by a factor of three) was that, if the opposing magnetic poles were separated about 5–6 millimetres further from each other than the length of the needle, which was to swing between them, the needles, whatever they were made of, disposed themselves exactly, on each occasion, in the direction of the two magnetic rods, and, when diverted from this direction, returned to it as before by way of numerous oscillations (often more than 30 per minute).

3. Since all the causes whereby the magnetism of a body is strengthened, under the influence of the earth's magnetism, like those whereby it can be destroyed, are obviously and without difficulty reducible to such as affect cohesion, it would be needless to append any special remark on the subject, while

4. The deviations of the magnetic needle and other peculiarities of its motions can be understood only in the context of a more general view of the planetary system, of axial rotations and other universal motions.

---

[8] In the *Introduction to the Outline of a Philosophy of Nature*, p. 75, and in the essay: "General Deduction of the Dynamic Process or of the Categories of Physics" in the *Journal*, vol. I, nos. 1 and 2 [1800].

6

General Considerations, as
Results of the Foregoing

Light and heat, which can set even inert matter in motion and throw dead substances out of equilibrium, both derive from a single source, and man has long thought of them both together – the one as cause and the other as effect. But light, this element of the heavens, is too generally distributed, too universally active, for the eye of the ordinary man, fettered to the soil, to *seek* it, in order to enjoy the *blessing of sight* with consciousness. Light, as such, touches only the more spiritual organ – and what we owe to it, insofar as it is *light,* are dramas, which the man, whose sense is turned towards the earth, has no capacity to receive. With the more abundant light of the spring sun, there also appears anew the ever-changing play of manifold deliquescent colours upon the surface of our earth, which but little earlier had still been wearing the monotonous garb of winter; and the rise and fall, the coming to be, changing, and passing away, of these colours is the measure of a time-reckoning which, everywhere present, accompanies us into the very midst of Nature. The youthful light of the stars appears to us from afar, and connects our being to the existence of a universe which, though unattainable for the imagination, yet is not altogether hidden from the eye.

But all the manifold spectacles which light vouchsafes to us have no immediate influence upon our *needs;* they are assigned to a nobler sense. Heat, already closer to the lower senses, is connected more nearly to the imperative needs of mankind; no wonder that for him who is directly receptive to all its effects, it is the first thing that draws him to sun-worship. It was already a very refined religion which taught the worship of that benign star as the origin of *light,* the purest, most unsullied element that we know, despite the fact that an earlier and widely distributed primitive folk-belief, which was never quite extinguished among any nation of antiquity, honoured the first power of Nature in the symbol of *fire.* Already the alternation of day and night, like the changes in living and non-living Nature that are linked with the return and departure of that star, were teaching mankind that light and heat are the sole animating forces of the universe; still more so did the change of the seasons, since the sun, as soon as its rays fall more vertically, seems to waken Nature herself from the sleep of death, and to recall to life what had previously been fettered in dead rigidity; but more than all, however, it was the dismal aspect of those regions where an eternal cold, among never melted ice-masses solidified into cliffs and crags, seems to stifle all stirrings of the force of life.

Everything which causes development, formation and expansion in inorganic matter appeared to man to be vital force. The phenomenon of the outward expansion of crude matter by heat is, as it were, a mere shadow of that inner living warmth which swells the bud, and preserves, advances and organizes, in embryo, the developing human child. The plant, brought out by the influence of heat, yet droops again as soon as light and heat cease to provide it with nourishment; at least it loses the beauty of its leaves, a proof that it has nothing more to give back, because it is no longer receiving anything. But the organism into which the spark of life has once fallen continues to bear within itself a source of inner warmth which ends only with life itself, and is so independent of external heat that it suffuses the body more strongly precisely when everything outside the body is stiff with cold. Nature herself has done everything to set the inner warmth into the most exact relation to zonal climate and temperature. Where she could not without danger make the measure of the inner heat excessive in proportion to the cold of the climate, she reduced the size of the organism itself, in order to concentrate in a smaller compass what, if distributed over a larger one, would have effected only half as much. The most mobile and lively creatures (such as birds) have also relatively the warmest blood, and the cold-blooded stand at the margins of animate Nature. The inner animal heat remains the same at every atmospheric temperature, and if that warmth is extinguished, external heat only accelerates the decay of the dead organism.

But Nature herself observes *degrees* with respect to this force, which she never exceeds without advantage to vital and organic Nature. A host of plants and animals are forever excluded from both hot and cold regions of the earth, while only a few are *entirely* alien to the temperate zones, to say nothing of the fact that only in the last has the noblest form of humanity flourished, evolved and become cultured. In the temperate zones themselves, Nature is obliged, as soon as the natural measure of heat is exceeded, to restore equilibrium by revolutions. Even light everywhere meets resistance on its way to us, and Nature allows no force ever to overstep its limits altogether. There is also the fact that heat itself is nothing *original*, that it exists only insofar as light meets resistance, and thus it is only against countervailing forces that even the active forces of Nature reveal their total might, which, if once it were limitless, would destroy everything by which it might find expression, and so abolish itself. No wonder that light and heat are always endeavouring to combine with opposites in proportion to their quantity, because only within this limitation are they what they are – expansive, repulsive, animating forces.

Thus it is necessary even for the preservation of these forces that inert, dead matters should work against them. For itself, therefore, the earth would rest and move only in accordance with its inertia, undeveloped in those forces and effects which it harbours within itself, if life-giving activities did not flow, as if from a higher order, to unfold earth's unity, and awaken therein the inner life and those forces which, operating against the laws of gravity, teach the dead mass itself to obey other laws than those of universal attraction.[1] For this is the character of whatever is ruled by higher forces, that laws of inertia and gravity have no power over it, as they do over everything else. Everything more ignoble inclines towards the earth; everything more noble raises itself, of its own accord, above it. The vegetative plant is already striving to distance itself from the soil; where it is itself incapable of holding its luxurious growth erect, at least it struggles towards the sun on the support of others, and sadly sinks its head, as soon as it is forsaken by the powers that drove it upward.[2] Through the action of heat the most solid bodies change their state; the majority become liquid, many evaporate altogether, only a few withstand its power, and even these seem to exist only to support the nobler bodies.

It is forces of attraction that are primarily at work, both within and on the surface of the earth. A secret affinity binds one material with another, or mutually attracts them as soon as a higher force (such as fire or heat) has severed their previous combination. These affinities all seem to have a common midpoint. Nature, in order to make possible the greatest multiplicity of phenomena, has everywhere set the heterogeneous against the heterogeneous. But in order that unity should prevail in that multiplicity, and harmony in this conflict, her wish was that heterogeneous should strive to combine with heterogeneous, and only in this combination become a *whole*. Thus Nature has everywhere distributed a variety of substances which are all related to

---

[1] [In the first edition the last sentence reads]: "The fixed earth rests below and moves only in accordance with its inertia; in itself, it contains no other than dead forces, and only from above, as if from another world, do vitalizing powers stream upon it and penetrate its interior, in opposition to the laws . . ."

[2] The more lively organization never consists in the relationship to the mass which it contains, and the aging body, even though it loses mass, does not lose weight in proportion. [This sentence is missing in the second edition.]

one another only in that they strive in common towards combination with a third. Even dead materials, which no longer show any affinities, are perhaps only those in which that combination has long been completed, and whose powers of attraction have thereby come to rest. The artifice of Nature seems, therefore, to have been *this:* to separate substances which were by nature homogeneous, and, so far as possible, to keep them separated, because, once combined, they are incapable of further separation, and are nothing but dead inert matter.

But where is it, that middle term which alone connects all these mutual affinities of bodies? It must be present everywhere and, as universal principle of partial attractions, be dispersed over the whole of Nature. Where else should we seek it than in the medium in which we ourselves live, which surrounds everything, permeates everything, is present to everything?

The air, daily rejuvenated, envelops our earth; itself the scene of constant changes, it is not only the medium that conducts to earth the higher forces (light and heat) by which combinations are broken up and attractions effected, but is simultaneously the mother of that remarkable basic material, which, as universal middle term of all affinities between bodies, intrudes, whether mediately or immediately, into every chemical process. And thus Nature has already made possible the greater part of her phenomena by the simplest means, in that she has set two orders of substances, the fluid and the solid, in opposition to each other. No chemical process gets under way without the presence of some fluid substance. While solid bodies provide the ponderable basic materials which belong to the chemical process, the fluids commonly provide both force and medium to the process, because they are just as much the vehicles of light or heat as they are of the basic material that pertains to the chemical process.

So as soon as the nature of different elastic fluids had been discovered, one could legitimately expect from these discoveries the most important consequences for the extension of our knowledge. Nature herself has separated these two classes of substances by boundaries too sharp for us not to be able to hope that we may find in this opposition the secret which enables her to produce the greatest effects by the simplest means. In vain would we labour to blur these boundaries, and to claim that the transition from fluid to solid bodies is continuous. Nature admittedly makes no leap; but it seems to me that this principle is much misunderstood if we try to bring into a single class things which Nature has not only separated, but has herself opposed to one another. That principle says no more than this, that nothing which *comes to be* in Nature *comes to be* by a leap; all *becoming* occurs in a continuous sequence. But it by no means follows from this that everything which exists is for that reason continuously connected – that there should also be no leap between what *exists*. From everything that is, therefore, nothing has *become* without steady progression, a steady transition from one state to another. But now, since it *is*, it stands between its own boundaries as a thing of a particular kind, which distinguishes itself from others by sharp determinations.

The sharpest boundary between solid and fluid substances is the exclusive determination of the latter as the vehicle of *positive* causes. Solid bodies, on the other hand, are either simply and solely obedient to the laws of gravity, or, if they obey higher (chemical) laws, they do so according to laws of (qualitative) attraction, that is, by *negative* forces.

That remarkable fluid (vital air), which seems, to us, to be the only source of light, is still more distinct from all other substances, whether solid or liquid. For while all other bodies contain only the *single* basic materials that are capable of chemical attraction, vital air possesses in itself the *universal* principle which lies at the root of *all* chemical attractions *collectively*.

Since this fluid unites in itself the most heterogeneous factors, it is already understandable from thence that it is capable of the most manifold appearances. Hence the electric attractions and repulsions, hence the phenomena of decompositions of air and of the combustion of bodies, hence the appearance of light, which gradually becomes more intelligible to us if we distinguish the phenomenon of light (its effect upon our organ) from what it is and must be for the understanding. And if perhaps the whole of Nature, if even the economy of the animal body, should depend on attractions and repulsions, then we understand why Nature diffuses that fluid everywhere, and why she has linked with its presence, not only the accomplishment of many chemical processes, but even the continuance of vegetable and animal life.

The heterogeneous principles which Nature has united in this fluid *can* only be known to us by their effect on the senses, and the feeling which this effect produces in us itself depends upon the expressions of which we make use. Light and heat are mere expressions of our feeling, not a designation of that which acts upon us. From the very fact that light and heat affect quite different senses, and work so utterly differently, we can already infer that in both cases we are designating mere modifications of our organ. An unusual oscillation of our cranial and optical nerves, a sudden fright, sudden astonishment, or any other disturbance of our eyes, makes us see light where there actually is none. Even people whose sight has been completely destroyed see light at night or in sudden agitations. And perhaps even the colour series is not the result of a splitting of the light-ray, but a sequence which is produced by our eye, and which the fatigued organ not infrequently runs through on its own. At least people have been known who were quite incapable of distinguishing colours even with seeing eyes.

The same is the case with the principle of all chemical attraction which modern chemistry has designated by the name *oxygen* (*Sauerstoff*). The name is taken from an effect upon our organ, which this substance never exercises on its own account, but only in its combination with bodies, and which no more designates than light and heat do, what this principle is *in itself*. But we can retain this expression without misgiving, the moment we have become accustomed to think, in that connection, of something more universal than a *contraction of the gustatory nerves*. Since this principle is of the *negative* kind, it is even dubious whether the hope will ever be fulfilled of presenting it for itself and in isolation. It is enough, meanwhile, for us to know that Nature is able to achieve the entire manifold of her phenomena, on the small scale as well as on the large, by means of opposing forces of attraction and repulsion.

Our view now expands. From individual laws whereby subordinate forces in smaller regions maintain the eternal commerce of Nature, we ascend to the laws which govern the universe, which impel worlds towards worlds, and forever keep bodies from colliding with bodies, or system from falling into system.

Universal Features of the
Dynamic Process
(Supplement to Chapter 6)

It would be futile to expect to understand the manifold effects of Nature, or the wonderful productions in which she reveals her innermost being, from merely external effects on matter, as in those systems for which matter is the absolutely dead and inanimate, and so too, at bottom, are all the influences from whose effect on matter the livelier phenomena and higher productions are explained. The germ of life, though still imprisoned, lies already within the mass, and although the purely corporeal portion of Nature appears in the series of bodies, while the spiritual portion, or universal soul, seems to project itself separately in light, yet both find themselves again in the organism, where the soul, or form, holds the matter so firmly and binds itself so closely thereto that in the whole of organic being, as in the individual action, the form is wholly matter and the matter wholly form.

If, of the two unities in the absolute, the one in which the universal becomes a particular is that of Nature, and the latter accordingly the universal realm of being-for-itself, then the world-structure is the total embodiment of the infinite into the finite, and thus itself again the unity which comprehends all others, so far as they recur in Nature. The material universe, and every world-body for itself, is therefore none of the particular unities which first proceed from it – not inorganic mass, not plant or animal – but the identity of this totality, as the normal eye can survey it. Only within the unity of every world-body, that is, of every such whole, which, *qua* appearing body and at the same time idea within the appearance, is a universe for itself, is there a repetition of that act of embodiment whereby the absolute identity entered into the particularities of world-bodies, into the outgrowth of the world-body's identity into the series of particular bodies, which here can appear, not as universes, but only as individual unities, because they are subordinate to the dominant unity.

In the state of primary identity of the matter of every world-body, all differentiations reside in it undistributed and undeveloped, but the

same eternal act, whereby it appears in particularity, also sets its efficacy going within itself. Every idea embodied in it itself becomes form,
just as the world-body does, and appears by way of an individual
actual thing.

The first potency of this unfolding of identity is, as we said, that of
the embodiment of unity into multiplicity, the absolute form of which
is absolute space, as its relative form is the line. All forms whereby
things are separated in this potency, become, therefore, mere forms
of space, and since space, in its identity as image of the absolute in
difference, simply includes the three unities again, these forms are the
three unities or dimensions of space. Now that, generally speaking, all
bodily differences must reduce uniquely to their relation to the three
dimensions of space, and that bodies in all qualities are divided into
the three classes, that they display the preponderance of the first
dimension and of absolute coherence, or that of the other dimensions
and of relative connection, or finally the greater or lesser indifference
of both in fluidity – this follows already from the general proof, but
can also be based on complete induction.

With this there is an end to all those absolute qualitative differences
of matter which a false physics fixes and makes permanent in the so-
called basic substance: All matter is intrinsically one, by nature pure
identity; all difference comes solely from the form and is therefore
merely ideal and quantitative.

The other unity within the absolute embodiment of the infinite
into the finite, which is the endeavour of all particularity to return
into universality, of all difference to return into identity, and (since
this appears here as light) into *light,* just as light in the first potency
had embodied itself in non-identity and been darkened therein – this
other unity, I say, embraces all forms within itself again, just as the
first did, only as forms of *activity,* just as the former were forms of
being. This reconstruction of individual things into light is what
appears universally as dynamic process, and all forms of it will have
to correspond, just like those of the first potency, to the three dimensions of space.

It has been demonstrated in the foregoing that magnetism, as a
process, as form of activity, is the process of length, electricity the
process of breadth, just as the chemical process, on the other hand, is
that which alone affects cohesion or form in all dimensions, and hence
in the third.

Here too by the construction itself, we have ruled out all fixed
qualitative oppositions of particular matters, whose action has for long
enough been vainly invoked for the comprehension of these phenomena. Their ground and source lies in the form and inner life of the

bodies themselves, although light, as universal, necessarily precedes every dynamic process. The difference of their forms rests only on the different relations of the same activity to the three dimensions, and so we can also, conversely, again make all qualitative differences of bodies in the first potency depend on their different relations to the three dimensions of the dynamic process.

It is simultaneously established in this construction that the chemical process as a totality comprehends the first two forms in itself.

Substance, the essence of absolute unity, is wholly presented in the organism, which denotes the third potency. Universal and particular are here rendered wholly indifferent, so that matter is entirely light, and light entirely matter, when seen from the outside, for instance, in colour, which is no longer a dead and inert thing, like that of the body in the first potency, but lively, mobile and intrinsic; regarded internally, through the fact that here the whole being is activity, and activity at the same time being. And even in this highest marriage of matter and form, that first type returns in the three forms of all organic life.

What was cohesion and magnetism in the first and second potency, returns here, after the ideal principle has identified itself with matter *for the first dimension,* as the formative impulse, as reproduction. What there presented itself as relative cohesion, or electricity, is here, in the absolute identification of form and matter *for the second dimension,* raised to irritability, to the living power of contraction. Finally, where the light takes the place of matter altogether, and presses into the *third dimension,* so that essence and form in this way become wholly one, the chemical process of the lower potency passes over into sensibility, into the inner absolute formative power.

With this comes the solution to the whole problem of each and every world-body, namely, to present as difference what it harboured in itself as identity. In it, the third unity is the first and absolute one. But it cannot appear as the *particular,* without appearing as the indifference of the two opposites, and *vice versa.*

Immediately with the production of the real indifference-point in the real world, it also emerges ideally therein as reason, as identity, as the true ideal original substance of all things.

If we again compare the different potencies with one another, we perceive that the first is subordinated as a whole to the first dimension, and the second to the second, but that in the organism the true third dimension is first attained, whereas in reason, without potency, the static mirror of absolute identity, as in its counterpart, fathomless space, which is identity erupting in the relativity of the embodiment of the infinite into the finite, all dimensions become indifferenced and lie in one.

This is the general articulation of the universe, which it is the true task of the Philosophy of Nature to demonstrate as the same for all potencies of Nature.

BOOK II

Though a strictly scientific format would not have allowed it, the freer form of our inquiries has permitted us, instead of gradually descending from pure to empirical principles, to ascend, on the contrary, by degrees, from experience and empirical laws towards pure principles that are prior to all experience.

Universal attraction and equilibrium have long been regarded as the law of the universe, and from then on every attempt to have the whole of Nature act, even in subordinate systems, according to the same laws by which she acts in the system of the whole has been viewed as a valuable achievement.

Our purpose is now to discover how the laws of attraction and repulsion in the parts may be connected with those of universal attraction and repulsion, whether they are not both, perhaps, united by a single common principle, and both equally necessary in the system of our knowledge – questions whose solution will perhaps be the prize of the investigations to follow.

1

On Attraction and Repulsion in General, as Principles of a System of Nature

We assume, for the time being, that the laws of reciprocal attraction and repulsion are *universal* laws of nature, and ask what would necessarily have to follow from this assumption.

If both are *universal laws of nature,* they have to be conditions for the possibility of a nature as such. But we begin by considering them only in regard to *matter,* insofar as it is an object of our knowledge *in general,* and apart from any specific or qualitative diversity it may possess. So these laws must first be considered as conditions for the possibility of matter as such, and there must be no matter originally conceivable, without there being attraction and repulsion between it and some other.

This we presuppose. Whether and why it should have to be so will be investigated later on.

Matter, for us, has hitherto been no more than just something extended in three dimensions, which *occupies* space.

Let us now postulate attraction and repulsion between two *original* masses, for this is the least that we can presuppose; we can imagine these masses as large or small as we please, but with the restriction that we take them to be *equal* (for as yet we have no reason to suppose them unequal). We then get the following result: Their attractive and repulsive forces would have to *cancel* one another (reciprocally *exhaust* each other); their attractive and repulsive power is merely a *communal* one, and since it is only by means of these forces that they reveal their presence in space, the ground of difference between them also lapses, and they cannot be regarded as opposing masses, but only as a single mass.

But no matter is, or can be, anything but forces attracting and repelling through action and reaction; so unless, in addition to these two basic masses, A and B, we have a third mass, C, upon which they now exert their common effect, A and B will in fact = 0, since their forces mutually cancel, and now present only a single common force; for there is nothing for them to act upon, and nothing that could act upon them; but if we posit a third mass (similar, again, to the first two), this will be the purest, fairest and most fundamental relationship.

For two equal masses cannot, as such, be external to one another, and therefore different, without again being one and internal to each other in a third, and this without being added together therein, or the one augmenting the other; for otherwise they would again be merely in this third, and this without being added together therein, or the one augmenting the other; for otherwise they would again be merely in this third, and not externally to each other, but in such a way that the two would be one among themselves, and with the third, and each of the first two would be simultaneously all of the third and one side of it. For, as Plato says in the *Timaeus,* two things cannot, in general, exist without a third, and the fairest bond is that which best unites itself and the bonded into one, so that the first is related to the second as the latter is to the one between.[1]

If, however, instead of the two *equal* masses, A and B, we suppose two *unequal* ones, then their forces on either side will not in fact be *reciprocal,* but the force of the one (say A) will entirely cancel that of the other (B), and thus we shall again have only one mass, having a surplus of force, which we cannot conceive of without at once giving it another object on which to use it.

So in both cases, in order to conceive the relationship between two basic masses, we are already obliged to append in thought a second relation, in which they both stand to a third mass, and this is as true of the smallest masses as it is of the largest.

If we consider the relationship between three primal and equal masses, which all mutually attract and repel each other, then no one of them will exhaust its power on the others, for each perturbs at every moment the effect of the one upon the other, since each (as presupposed) is centred in like fashion on each of the others, and in like fashion is external to it. For the same reason that A or B would have to undergo an effect from C, the latter undergoes the same from A and B, and conversely; so, given such an equality in the grounds of determination, there is no effect anywhere, and since the latter is expressed in the physical world as motion, there is no motion anywhere either. We could only conceive of this among the supposed masses, if A and B, in the same way that C is divided among them, were in turn divided among others, and in such a manner that the equality with the third

---

[1] [In place of the last passage, the first edition runs]: But if we posit a third mass (still equal to the first two), what follows? The latter, in virtue of its original powers of attraction and repulsion, will now compel A and B to direct their common force towards it; the power of each one acts jointly on the other two, and each one now prevents the other two from exhausing their original forces upon each other.

existed only collectively, and not in the individual parts; there would be motion only in these secondary masses, since only of them is each, for itself, unequal to the third, although collectively they exhibit the most perfect unity with the latter.[2]

So if *motion* is to arise in a system, the masses have to be supposed *unequal*. And it follows already, from this very fact, that the most primal motion by means of dynamic forces cannot be rectilinear. This must also be the case, if a *system* of bodies is ever to be possible at all. For since the concept of *system* implies it to be a self-contained whole, the motion in the system must likewise be conceivable only as *relative,* without being connected with anything present outside the system. But this would be impossible if all the bodies in the system were moving in a straight line. A system, on the other hand, in which subordinate bodies describe orbits, approximating more or less to circles, about a common immovable centre, has no need of an empirical space existing outside it, even with respect to possible experience (so that its motion may be conceived as relative). For in fact (as has been shown by Newton already, and by Kant), the motion in such a system bears no relation to any empirical space existing outside it; yet it is not an absolute, but a relative, motion – relative, that is, with respect to the system itself, in which the bodies belonging to it constantly change their relationships to one another, but always with respect only to the space which they themselves enclose by their motions (around the common centre). With respect to any other possible system, the system presupposed is absolutely one.

So even if we supposed such a system to be subordinated to one still higher, that would not alter *among themselves* the relationships of the system, as a self-contained whole. All motion *in* this system occurs only with respect to the system itself. So any motion that might accrue to it with reference to another system would necessarily be a motion of the *whole* system (regarded as a unity). Such a motion of *the whole system* (in

---

[2] [In the first edition the last passage runs]: If we consider the relationship between three original, equal masses, which all mutually attract and repel, then no one of them will exhaust its powers on the others, for each one perturbs at every moment the action of any one upon the rest. Thus according to the same law by which, for example, C perturbs the effect of B upon A, A in turn perturbs the effect of C upon B. But at this instant the effect of A upon C is perturbed by B, and so this interchange continues indefinitely, since it is forever reconstituting itself. Thus the action of each one upon the other two must constantly persist, indeed, since it is constantly reconstituted, but it has to be thought of at every single instant as infinitely small, since it is forever being perturbed; and since the original forces of matter can only act as *moving* forces, the motion which each one occasions in the other two will be conceived as infinitely small. So in a system of bodies which are all assumed to be *equal,* no motion occurs.

relation to a system outside it) would, with respect to the system itself, be *absolute*, i.e., no motion at all (and so it must be, if the system is to be a system). So wherever the whole moves in the universe, the system in itself remains the same, its bodies forever describe the same orbits, and the inner relationships which govern, for example, the change of seasons, of climate, etc., on the individual body, also accompany the system throughout a career for which millennia provide no measure.

Since, therefore, the subordinate system is equivalent to *one* body, in relation to the higher one, and since the attractive forces of the whole system can be thought of as united at the centre, the central body would have at the same time to belong to a higher system (as a planet, carrying the other bodies along with it as satellites), without this relationship having any influence on the internal relations of the subordinate system. For the force whereby the central body is drawn towards the midpoint of another system is at the same time also the force whereby it attracts the planets of *its own* system. Thus it is subject to the same laws as those governing the single system of the world, and in resolving the problem of how matter as such is *originally* possible, the problem of a possible universe has also been solved.

Having once pursued the principles of universal attraction up to their full height,[3] we can now descend again to individual bodies of the system. By the same law which keeps such a body in its orbit, everything upon it must tend towards the centre. This motion towards the centre of the larger body is called *dynamic*, because it occurs by means of dynamic forces. But every motion is merely *relative*, and the apagogic proof of a principle that would have to conclude from its opposite to an *absolute* motion holds everywhere with the same degree of assurance. That every motion is relative, means that in order to perceive motion I must posit outside the moving body another which – at least in relation to *this* motion – is *at rest*, even though it may in turn be itself moving in relation to a third body, which *to that extent* is likewise *at rest*, and so on *ad infinitum*. Hence the sensory illusions necessary for experience to be possible, such as the stability of the earth and the motion of the heavens, which understanding can discover, indeed, but never eliminate.

Nay more: In the body that is *moving*, there must likewise be *relative rest*, that is, the parts of the body, while they are all changing their relation to other bodies in space, must not alter their relation *among themselves*, and if they *do* change it, then for this to be perceptible,

---

[3] That a world-system is possible *at all* can have no reason other than the principles of attraction and repulsion. But that it should be *this particular* system can and must be explained solely by the laws of universal attraction; why? – more on the subject later.

there must be others that do *not* change it, i.e., the body must at least be *persistent*, even if it is not in a *persisting state*.

Matter (as such) is incapable of any change in its state without the action of external causes. This is the law of the *inertia* of matter, and is equally applicable to states of both motion and rest. But matter cannot be moved by external causes without opposing thereto its active, moving forces (impenetrability). So whether the body is at rest, or is moving under the influence of external forces (for both, in this respect, are completely equivalent), the effect of its *individual* powers of movement must be thought of as *infinitely small* – in the first case, because it *persists* in its state, and in the second, because it is expressly supposed to be set in motion by *external* causes. So the relative rest, which attaches to the body *with respect to itself*, occurs whether that body be thought of in relation to bodies at rest or in motion outside it.

But I am no more able to imagine motion without rest than rest without motion. Everything at rest is only so insofar as something else is in motion. I only perceive the universal motion of the heavens insofar as I take the earth to be at rest. Thus I relate even the *universal motion to rest in the parts*. But just as the universal motion presupposes partial rest, so the latter in turn presupposes a still more partial motion, which again presupposes a more partial rest, and so *ad infinitum*. I cannot conceive the earth to be *at rest* relative to the heavens, unless there again be motion of parts upon it, and this partial motion, e.g., of the air, of rivers, of solid bodies, is again inconceivable without presupposing rest of the parts in these things themselves, and so on.

So in every body that is moving, I suppose *internal rest,* that is, an equilibrium of the inner forces; for it moves only insofar as it is matter *within specific boundaries.* But specific boundaries can be thought of only as the product of opposing forces that reciprocally limit each other.

But this equilibrium of forces, this rest in the parts of the body, I cannot envisage save by reference to the opposite – absence of equilibrium and motion of the parts. But in that the body is *moving*, this is *now* not supposed to occur, for it is taken to move as a body, i.e., as matter within specific confines (in a mass). So again I cannot think of this disturbed equilibrium (the movement of parts in the moving) body as *real*, though I must necessarily think of it as *possible*. But this possibility is not to be merely an *imagined* one; it has to be a *real* possibility, having its ground in the matter itself.

But matter is *inert*. Motion of matter without external causes is impossible. So even this motion *of the parts* cannot occur without external causes. But now, so far as we know at present, only a *moving* body can *communicate* motion to another. But the motion of the *parts* that we are talking of is supposed to be quite different from that produced by impact, by communication – it is meant, indeed, to be the opposite of this. Since it cannot, therefore, be a motion communicated to another by a *moving* body, then – as necessarily follows – it must be a motion which even the body at rest communicates to what is at rest. Now every motion produced by *impact* is called *mechanical,* but motion produced by the body *at rest* in *what is at rest* is called *chemical;* so we would have a hierarchy of motions, as follows:

All other motions are necessarily preceded by the original *dynamical* motion (that is possible only through forces of attraction and repulsion). For even *mechanical* motion, communicated, that is, by impact, cannot occur without action and reaction of attractive and repulsive forces in the body. No body can be struck without itself exerting *repulsive* force, and none can move *en masse,* without *attractive* forces operating within it. And still less can a *chemical* motion occur without a free play of the dynamical forces.

Chemical motion is just the opposite of *mechanical* motion. The latter is communicated to a body by *external forces,* the former occasioned in the body by *external causes,* indeed, but yet, so it seems, by internal *forces.* Mechanical motion presupposes *parts at rest* in the *moving body;* chemical motion, on the contrary, *motion of the parts* in a body that *does not move.*

How chemical motion is related to *universal* dynamic motion, is not so readily determined. This much is certain, that both are possible only through attractive and repulsive forces. But the universal forces of attraction and repulsion, insofar as they are conditions for the possibility of matter as such,[4] lie beyond all experience. The forces of chemical attraction and repulsion, on the other hand, already presuppose matter, and so cannot be known at all except by experience. Since they precede all experience, the universal forces are considered *absolutely necessary,* while the chemical forces are viewed as *contingent.*

But the dynamical forces cannot be thought in their *necessity,* save insofar as they simultaneously *appear,* in their *contingency.* In every individual body, attractive and repulsive forces are *necessarily* in *equilibrium.* But this necessity is *felt* only in contrast to the *possibility* that this equilibrium should be disturbed. This possibility we must now look for in matter itself. The ground of it can indeed be thought of as an *endeavour* of matter to escape from the equilibrium and yield to the free play of its forces. Matter, at any rate, in which we presuppose no such possibility (which is incapable of chemical treatment), is called, in the special sense of the word, *dead* matter.

---

[4] This was expressly presupposed above.

But inert matter, in order to forsake the equilibrium of its basic forces, is in need of an external influence. As soon as this ceases, it sinks back into its previous state of rest, and the whole chemical phenomenon is not so much an endeavour to abandon equilibrium, as an effort to maintain it. But because the essence of matter consists in the equilibrium of its forces, Nature was necessarily obliged to ascend above this level, to higher stages.

For when once the first step has been taken, from the necessary to the contingent, it is certain that Nature does not remain on any lower level, if she can advance to a higher one. But for this it is sufficient that she simply permits a free play of the forces in matter, for when once the latter emerges from the equilibrium that sustains it, it is also not impossible that some third thing (whatever it may be) should make this conflict of free forces *permanent,* and that matter (now a *work of Nature*) should thereby find its continuance in this very conflict itself. Thus already in the chemical properties of matter there are actually lying the first seeds, albeit still quite undeveloped, of a future system of Nature, which in its most diversified forms and structures can evolve up to the point at which creative Nature seems to return back into herself. Thus the way is at once pointed out for further inquiries as to where in Nature the necessary and the contingent, the mechanical and the free, part company. Chemical phenomena constitute the middle term between the two.

It is this far, then, that the principles of attraction and repulsion actually lead us, as soon as we regard them as principles of a *universal system of Nature.* It is all the more important to look more deeply into the reason for these principles, and our right to the unrestricted use of them.

Since the force of *universal* attraction is everywhere proportional to the *quantity* of matter, it may also hereafter be called *quantitative,* just as the force of (chemical) attraction *among the parts* can be called *qualitative,* since it seems to depend on the qualities of bodies.

General View of the System
of the World
(Supplement to Chapter 1)

Very significantly did the ancients, and after them the moderns, describe the real world as *natura rerum,* or the birth *of things;* for it is that part in which the eternal things, or Ideas, come into existence. This does not take place through the intervention of a stuff or matter, but through the eternal self-division of the absolute into subject and object, whereby its subjectivity, and the unknowable infinitude hidden therein, is made known in objectivity and finitude, and turned into something. As we know from the foregoing, this act is not separated, in the in-itself, from its opposite, and appears *as this* act at all only to that which itself lies therein, and does not integrate itself through the opposite unity, whereby it reconstructed itself in its in-itself or absolute existence.

For through the very act in which the absolute makes known its unity in diversity, every unity formed in the particular has the necessary endeavour to be *in itself,* and to make knowable the essence in the particularity or nature of its identity as such. Hence, as with the universe in general, so every thing in Nature is known only from its one side, namely that of the clothing of its essence in form.

Now since the thing cannot exist *as such* in the sphere of being for-itself and in-itself, without being in its particularity, though the latter is knowable only in a merely relative and imperfect identity (since in the absolute form everything is one), it necessarily appears with merely relative identity of the infinite and finite; and since this is always and necessarily a mere part of the absolute identity, or Idea, the thing necessarily appears *in time;* for in regard to any thing, temporality is posited by the very fact that it is not, in fact and by form or reality, everything that it can be, by its nature or the Idea.

Now the form in which the infinite is objectified in the finite, taken purely as such in its diversity, as a form in which the *in-itself* or *nature* appears, is bodiliness or corporeality as such. So insofar as the Ideas, clothed in this objectification of finitude, appear, to that extent they are necessarily corporeal; but insofar as the whole is likewise reflected as form in this relative identity, so that even in appearance they are still Ideas, they are bodies which are simultaneously worlds, that is, *world-bodies*. The system of world-bodies is therefore nothing else but the realm of Ideas, visibly knowable in finitude.

The relationship of the Ideas to one another is that they are in each other, and yet each is absolute for itself, so that they are at once dependent and independent – a relationship that we can express only by the symbol of procreation. Among the world-bodies there will thus be a subordination, as among the Ideas themselves, namely, one that does not abolish their absoluteness in itself. For every Idea, that in which it exists is the centre: The centre of all Ideas is the absolute. The same relationship is manifested in appearance. The whole material Universe branches out from the highest unities into particular universes, because every possible unity again breaks up into other unities, of which each can appear as *the particular one* only through continued differentiation. But world-bodies must be seen as the first identity, in which nothing as yet is particularized, although with the first particularizing of the world-body, as finite, there is also posited the further particularizing of what lies within it, so that, being itself finite, it can also bear nothing but finite fruits. For just as it is in itself an Idea, which appears, through itself, as particular form, so all other Ideas that are built into it, and which it produces from itself, can become objective, not in their *in-itself*, but only through individual real things. So what we call organic and inorganic matter are themselves, in turn, mere potencies of that first identity. To that extent the world-body, in its first identity, is not inorganic, since it is at the same time organic; not organic, in the sense that it would simultaneously have in itself the inorganic, or the material which the organic has outside it. We call animal only the relatively animal, for which the material of its existence lies in inorganic matter; but the world-body is the absolute animal, which possesses everything it has need of in itself, including, therefore, that which for the relatively animal is still outside it, as inorganic material.

Now the being and life of all world-bodies, which in appearance is similar to that of the Ideas, rests in the double unity of all Ideas – that whereby they are in themselves, and that whereby they are in the absolute. But these two unities are again one and the same unity. The first is that in which the infinite in its particularity *expands;* the second that in which its particularity *reverts* into absoluteness; the former, that whereby those unities are in themselves, outside the centre; the latter, that whereby they are in the centre.

In the supplements to follow, we shall determine more exactly the extent to which these two unities are comparable with those of the expansive and attractive forces, which physics until now has made the basis of its theories, as universal principles of a system of Nature. In the meantime, we refer the reader who wishes further information about the laws of the world-system, according to the doctrines of Nature-philosophy, to the dialogue: *Bruno, or On the Divine and Natural Principle of Things* (Berlin: Unger, 1802),⁵ as also to our *Further Outlines from the System of Philosophy,* § VII in the *Neue Zeitschrift für spekulative Physik,* vol. I, no. 2.

⁵ [English translation by Michael G. Vater, Albany, N.Y., 1984.]

2

On the Fictitious Use of These Two Principles

Although Newton, it seems, was in two minds about the meaning of the principle of universal attraction, established by himself, his followers very soon began to regard the attraction of world-bodies, one to another, no longer as a merely seeming thing, but as a *dynamic* attraction, inherent in matter from the beginning. This attraction would in fact be *seeming*, if it was produced by the action of some third matter (such as the aether), which drove bodies mutually against one another, and pushed them apart. So if, as he says in some passages (though elsewhere he expressly maintains the opposite), Newton was genuinely doubtful as to what "the *effective cause* of attraction" might be, whether it perhaps was not occasioned by an impact, or in some other way unknown to us, then the use that he made of this principle in the erection of a world-system was in fact a merely *seeming use*, or rather the force of attraction itself was to him a scientific fiction, which he used simply in order to reduce the *phenomenon*, as such, to *laws*, without wishing to *explain* it thereby.

But in so doing, Newton was most probably anxious to avoid another possible seeming use of this principle, into which a large proportion of his followers soon afterwards fell. To avert the illusion of his having really wished to give a *physical explanation* of universal gravitation by means of this basic force, he preferred, for a time, to treat the whole phenomenon of attraction as seeming, and therefore himself in turn sought for a *physical explanation* of it in the mechanical action of a hypothetically assumed fluid which he called the *aether;* but soon after, he again contradicted this assumption just as strongly as he had previously maintained it—an obvious proof that he was not satisfied with either the one or the other, and that he considered a third way out to be possible.

If the principle of universal attraction is supposed to *explain* anything, then it amounts to neither more nor less than some occult quality of the Scholastics—than the abhorrence of a vacuum, and other things of that kind. But if this principle itself stands at the limits of all physical explanation – if it is that which first makes possible any sort of inquiry into cause and effect – then we must desist from looking for any further cause of it, or from establishing it in turn as a cause (i.e., as something that is possible only in the context of natural phenomena).

When Newton himself said of the force of attraction that it was *materiae vis insita, innata,* etc., he was mentally attributing to matter an existence independent of the attractive force. Matter could thus also be *real,* without any attractive forces; that it has them (that, as some of Newton's disciples said, a higher hand has impressed this tendency upon it, so to speak) is a *contingent* thing, as regards the existence of matter itself.

But if attractive and repulsive forces are themselves conditions of the *possibility* of matter – or rather, if matter itself is nothing else but these forces, conceived in conflict, then these principles stand at the apex of all natural science, either as lemmas from a higher science, or as axioms that must be presupposed before all else, if physical explanation is to be otherwise possible at all.

But because, in *reflection,* it is possible to conceive of attractive and repulsive forces as distinct from matter, people suppose (through a deception by no means uncommon) that what can be separated *in thought* is also separate *in fact.* If we succumb to this deception, then matter is just there, without any attractive or repulsive forces.

If so, they can no longer lay claim to the dignity of first principles, and now themselves enter into the sequence of natural causes and effects – but when thought of as *causes,* they present to the understanding nothing but obscure qualities of matter which, instead of promoting inquiry into Nature, are actually an obstacle to it.

The same illusion of reflection which led people astray about these principles, extends its influence over all the sciences. Leibniz rejected Newtonian attraction, because he held it to be the fiction of an inert philosophy, which instead of laboriously researching into physical causes, prefers to take refuge at once in dark unknown forces (as the goal of all natural knowledge). But when Newton explained universal attraction by a force implanted in matter itself, he was doing no other than Leibniz, as generally understood, was himself doing, in another field, when he explained the original and necessary acts of the human mind by *innate* powers. Just as Newton separated matter from its forces, as if one could exist without the other, or as if matter were something other than its forces, so the Leibnizians separated the human mind (as a thing-in-itself) from its original powers and activities, as though the mind could be actual in any way other than through its powers and in its activities alone.

Long before Newton, it was Kepler, that creative spirit, who affirmed in poetic images what Newton later expressed in more prosaic form. When the former first spoke of the longing which drives matter towards matter, and the latter of the attraction between body and body, neither of them supposed that these expressions should ever be taken for *explanations,* either to themselves or others. For to them, matter and attractive or repulsive forces were one and the same – both being merely two equivalent expressions for the same thing, the one valid for the senses, the other for the understanding.

Even when Newton found himself faced with the alternatives, of regarding the universal force of attraction either as an occult quality (which he did not want and could not do) or as merely seeming, i.e., as the effect of an alien cause, he never, so it seems, himself worked out the reason which drove him back and forth uncertainly between two contradictory claims. Why should he even have needed to do so? That reason concerned only the possibility of the principles; the system, certain in itself, had no part in it.

Our age, which not only discovers itself, but also investigates the *possibility* of earlier discoveries, has found out this error of reflection, which runs through all the sciences. To the theory of Nature, within its prescribed limits, this can be very much a matter of indifference. It goes its own appointed way, even when it is not clear about principles. The discovery in question is all the more important to philosophy, at whose tribunal there must ultimately be a settlement of all those disputes that other sciences do not care to meddle with, trusting as they do to the perspicuity of their concepts, or to the touchstone of experience, which at every moment lies ready to their hand.

Philosophy itself, in the meantime, however much its principles agree with what is generally known to and assumed by common sense, has still not succeeded, as yet, in getting rid of that obscure scholasticism, which carries over to sensory things what is valid only in an absolute sphere, that of reason; which degrades Ideas into physical causes; and which, while in actuality not advancing a step beyond the world of experience, still prides itself on a real acquaintance with things supersensible.[1] People have not yet seen, for the most part, that the ideality of things is also the only reality, and are preoccupied with fancies about things external to sensory objects, which still retain their properties about them, nonetheless.[2] Because reflection is able to sepa-

---

[1] . . . getting rid of that obscure scholasticism which, ignorant in regard to all the demands which experience and the empirical sciences make upon philosophy, continues even now to indulge its speculative illusions, and, priding itself upon a supposed knowledge of the *real,* to look down with disdain upon all attempts to confine our knowledge solely to the world of experience. [1st Edn.]

[2] . . . not seen, that things are not distinct from their effects, and are preoccupied even now with fancies about things that are supposed to be present externally to things themselves. [1st Edn.]

rate what in itself is never separated, because the fancy can divide the object from its property, the actual from its action, and thereby keep a hold upon them, the supposition is that these real objects without properties, things without action, can also exist outside the fancy – regardless of the fact that, apart from reflection, every object is present for us only through its properties, every thing through its action alone.

Philosophy has taught that the *self* in us – abstracted from its doings – is *nothing;* regardless of this, there are philosophers who continue to believe, with the general public, that the soul is some sort of thing – they do not themselves know what sort – which might very well *exist,* even if it neither felt, nor thought, nor willed, nor acted. This they express as follows: The soul is something that exists *in itself.* That it actually does think and will and act is *contingent,* and does not constitute its *essence,* but is merely implanted in it; and if somebody asks why it thinks, wills and acts, he is told that this just is so, and that it could doubtless also *not* be so, too.

Now the same spirit prevails in the common ideas about attractive and repulsive forces in matter. For what people want is, not that these forces be matter itself, but rather that they should merely be *in* matter. As soon as they have been granted an existence independent of matter, people also go on to ask what these forces may be *in themselves,* and no longer what they are in relation *to us;* and here lies the πρωτον ψευδος of all *dogmatism.* People forget that these forces are the primary conditions of *our knowledge,* which we attempt in vain to account for from *out* of our knowledge (either physical or mechanical); that by nature they already lie beyond all knowledge; that as soon as we ask the reason for them, we have to leave the realm of experience, which *presupposes* those forces; and that only in the nature of our cognition *as such,* in the first and most primal possibility of our knowing, can we find a justification for setting them ahead of all natural science, as principles that are utterly indemonstrable in science itself.

Matter and bodies, therefore, are themselves nothing but products of opposing forces, or rather, are themselves nothing else but these forces. How, then, do we come to employ the concept of force, which cannot be presented in any intuition, and thereby already betrays the fact that it expresses something whose origin lies beyond all consciousness – that all consciousness and cognition are first made possible thereby, and hence, too, all explanation, by laws of cause and effect? Why, then, are we obliged in our knowing to come finally to a halt at *forces,* when these are themselves supposed to be either *explanations* of natural phenomena or the *object* of a physical explanation?

There is thus a twofold *illusory use* of these principles.

First, in that we begin by presupposing the independence of matter in thought, and then afterwards in reality, so that the forces of attraction and repulsion may only thereafter (we know not how) be implanted into it. For since these forces have reality only as conditions of the *possibility* of matter, they can now, if matter is real independently of them (if they are merely implanted in matter), no longer elude our physical investigations on this score; but in the sequence of natural causes and effects they represent nothing else but hidden qualities, which are not allowed to figure in any reputable natural science.

It is therefore wiser, in this case, to explain the whole phenomenon of attraction to be an *illusion*. But such an assumption has this in common with the foregoing, that it has to *presuppose* matter, in order thereafter to *explain* it. For in general all explanation is impossible without *presup*-posing something else, which underlies all subsequent explanation as a substrate. Thus even a mechanistic physics presupposes as a datum for its explanations empty space, atoms and a more rarefied matter that drives the latter against each other and pushes them apart.

Now as to these presuppositions, it is sufficient to remark that the mechanistic physics, in that it undertakes to explain the physical world by mechanical laws, is obliged, against its will, to presuppose bodies, and thus attractive and repulsive forces. For the fact that it views the original particles (*corpuscula*) as absolutely impenetrable and absolutely indivisible, so that it may thereby dispense with such forces, is nothing else but the expedient of a lazy philosophy, which because it does not want to admit something, which in fact it is bound to admit, as soon as it embarks on investigation, prefers to cut off all inquiry in advance, by a dictatorial fiat, and so forces reason, under protest, to acknowledge restrictions, where it is by nature unable to acknowledge any such thing.

Thus even the atomist is unable to get on without an illusory use of these two principles, which he is nonetheless wary of confessing, since if he did so, his whole enterprise would be in vain. For (contrary to his knowledge) he presupposes those principles so far as he has need to, in order to be able to represent them as dispensable, and uses them himself, in order thereafter to deprive them of their worth. They alone provide him with the fixed point to which he must apply his own lever in order to displace them, and in seeking to represent them as *dispensable* for an explanation of the world-system, he shows that they were at least *indispensable* to his own system of ideas.

Since another new attempt is now expected, whereby the mechanistic physics (honourable at least for its antiquity) is to be put completely beyond doubt, and upheld as the only possible system of the universe, it is not inexpedient to see what may well be promised in advance from such an attempt (so far as it is at present possible to judge it).

On the Concept of Forces in General and More Especially in Newtonianism (Supplement to Chapter 2)

Since we are anxious here to achieve general clarity about the concept of forces, we remark right away, though also for purposes of future inquiry, that although matter, for Kant, may have been constructible out of the two countervailing forces of attraction and repulsion, we, however, have no more been able to admit a purely expansive or attractive force than we are able to grant a pure finite or infinite (in that these are mere formal factors, and *identity* is the absolutely one and primal real); and we also observe that in the case supposed, that which we designated the first has to be thought of as the first of our two unities, namely expansion of identity into difference, while the second must be taken as the other unity, namely reversion of difference into identity, so that each of the two opposing forces comprehends the other.

But with this the concept of forces would already be abolished as such, since the implication is that on such a view they are *simply* conceived as purely ideal factors, whereas what we would call expansive force would in fact be already a whole or identity of expansive and attractive force (both taken in the formal sense), just as would that which we have referred to as attractive force.

So the concept of these two forces, as Kant defines it, is a purely formal concept engendered by reflection.

If we consider this concept in the higher application given to it by Newtonianism, in explaining the orbital motions of world-bodies by a force of attraction and repulsion conceived in relation to the centre, these forces in fact have no higher significance in this explanation than that of a hypothesis; and if Kepler, by the words centrifugal and centripetal force, was really designating nothing else but the pure phenomenon, it is undeniable, on the other hand, that in Newtonianism both have in fact acquired the sense of physical causes and grounds of explanation.

It has to be said that in the above-mentioned system the concept of force is designating, not only in general, but also in particular, a one-sided causality relationship that is intrinsically objectionable for philosophy. Not as though Newton did not teach that even the attracted body exerts a pull on the one attracting it, and that in this relationship action and reaction are again equal; the objection, rather, is that he locates the pull quite passively in the *quality of being attracted,* and conceals under an appearance of dynamism the purely mechanical style of explanation. The cause of centripetal motion in the attracted body as such lies, according to Newton, in the attracting one, whereas it is actually an inherent principle of the attracted body itself, which is as necessarily also in the centre, as it is absolutely in itself. Centrifugal force, as a ground of explanation, is no less a hypothesis; but the relationship of the two causes in bringing about the orbit is again conceived as a purely formal one, and all absoluteness is abolished therein.

We set forth briefly the main conceptions whereby all so-called physical explanations of the higher relationships of things must be evaluated.

In the sphere of pure finitude as such, everything is endlessly determined by some other particular, in itself devoid of life; this is the region of pure mechanism, which for philosophy has no existence anywhere, and in which it apprehends nothing of what it apprehends at all.

In that sphere wherein alone philosophy is acquainted with all things, the mechanistic thread is completely broken off; here dependency is at once absoluteness, and absoluteness dependency. Nothing therein is merely determined or merely determinant, for everything is absolutely one, and all activity springs forth directly from absolute identity. Substance, unity, is not divided by being dispersed into a multiplicity; for it is one, not through negation of multiplicity, but in virtue of its essence or Idea, and does not cease to be so even in multiplicity. In every thing, therefore, there dwells the undivided and indivisible substance, which in keeping with the limitations of its form produces, directly from itself and with no external intervention, everything that is posited in this thing, as if there were nothing outside it; for as surely as every thing is for-itself in absoluteness, so surely is it also one with every other, without any other intermediacy but that of substance. It is coupled, therefore, to another thing (under gravity, for example), not by an external cause (a pull), but through the universal pre-established harmony, whereby all is one and one is all. There is consequently nothing in the universe oppressed, purely dependent or in subjection, for everything is in itself absolute, and hence also in the absolute, and because this one and all is at once in every other. The earth, if it seems to have an endeavour towards the sun or any other body, gravitates, not towards the *body* of the sun or any other star, but solely towards substance; and this, not by way of a causality-relationship, but in virtue of the universal identity.

To apply this to the so-called centrifugal tendency, the latter is the same inherent principle or essence of the world-body as the centripetal; for by the former the body is in itself absolute, a universe in its particularity, and by the latter it is in the absolute: As we have seen, this duality is itself one. These two forces, falsely so designated, are thus in truth merely the two unities of the Ideas, just as rhythm and the harmony of the motions arising from them are the reflex of the absolute life of all things. For knowledge of these exalted relationships, the understanding is thus wholly dead – they are evident only to reason; to deduce them, as Newton did with centrifugal force, in a still merely mechanist fashion from the action of God is quite literally – to borrow, with Spinoza, the term of an old writer – to rave with the understanding.

3

Some Remarks on the Mechanical Physics of M. le Sage

The *mechanical physics* of M. le Sage has been known to us, till now, in part from certain writings of its founder, namely, the *Lucrèce New-tonien* and his prize essay, *Attempt at a Mechnical Chemistry,* and in part from what some of his friends have told us about it, for example, M. de Luc in his two works *On the Atmosphere,* and in far more connected and systematic a fashion, M. Prévost, in his treatise *On the Origin of the Magnetic Forces.*[1] The remarks that follow have been based throughout on the last-mentioned piece.

What seems most surprising is that the mechanical physics begins with *postulates,* then erects *possibilities* upon these postulates, and finally purports to have constructed a system that is beyond all doubt.

According to its first postulate, there are many *primary bodies (corpuscules)* distributed in a certain space, all of equal mass, but small enough to be not very noticeably distinct from one another when in contact, and moreover so constituted that each of them attracts the particles of its kind less than it does those of the other kind.[2]

Thus the mechanical physics conceives of its *primary particles* as *points;* but as *occupied* (material or physical) points. But if these points are still material, then the question is: what entitles the atomist to stop short at these points? For mathematics proceeds, for that very reason, to dwell upon the infinite divisibility of *space,* and philosophy, though it may be wary of saying that *matter* (considered in itself) *consists* of infinitely many parts, does not cease, on that account, to insist upon an infinite *divisibility,* i.e., the *impossibility* of any *completed* division. So if the mechanical physics presupposes first (or last) particles, it cannot borrow the ground for this assumption from either mathematics or philosophy. So the ground can only be a *physical* one; that is, the theory has, if not to prove, at least to maintain, that these are particles which are *physically* impossible to divide any further. But having first

---

[1] *De l'origine des forces magnétiques,* Geneva, 1788; German translation, Halle, 1794.
[2] *Ibid.,* §§ 1, 2.

of all withdrawn the object from all possible experience, as we do in postulating physically indivisible particles, we then have no subsequent right of appeal to experience, i.e., to a physical ground (as in this case to *physical* impossibility). Hence this assumption is a perfectly *arbitrary* one, it being imagined possible, that is, in dividing up matter, to light upon particles which it is impossible, by the very *nature* of these particles, to divide any further. But there is no *physical* impossibility which could, *as such*, be *absolute*. Every physical impossibility is *relative*, i.e., valid only in relation to certain forces or causes in Nature, unless of course we take refuge in occult qualities. So as to the physical indivisibility of these primary particles, the claim amounts only to this: that there exists in Nature no (moving) force that could overcome the bonding of these particles together. But for this claim, likewise, no ground can be offered, save one extracted from the system itself, namely that without it the system could not survive. So it has to be restricted to saying that we cannot *think* of any natural force that would be capable of dividing these particles. But when stated in this fashion, the falsity of the claim is obvious. For every bond in the world has *degrees*, and as soon as it becomes a question of what I am able to *think*, I can imagine no degree of bonding for which I could not also think of a force that would be sufficient to overcome it.

But perhaps the mechanical physics disdains these objections, as the futile pedantries of a presumptuous metaphysics, and seeks to cut short any further inquiries, once and for all, by declaring: *So be it.* This decree, however, is valid only so long as we remain on the territory of experience, where all proofs of a thing's possibility or impossibility must fall mute in face of its *reality;* yet not so, once we have ourselves ventured into a field where there can be no further teaching from experience about possibility and impossibility, and where the mind recognizes only what it knows as *absolute* possibility to be absolute reality as well.[3]

So what right, we may ask the corpuscular philosopher, did you have to postulate any infinite divisibility of matter at all, and not merely to assume as possible, but actually to attempt, the dissolution of matter into its elements? The experience that matter is a composite thing? But if you have no other ground to offer, then you must likewise pursue the division of matter only so far as you are confronted with a composite in *experience*. But this conflicts with your enterprise of resolving matter into its elements. So somewhere you must come to a point where experience no longer compels you to go

---

[3] . . . where the mind surrenders wholly to its freedom, caring only that nothing should restrict this. [1st Edn.].

on dividing, and where you abandon yourself wholly to the freedom of your imagination, which continues to *assume* parts, even where they are no longer knowable. But once you have permitted full freedom to your mind, to go on dividing even where experience no longer requires it, you then have no ground for restricting this freedom anywhere. In the human mind itself there can be no ground for leaving off at any point, so the ground would have to lie outside it; that is, we would have to light somewhere in experience upon elements that set absolute limits to our freedom in subdividing matter. But we thereby find ourselves once more under the necessity of assuming an absolute impossibility, which is yet at the same time to be a *physical* one, an impossibility, that is, for which no further ground can be given, and yet one which resides in Nature, where everything must have a ground and a cause—an impossibility, therefore, which is itself impossible, because it contradicts itself.

If the mechanical physics is thus constrained to admit that there is no longer any ground for its assumption of original, absolutely indivisible particles, there is no seeing why it still has any concern for the possibility of matter as such. And in fact, it cares not at all about this either, but confines itself to explaining the possibility of a *determinate* matter, or what comes to the same, the specific diversity of matter, by way of these elements and their relation to empty space. In so doing, it has the advantage of presuming matter to be wholly uniform in its elements. But the latter, since they are assumed to be absolutely impenetrable, can still differ from one another in their *shape*, which now has to be regarded as *unalterable*. Hence there is already a possibility, despite all the original uniformity of the elements, of still asserting a specific diversity of the basic masses, according to whether they are composed of particles of the same or a different shape. And finally, we also have the addition of empty space, which allows complete freedom to the imagination in accounting for even the greatest diversity of matter, with respect to its specific density, by arbitrary relationships of emptiness to fullness in bodies, and *vice versa*.

This, then, is also the greatest advantage of all mechanical physics, that it can render intuitable to the senses that which can never be presented in sensory intuition by a *dynamical* physics (a physics, that is, which undertakes to explain the specific diversity of matter solely by degrees of relationship among attractive and repulsive forces). Thus, considered *within its limits,* the mechanical physics can itself become a masterpiece of cleverness and mathematical precision, even though it is utterly groundless in its *principles.* So we are not here concerned with what M. le Sage's system can accomplish, from a mathematical viewpoint, as soon as its presuppositions are granted, it being a question, rather, of examining those *presuppositions* themselves, and the *application* of his system to physics and natural science as such; for as to the system itself, it lies so far beyond the bounds of our experience that it could be perfectly convincing in itself, and yet become exceedingly doubtful in application to experience.

M. le Sage's system assumes, therefore, that an infinite number of *hard, very small and well-nigh identical particles* are uniformly distributed in an *empty space*.[4] Now so far as *empty space* is concerned, it is something that cannot be presented in any experience. For if we think it needed, in order to be able to explain the unimpeded motion of stable bodies (much as Newton took cosmic space to be empty, simply so as not to be distracted in his calculations of celestial motions by the interpolation of a material that could impede them), it is also possible to envisage a material whose resistance to the motion of these bodies (in regard to a possible experience) can be assumed to = o. But in general this system allows completely free play to the imagination from the very outset. An *infinite* number of *very* small, *well-nigh* identical bodies! Here we cannot help but ask *how* small they are then, or *to what extent* they are identical. At least we ought to suppose that atoms must be neither *very* small nor *well-nigh* identical, but absolutely alike and absolutely small. Moreover, the concept of *hard* has only *relative* validity, in respect of the force that is applied to separate the *individual* parts of a body, or to displace them. Thus even the primary particles would have to possess only relative hardness; i.e., there would have to be some possible force that could abolish the connection of their parts, which is inconsistent with the concept of primary particles.

Now these particles move in a straight, undeviating line, but in the most varied directions; their motion is so much *alike* in velocity that every point in space can be taken, for a moment at least, as the centre.

This is the second presupposition of the mechanical physics—at which it cannot arrive, however, except by way of a leap. For since it derives all phenomena, and even the gravitation of bodies, from an impact, it renders itself incapable of providing any further ground for this impact (the original motion). For even if the elements of the weight-producing fluid were assumed to be originally unlike, i.e., of a different shape, it would still be impossible for any *motion to arise* through this unlikeness, though it must equally be granted that if motion has once arisen between unlike elements, seeming attraction can take place.

So if the mechanical physics objects to the dynamical, that the latter is unable to explain *attraction*, as the basis of universal motion, it must

[4] Prévost, *op. cit.*, § 31.

itself, since it wishes to know nothing of universal attraction, in turn forgo any explanation of the original motion. But since (according to the dynamical philosophy), attractive and repulsive forces constitute the *essence* of matter itself, it is more intelligible that we should be able to give no further reason for these forces than that we should *not* be in a position to explain motion by impact, which already *presupposes* the existence of matter and thus has to be capable of being explained. Moreover, it is not enough for the mechanical physics to postulate the motion of the weight-producing fluid as such; it also postulates a specific sort of motion, namely, motion in an undeviatingly straight line, though of such a kind that the directions of the individual motions are to be as manifold as possible.

The *third* postulate of the mechanical physics is, finally, that at any given point of space in which the atoms are moving, there is a spherical body *much larger* than the primary particles.[5] We have to marvel that, if it is possible to make do with such assumptions, anyone would take upon himself the thankless task of asking how *matter as such* can be possible. For it ought to be considered that, if it is permissible simply to presuppose solid bodies, which are furthermore different from one another in mass, and on top of that a fluid which moves itself and strikes upon the larger bodies, there is no understanding how a man of Newton's genius would want to go back to forces in matter itself, in order to explain the possibility of a material world. In truth the mechanical physics, having once put its three postulates behind it, goes irresistibly upon its way.

Yet at once we fail to understand how the mechanical physics proposes to explain the communication of motion. For motion can in general be *communicated* only by means of the action and reaction of *repulsive* or *attractive* forces. A matter which does not possess originally motive forces could not, even if it chanced to have motion, be receptive of any force, which originally does not attach to it at all. If matter has no originally motive forces, which attach to it even when it is at rest, we must posit its essence in an absolute inertness, i.e., in a total absence of force. But this is a concept without sense or significance. To such a non-entity as matter is in this case, it is no more possible to communicate anything than it is to take anything away. The mechanical physics itself is therefore constrained to attribute *original* repulsive and attractive forces to matter *as such*, and merely refuses to accept the name (though not the thing).

Moreover, there is no communication of motion without an interaction of impenetrability (without pressure and resistance). Now the

[5] *Ibid.*

mechanical physics can offer no further reason for the impenetrability of its primary particles, and of matter as such. So it has to suppose the primary particles to be absolutely impenetrable; only secondary bodies, insofar as they are not absolutely dense, and contain empty spaces, possess *relative* impenetrability (which permits of degree). So again there is no seeing how the primary particles, insofar as they are absolutely impenetrable, and are thus incapable of compression, can communicate motion to another body.

These are all metaphysical objections, if you will, but they are perfectly in order against a hyperphysical physics. For this system in fact proceeds from hyperphysical fabrications (primary bodies of absolute impenetrability and density), which cannot be realized by any experience, and which it treats nonetheless according to laws of experience.

The mechanical physics thus has the primary particles acting upon the spherical body which it postulates. The latter naturally retards their motion, and the collective impact of all the particles must endow it with a certain velocity. But all the streams of atoms have their antagonists, i.e., atoms that are moving against the body in an opposite direction. So the latter will be at rest and in equilibrium.[6]

Let us therefore posit in space another large spherical body. The particles impinging on the one do not now impinge upon the other, and hence these two bodies will move towards each other; the streams of little particles drive them against one another, and thus become — the *cause of universal gravitation*. These particles may thus be called *gravity-producing particles* (*corpuscules gravifiques*).[7]

M. Prévost fears that at first sight a difficulty will perhaps be found in this way of looking at things, since correct concepts will not be formed either of the *size* of the gravity-producing particles or of their *velocity*, or of the *permeability* of the bodies exposed to their action.[8] But I think that these difficulties would be very easily removed, if only another much greater one were to be disposed of, viz., that the mechanical physics already assumes the *main point* — that which has always given the most trouble to all philosophers and physicists — namely, the possibility of matter and motion *as such*. For the first problem of all Nature-philosophy is not how *this or that particular* matter, *this or that specific* motion, may be possible. But if once we assume that matter is itself nothing else but the product of original, reciprocally self-limiting forces, and moreover that no motion whatever is possible without primally *motive* forces which necessarily attach to *matter*, not only in a

[6] *Ibid.*
[7] *Ibid.*, § 32.
[8] *Ibid.*

particular state, but insofar as it is *matter* at all (whether it be at rest or in motion) – if once, I say, we make this assumption, then the question arises, What *necessity* are we under to go on calling upon *mechanical* causes to explain universal motion, so long, at least, as we can make do with those *original dynamical* forces which are already required for the possibility of matter as such?

The mechanical physics itself, for that very reason, avoids all such questions concerning the possibility of a motion and matter as such. This is also necessary, if it is to sustain its point of view. For if it is already part of the *essence* of matter, if matter only *is* such, in that it reciprocally attracts and repels, and if these very forces of attraction and repulsion must themselves in turn be presupposed, in order for *mechanical* motion to be intelligible, then we shall also find ourselves inclined from the outset to explain the motion of the Universe itself from the general forces of matter as such, and not from mechanical causes, since even if we were willing to allow the latter, we should still have to keep coming back to the former in the end. Now if it eventually turns out, as M. Prévost himself so honourably concedes, that a (large) part of the phenomena of Nature, namely those of astronomy, are very readily explicable by the purely dynamical hypothesis of universal attraction, without any regard to a possible mechanical cause of this force,[9] it is very easy to see why we do not at once give assent to a system which, however admirable it may be – within its specific limits – is still erected on mere possibilities. By M. Prévost's own admission, it is only certain phenomena of the special theory of Nature (such as cohesion, for example, the specific differences of matter, etc.) which remain unexplained in the dynamical system.[10] Now to these we can as yet give no attention here (though we shall later on). I therefore content myself with adding some further remarks concerning this system as a whole.

The mechanical physics is a *purely ratiocinatory* system. It does not ask what *is*, and what can be determined from experience, but makes assumptions of its own, and then asks: If this or that were the case, as I take it to be, what would follow from that? Now it is perfectly understandable, of course, that given *certain assumptions*, it is also possible to explain by mechanical causes everything that has otherwise been explained by the laws of a dynamical attraction. Thus M. le Sage deduces Galileo's law of falling bodies from his hypothesis of weight-producing particles. But for this purpose he first of all assumes "a particle of time which has an unalterable size, which is, in a quite specific sense, a

---

[9] *Ibid.*, § 33.
[10] *Ibid.*

temporal atom, and cannot in any way be broken up." Such a view seems to presuppose conceptions of time of a kind that cannot be tolerated in any sound philosophy, and still less so in mathematics. Time would be a sort of discrete fluid, existing outside us, in much the same way that M. le Sage conceives of the weight-producing fluid. Furthermore, "the weight-producing cause strikes the body only at the *outset* of each such atom of time (which is supposed, however, to be *indivisible*); while the latter is *in passage,* it does not act upon the body, but renews its impact only when the next instant begins." I know not whether a famous argument of the old sceptics might not be aptly employed against this supposition: Either the impact operates at the last moment preceding the atom of time or in the first moment of the time-atom itself. But the first alternative is contrary to the supposition, and in the second case the time-atom, which is of course indivisible, has already gone by while the impact is at work, which equally contradicts the assumption. From these subtleties M. le Sage extracts a law that comes very close to the familiar rule (that the distances of fall are related as the square of the times). However, we must strictly adhere to M. le Sage's temporal atom. For if, like Councillor Kästner,[11] we calculate the law for a divisible time, we run into contradictions, which M. le Sage assuredly does not want, "since he calculates only for whole times, and not for parts of them."[12]

What Councillor Kästner says, in this connection, of M. le Sage's procedure, can be applied to his entire system. "What M. le Sage," he says, "is opposing to the Galilean law, can be stated approximately as follows: There are certain small particles of time, of a particular size, though we do not know how large; at the beginning of each such time-particle, and never otherwise, something, we know not what, or how strongly, strikes a falling body, so that in this time it goes a distance, we know not how far, and now it falls further, not according to the law that people claim to have discovered, but according to an altogether different law, which cannot, however, be known by experience to differ from the previous one. And taking this all together, what do we learn? *That the fall of bodies can be very intelligibly explained by reference to things that we know nothing whatever about.* The law discovered is this: The spaces traversed by any falling body are proportional[13] to x multiples of an x time-atom. Le Sage explains everything by *conjecturing* how the weight-producing matter *might* be, etc."

The greatest advantage to M. le Sage's system is that it lies in a

---

[11] Cf. his essay at the end of De Luc's *Investigations on the Atmosphere,* translated by Gehler, p. 662.

[12] *Ibid.,* p. 663.

[13] *Ibid.,* pp. 664ff.

region where no experience can either confirm or confute it. In such a field, assuredly, the purest exercise of the mathematical method is possible. M. de Luc observes, of the new law of falling bodies, that "although this law may deviate considerably (here, by 100 such time-particles) from the long-familiar and demonstrated law of Galileo, this difference is nevertheless so small *that it proves impossible, by observation, to distinguish the one from the other*." In my opinion, this can be stated more generally as follows: A major merit of the system lies in the subtlety of its objects, which is so great that the most considerable divergencies of calculation are still not even noticeable in experience.

The whole system proceeds from abstract concepts,[14] which cannot be represented in any intuition. If appeal is made to *ultimate forces,* we thereby admit unreservedly that we stand at the limits of possible explanation. But if first *particles,* and the like, are spoken of, this is something of which I still have the right to demand an account. In Nature there is nothing either absolutely impenetrable or absolutely dense or absolutely hard. All conceptions of impenetrability, density and so on are always merely conceptions of *degrees,* and just as no possible degree can be the *last* for me, so equally little is any degree the *first* for me, beyond which no other or higher could be conceived. We therefore attain to the idea of an absolute impenetrability, and suchlike, no otherwise than by setting absolute bounds to the imagination. Because it now becomes so easy, once the imagination has been deadened, to conceive of something absolutely impenetrable, and so forth, people thereby believe that they have also ensured the reality of this idea, though it is forever incapable of realization in any experience.

The dynamical system is ultimately its own best defender against any project for a mechanistic physics. The latter can make no headway without presupposing bodies, motion and impact, i.e., precisely the main issue. It thereby acknowledges that the question concerning the possibility of matter and motion as such is a question incapable of a physical answer, and must therefore be already assumed to have been answered in every system of physics.

[14] [The first edition has "speculative concepts" (and likewise "purely *speculative* system," three paragraphs above). Cf. the Introduction, notes 3 and 4.]

General Remark on Atomism
(Supplement to Chapter 3)

What has been said in the preceding chapter, about the value of atomism in itself, excuses us from further explanations on the subject; as for its relative value, we recall merely that atomism as such is the only consistent system of empiricism; that for one who views Nature merely as a given, and strictly adheres to this standpoint, no other ultimate assumption is possible save that of atoms and the composite character of matter; and that it is due only to the thoughtlessness of an empirical age, and the incapacity for general views within empiricism itself, if the system of le Sage, for example, has not met with general approval and undergone further development. Who, with any feeling at all for science, will not candidly confess that he is mentally more at home in the purity of le Sage's atomism than in the impure farrago of the customary physics, pieced together from mechanical and semi-dynamical modes of thought? In the former everything is clear and comprehensible, as soon as we are agreed about the primary conceptions, which it is easy for the empirical approach to do; here, by contrast, everything is embroiled in unstable and unknowable circumstances. It can be argued that those physicists, like de Luc and Lichtenberg, who have for a long period exclusively enriched the theory of Nature with ideas were committed to this system [of atomism], or at least inclined to it. If we rise, indeed, above the standpoint of givenness, and to the Idea of the universe, then all atomism really collapses; but those who cannot do this might be expected, at least in that sphere (which is indeed their true and only one), to bring it to some sort of completion.

4

First Origin of the Concept of Matter, from the Nature of Perception and the Human Mind

The abortive attempt to explain universal attraction by way of physical causes can at least serve the purpose of alerting natural science to the fact that it is here employing a concept which, not having grown up on its own soil, must seek its credentials elsewhere, in a higher science. For natural science cannot be allowed simply to assume something, for which it can point to no further ground. It has to confess that it is relying on principles which have been borrowed from another science; but in so doing it is confessing no more than what every other subordinate science must likewise confess, and is simultaneously ridding itself of a demand that it could never wholly reject, yet was equally unable to fulfil.

But the presumption which seems to reside in the claim that attractive and repulsive forces pertain to the *essence of matter*, as such, might long ago have made the scientist aware that it is here a question of pursuing to its first origins the concept of matter itself. For forces, after all, are nothing that can be presented in intuition. Yet there is so much reliance on these concepts of universal attraction and repulsion, they are everywhere so openly and definitely assumed, that we are automatically led to the idea that, if not themselves *objects* of possible intuition, they must nevertheless be *conditions* for the possibility of all objective knowledge.

We therefore set out upon a search for the birthplace of these principles, and the *locale* where they are truly and originally at home. And since we know that they necessarily precede everything that we can claim or assert about the things of experience, we must surmise from the outset that their origin is to be sought among the conditions of human knowledge as such, and to that extent our inquiry will be a *transcendental discussion* of the concept of a matter in general.

Now here there are two roads open to us. Either we analyse the concept of matter itself, and show, maybe, that it absolutely has to be thought of as something that occupies space, albeit within certain bounds, and that we therefore have to presuppose as a condition for

its possibility a force, which occupies space, and another force opposed to this, which sets bounds and limits to that space. But in this
analytical procedure, as in all such, it happens only too readily that the
necessity originally attaching to the concept vanishes from our grasp,
and that we are misled, by the ease of resolving the concept into its
components, into considering it as itself an arbitrary *self-created* concept, so that in the end it is left with nothing more than a merely
logical significance.

It is safer, therefore, to allow the concept to arise, as it were, before
our eyes, and thus to find the ground of its necessity in its own origin.
This is the synthetic procedure.

Since we are therefore obliged to ascend to philosophical axioms,
we need to establish, once and for all, the principles to which we shall
be constantly recurring in the course of our inquiries. For let it be
remembered that we are not concerned merely with the concept of
(dead) matter, but that very much remoter concepts await us, to all of
which the influence of these principles must extend. Dead matter is
only the first stage of reality, over which we gradually clamber up to
the Idea of a *Nature*. *This* is the final goal of our inquiries, which we
must now already have in view.

The question is, Whence the concepts of attraction and repulsive
force in matter? From inference, somebody may perhaps reply, and
think that with this he has thereupon settled the issue. The *concepts* of
those forces I do indeed owe to the inferences I have performed. But
concepts are mere silhouettes of reality. *They* are projected by a subservi-
ent faculty, the understanding, which enters only when reality is already present, which apprehends, grasps and retains what only a creative faculty was in a position to *engender*. Because understanding does
everything it does with *consciousness* (hence the illusion of its freedom),
everything—including reality itself—becomes, under its hands, *ideal*;
the man whose whole mental power has been reduced to the capacity
for making and analysing concepts knows *no* reality—the very question
of it seems nonsense to him.[1] The *mere* concept is a word without

---

[1] In our age the question has first been raised, in its highest generality and determinacy: Where does the real in our presentations actually come from? How
comes it that, although we are only aware of it through *our presentation*, we are
nevertheless convinced of an *existence outside us*, as unconquerably and unshakeably
firmly as we are of our own existence? One would have thought that anybody who
believed this a futile question would have refrained from discussion upon it. No
such thing! The attempt has been made to represent this question as a purely
speculative one. But it is a question of concern to *man*, and one to which a purely
speculative cognition does *not* lead. "A person who feels and knows nothing real
within him or without—who lives upon concepts only, and plays with concepts—to
whom even his own existence is nothing but an *insipid thought*—how can such a
person speak about reality (any more than the blind man about colours)?"

significance, a sound to the ear, without meaning for the mind. All the reality that can accrue to it is lent to it solely by the *intuition* that preceded it. And hence, in the human mind, concept and intuition, thought and image, can and should never be separated.

If all our knowing depended on concepts, there would be no possibility of persuading ourselves of any *reality*. That we envisage attractive and repulsive forces – or are even merely *able* to do so – makes them at most into a work of thought. But we maintain that matter is real *outside us,* and matter itself, insofar as it is real outside us (and not merely present in our concepts), is possessed of attractive and repulsive forces.

But nothing is *real* for us save what is *directly* given to us, without any mediation by concepts, or any consciousness of our freedom. Yet nothing reaches us *directly* except by *intuition,* and intuition is therefore the highest element in our knowledge. So the reason why matter is *necessarily* possessed of those forces would have to lie in *intuition itself.* It would have to be demonstrable, from the *nature of our external intuition,* that whatever is an *object* of this intuition must be intuited as *matter,* i.e., as the product of attractive and repulsive forces. They would thus be *conditions of the possibility of outer intuition,* and from this, indeed, would stem the *necessity* with which we think them.

With this we now return to the question, What is intuition? The answer to it is given by pure theoretical philosophy; here, since we are concerned with its application, only its results can be briefly recapitulated.

Intuition, it is said, must be preceded by an external impression. Whence this impression? More of that later.[2] It is more important, for our purpose, to ask how an impression upon us is possible. Even upon the dead mass, from which that expression is taken, there can be no action, unless it reacts in turn. But I am not to be acted upon as dead matter is; such action, rather, is supposed to come to consciousness. If so, the impression must not only take place upon an original activity in me, but this activity must also continue to remain *free, after* the impression, in order that it may be able to *raise* the latter to consciousness.

There are philosophers who think they have plumbed the essence (the depths) of humanity, if they trace back everything in us to *thinking* and *representing.* But for a being that originally only *thinks* and *represents,* there is no seeing how anything outside him can have reality. For such a being, the entire real world (which exists, of course, only in his presentations) would have to be a mere thought. That something

---

[2] But yet I cannot refrain from already asking, at this point, what this expression is supposed to mean. For generations expressions have often been in use, in whose reality no man doubts – commonly much greater obstacles to progress than even false concepts, which do not stick in the memory so firmly as words.

exists, and is independent of me, I can know only in that I feel myself absolutely *necessitated* to represent this something to myself; but how can I feel this necessitation without the simultaneous feeling that in regard to all presenting I am *originally free,* and that presentation constitutes, not my essence itself, but merely a *modification of my being?*

Only by contrast to a free activity in myself does that which freely acts upon me take on the attributes of reality; only upon the original force of my *self* does the force of an outer world break in. But conversely also (as the light-ray becomes colour only in falling upon a body),[3] it is only vis-à-vis the object that the original activity in me first becomes *thinking,* or self-conscious *presentation.*

With the first consciousness of an external world, the consciousness of myself is also present, and conversely, with the first moment of my self-consciousness, the real world appears before me. The belief in the reality outside me arises and grows with the belief in my own self; one is as necessary as the other; both – not speculatively separated, but in their fullest, *most intimate* co-operation – are the element of my life and all my activity.

There are those who believe that one can have assurance of reality only through the most absolute passivity. It is, however, the mark of man's nature (whereby it differs from that of the animal) that he knows and enjoys the real only to the extent that he is able to raise himself above it. Experience, too, speaks loudly against this view, demonstrating by numerous examples that, in the highest moments of intuition, knowing and enjoyment, activity and passivity are in the fullest interaction; for I know that I am *passive* only through the fact that I am *active,* and that I am *active* only through the fact that I am *passive.* The more active the *mind,* the more heightened the *sense,* and conversely, the duller the *sense,* the more oppressed the *mind.* He who *is* otherwise *intuits* otherwise also, and he who *intuits* differently *is* differently also. The free man alone *knows* that there *is* a world outside him; to the other it is nothing but a *dream,* from which he never awakes.

All *thinking* and presentation in us is therefore necessarily preceded by an *original activity,* which, *because it precedes* all thinking, is to that extent absolutely *undetermined* and *unconfined.* Only once an opposing element is present does it become a *restricted* and, for that very reason, a *determinant* (thinkable) activity. If this activity of our mind were

---

[3] This image is an ancient one – (the same philosopher who employed it uttered the telling words: λόγου 'αϱχὴ οὐ λόγος, 'αλλά τι ϰϱεῖττον [The foundation of arguments is not an argument, but something superior]). There are yet other familiar things that can be used to elucidate the above. Thus the free will is only broken, becomes *law,* etc, upon the will of another.

originally restricted (as is imagined by the philosophers who reduce everything to thinking and presentation), the mind could never *feel* itself to be *confined*. It *feels* its *confinement* only insofar as it feels at the same time its original *lack of confinement*.[4]

Now upon this original activity there *works* (or so at least it seems to us, from the standpoint we here occupy) an activity *opposed* to it, which has hitherto been no less completely undetermined, and thus we have *two mutually contradictory activities as necessary conditions for the possibility of an intuition*.

Whence this opposing activity? This question is a problem that we must forever struggle to resolve, but will never resolve in a *real* sense. Our whole knowing, and with it Nature in all its multiplicity, arises out of unending approximations to this X, and only in our everlasting struggle to determine it does the world find its continuance. With this our whole further course is mapped out for us. Our entire enterprise will be nothing but a progressive attempt to determine this X, or rather, to follow out our own mind in its never-ending productions. For in this lies the secret of our mental activity, that we are necessitated forever to approach a point which forever eludes every determination. It is the point upon which all our mental endeavour is directed, and which, for that very reason, continually recedes, the closer we try to approach it. Were we ever to have reached it, the whole system of our mind – this world which finds its continuance only in the conflict of opposing endeavours – would sink back into nothingness, and the final consciousness of our existence would lose itself in its own infinitude.

As the first attempt to determine this X, we shall at once encounter the concept of *force*. Objects themselves we can regard only as *products of forces*, and with this there vanishes of itself the chimera of *things-in-themselves*, which are supposed to be the causes of our ideas. What, after all, can work upon the mind, other than itself, or that which is akin to its nature? It is therefore *necessary* to conceive of matter as a product of *forces; for force* alone is the non-sensory in objects, and the mind can oppose *to itself* only what is analogous to itself.

Now that the first incursion has taken place, what follows? By means of it the original activity cannot be *annihilated,* but only *restricted,* or – if we wish to borrow a second term from the world of experience – *reflected.* But the mind is to *feel* itself *as* restricted, and this it cannot do unless it continues to operate quite freely, and to react against the point of this resistance.

---

[4] Does the source of the Platonic myths lie here?

In the mind, therefore, there is a union of activity and passivity, an originally free and, to that extent, unlimited activity outwards, and another activity extorted from (reflected by) the mind *upon itself*. The latter can be regarded as the *restriction* of the former. But every restriction can be thought of only as the *negation* of a *positive*. Hence the former activity is *positive* in nature, the latter *negative*. The former is vented quite *indeterminately*, and to that extent tends towards the *infinite*, while the latter supplies *goal, limits and determinacy* to the former, and to that extent necessarily tends to a *finite*.

If the mind is to feel itself as restricted, it must freely couple together these two opposed activities, the *unrestricted* and the *restricting*. Only in that it relates the one to the other, and conversely, does it feel its present restrictedness, along with its original unrestrictedness.

If the mind therefore couples together activity and passivity within it, positive and negative activity in a single moment, what will the product of this action be?[5]

The product of *opposing* activities is always something *finite*. So the product will be a *finite* one.

Moreover, since it is to be the *joint* product of unrestricted and restricting activity, it will first of all incorporate an activity that *in itself* (and by nature) is *not* restricted, but if it is to be restricted, must be confined only by a counterstriving factor. The product, however, is to be a finite one—is to be a *joint* product of opposed activities—and thus it will also contain the opposed activity, which originally and by nature is *restricting*. So, by the common action of an originally positive and an originally negative activity, the joint product that we were looking for will arise.

Note also the following. The negative activity, which originally and by nature is for us a merely *restricting* activity, is quite unable to function, save in the presence of a *positive* activity that it restricts. But the positive activity is likewise *positive* only in contrast to an original negation. For if it were *absolute* (boundless), it could itself be conceived as negative merely (as the absolute negation of all negation). Both, therefore, the unrestricted and the restricting activities, presuppose their opposites. So in that product the two activities must be united with *equal necessity*.

[5] There may be readers who are still, perhaps, able to *think* of opposing activities within us, but have never *felt* that the whole machinery of our mental activity rests, in fact, upon that original conflict inside us. These will now not be able to grasp how from two merely *thought* activities, anything other than something else merely *thought* can arise. In this, too, they are perfectly correct. But *here* we are talking of opposing activities in us, insofar as they are *felt* and *sensed*. And it is from this felt and originally sensed conflict in ourselves that we want the *actual* to come forth.

Now that act of the mind wherein, from activity and passivity, from unrestricted and restricting activity, it fashions in itself a joint product, is called *intuition.*

Hence – and this is the conclusion we are entitled to draw from the preceding – *the nature of intuition, that which makes it intuition, is that in it absolutely opposite, mutually restricting activities are united.* Or to put it otherwise: *The product of intuition is necessarily a finite one, which proceeds from opposing, mutually restricting activities.*[6]

From this it is clear why intuition is not – as many pretended philosophers have imagined – the lowest level of knowledge, but the *primary one,* the *highest* in the human mind, that which truly constitutes its mental nature. For a *mind* is that which is able, from the original conflict of its self-consciousness, to create an objective world, and to give continuance to the product in this conflict itself. In the *dead object* everything is *at rest* – there is in it no conflict, but eternal equilibrium. Where physical forces divide, living matter is gradually formed; in this struggle of divided forces the living continues, and for that reason alone we regard it as a visible analogue of the mind. But in the *mental being* there is an *original* conflict of opposed activities, and from this conflict there first proceeds – (a creation out of nothing) – a real world. Only with the infinite mind does a world first also exist (the mirror of its infinitude), and the whole of reality is in fact nothing else but this original conflict in unending productions and reproductions. No objective existence is possible without a mind to know it, and conversely, no mind is possible without a world existing for it.

It is thus now presupposed that intuition itself is impossible without originally conflicting activities, and conversely, that the mind is only able to terminate in intuition the original conflict of its self-consciousness.[7]

---

[6] This whole derivation follows the principles of a philosophy which, remarkable for the range and depth of its investigations, after having been familiarized *ad nauseam* in the *letter* by a host of largely bad writings, revolving eternally in the same words and circles, at length found a more original interpreter, who by being the first who undertook to present the *spirit* of this philosophy, became its second creator. But till now only partisan, or weak-minded, or ultimately quite facetious authors have presented their respective judgements on this undertaking to the public.

[7] This is confirmed by the most ordinary attention to what goes on in intuition. What we feel at the sight of mountains lost in the clouds, at the thundering descent of a cataract, at everything, indeed, which is grand and glorious in Nature – that attraction and repulsion between the object and the contemplating mind, that conflict of opposing tendencies which is ended only in intuition – all this is occurring, only transcendentally and without consciousness, in intuition generally. Those who do not grasp such a thing have commonly nothing before them but their petty objects – their books, their papers and their dust. But who would even want men,

It is now self-evidently clear that even the product of intuition must unite these opposed activities within it. Only because a creative power within us allowed it to emerge from this conflict can *understanding* now grasp it, as a product which has become real, independently of understanding, through the clash of opposing forces. This product does not exist, therefore, through *composition of its parts;* on the contrary, its parts exist only after the whole–only now a possible object of the dividing understanding–has become real through a creative power (which alone can bring forth a *whole*). And thus we proceed towards the specific derivation of the basic dynamical principles.

whose imagination has been killed by rote-learning, dead speculation, or the analysis of abstract concepts–who would want scientifically–or socially–degenerate men to be thrust forward as the standard of *human nature* (so rich, so deep, so powerful in itself)? To exercise this power of *intuition* must be the first aim of all education. For it is that which makes man into a man. To nobody but a blind man can it be denied *that he sees*. But that he *intuits* with consciousness–that calls for a free mind and a spiritual organ which are withheld from so many.

The Construction of Matter
(Supplement to Chapter 4)

No inquiry has been surrounded, for the philosophers of every age, by so much darkness as that concerning the nature of matter. And yet insight into this question is necessary for true philosophy, just as all false systems are shipwrecked from the very outset on this reef. Matter is the general seed-corn of the universe, in which is hidden everything that unfolds in the later developments. "Give me an atom of matter," the philosopher and physicist might say, "and I will teach you from thence to apprehend the universe." The great difficulty of this inquiry might also be inferred from the very fact that, from the inception of philosophy up to the present day, in very different forms, admittedly, but always recognizably enough, matter, in by far the majority of so-called systems, has been assumed as a mere given, or postulated as a manifold, which has to be subordinated to the supreme unity, as an existing stuff, in order to comprehend the formed universe in terms of the action of the one upon the other. As surely as all those systems which forsake that opposition on which the whole of philosophy turns, leaving it unresolved and absolute precisely in its utmost boundaries, have never even attained to the *Idea* or *task* of philosophy, so equally is it obvious, from the other side, that in all systems of philosophy hitherto, including those which express, more or less, the archetype of truth, the still-undeveloped and merely imperfectly grasped relationship of the absolute world to the world of appearance, of Ideas to things, has also made unrecognizable the seeds of true insight into the nature of matter that were contained in them.

Matter, too, like everything that exists, streams out from the eternal essence, and represents in appearance an effect, albeit indirect and mediate only, of the eternal dichotomizing into subject and object, and of the fashioning of its infinite unity into finitude and multiplicity. But this fashioning in eternity contains nothing of the corporeality or materiality of the matter that appears; the latter is the *in-itself* of that eternal unity, but appearing through itself as merely *relative unity*, in which it takes on corporeal form. The in-itself appears to us through individual real things, insofar as we ourselves reside in this act of fashioning only as singularities or transit-points, on which the eternal stream deposits so much of that which in it is absolute identity, as is coupled with its particularity; for insofar as we also know the in-itself in the one direction only, that means that we do not know it as such, since it is simply the eternal act of knowledge, in its two undivided aspects, and as absolute identity.

Matter, absolutely considered, is therefore nothing else but the real aspect of absolute knowing, and as such is one with eternal Nature herself, wherein the mind of God, in eternal fashion, works infinitude into finitude; to that extent, as the whole begetting of unity in difference, matter again incorporates all forms, without itself being like or unlike any one of them, and as the substrate of all potencies is not a potency itself. The absolute would truly divide itself, if it did not also, in the real unity with matter, portray at the same time the ideal unity, and that in which both are one, for only the latter is the true reflection of the absolute itself. So matter, too, can no more divide itself than the absolute divides itself into matter (the real aspect of the eternal producing), in that, just as the absolute is symbolized in matter, so matter now in turn symbolizes itself, as the in-itself, through the individual potencies within it, and thus, in whatever potency it may appear, still always and necessarily appears once more as the totality (of the three potencies).

Now the first potency within matter is the fashioning of unity into multiplicity, as relative unity, or into distinguishability, and as the latter, indeed, it is the potency of appearing matter purely as such. The in-itself, which implants itself into this form of relative unity, is again the absolute unity itself, save that in subordination under the potency whose dominant element is difference or non-identity (for what dominates in every potency is that which takes up the other), it transforms itself out of absolute unity into the mutually external as *depth*, and appears as the third dimension. And again the two other unities, the first that of the implanting of unity into difference, which defines the first dimension, and the other that of the converse formation of difference into unity, which defines the second, are the ideal forms of this real of appearance, which in the complete production of the third dimension appear as undifferentiated.

The same potencies are also present in the corresponding potency of the ideal series, but there they exist as potencies of an act of knowledge, whereas *here* they appear displaced into an other, namely a being.

The first, which is transformation of the infinite into the finite, is in the ideal series *self-consciousness,* which is the living unity in multiplicity that appears deadened, as it were, in the real series, expressed in being as the *line,* or pure length.

The second, which is the opposite of the first, appears in the ideal as sensation; in the real it is sensation become objective, made rigid, as it were, the purely sensible, or quality.

The two first dimensions in physical things are related as quantity and quality; the first is their determination for reflection or the concept, the other for judgement. The third, which in the ideal is *intuition,* is the positor of relation; substance is the unity as unity itself; accident is the form of the two unities.

In both series the three potencies are one: The eternal act of knowledge leaves behind in the one only the purely real aspect, in the other the purely ideal, but precisely for that reason, in both it leaves the essence, albeit only in the form of appearance. Hence Nature is only intelligence congealed into a being, its qualities are sensations faded out into a being, while bodies, as it were, are its deadened intuitions. The highest life here conceals itself in death, and only through many barriers does it again break through to itself. Nature is the plastic aspect of the universe; even the pictorial art kills its Ideas, and transforms them into corpses.

It should be noted that the three potencies must be viewed, not as successive, but in their simultaneity. The third dimension is third, and real as such, only insofar as it is itself posited in subordination under the first (as a relative implanting of unity into multiplicity), and conversely, the first two can emerge as form-determinations only by reference to the third, which to that extent is again the first.

We still have to speak here of the relationship of matter and space. For just because in the former the whole is indeed embedded, but only in the *relative* unity of unity and multiplicity, and only the absolutely-real is also the absolutely-ideal, the latter [space] appears, for the present potency, as distinct from the real, as that *in which* this real exists; but precisely because this ideal, simply for its own part, is without reality, it also appears as *sheerly* ideal, as space.

From this it is evident that matter and space alike are pure abstractions, that one gives proof of the inessential nature of the other, and conversely, that in the identity or common root of both, precisely because they are what they are only as opposites, the one is not space, and the other not matter.

Those who require further details of this construction will find them in the works often cited, but especially in the *Darstellungen aus dem System der Philosophie,* in the second number of volume 1 of the *Neue Zeitschrift für spekulative Physik.*

5

Basic Principles of Dynamics

In intuition itself there was a constant interchange and constant encounter of opposing activities. This interchange is ended by the mind, in that *freely*, as it is, it returns to itself. Now it enters once more into its rights, and feels itself to be a free, self-subsistent entity. But this it cannot do without simultaneously granting *self-existence* and *independence* to the product that held it captive. Now for the first time it stations itself, as a freely contemplating entity, over against the real, and now for the first time the latter stands, as *object*, before the tribunal of the understanding. Subjective and objective worlds divide; intuition becomes presentation.

In the object, however,[1] those *opposing activities*, from which it emerged in intuition, have at the same time become permanent. The mental origin of the object lies beyond consciousness. For with it consciousness first arose. It therefore appears as something that exists quite independently of our freedom. So those opposing activities, which intuition has united in it, appear as *forces* attaching to the object in itself, without any reference to a possible cognition. For the *understanding* they are something merely *excogitated* and found by inference. But it presupposes them to be *real*, since they necessarily proceed from the *nature* of our mind, and of intuition itself.

Here now is the place to assure its reality, but also its limits, to the concept of basic forces in matter. *Force,* as such, is a mere concept of the understanding, and hence something that cannot, directly, be any sort of object of intuition. This indicates not only the origin of this concept, but also its use. Having sprung from the understanding, it leaves wholly undetermined that which has originally acted upon us. For it is only valid of the product of intuition, insofar as the understanding has accorded *substantiality* (self-existence) to the latter. But

---

[1] Only now, when the product of intuition has self-existence, can the *understanding* enter, to grasp and fixate it as object. The object stands before it as something that is there independently of itself. In the object, however . . . [1st Edn.].

the product of intuition is itself nothing original, but a *communal* product of objective and subjective activity (we express ourselves thus for
the sake of brevity, now that the situation has itself been made clear
enough to preclude possible misunderstandings). The basic forces of
matter are thus nothing else but the expression of those original activities *for the understanding,* for reflection; not the true in-itself, which
exists only in intuition;[2] and thus it will be easy for us to *specify* them
with perfect completeness.

Now one of those activities which intuition has united is *inherently
positive,* by its *nature unrestricted,* capable of restriction only by an *opposite* activity. The force, therefore, which corresponds to it in the object
will likewise be a positive force, which, if it is also restricted, at least
exerts against the restriction a resistance that is *infinite,* and can never
be totally abolished or destroyed by any opposing force. So I cannot
assure myself of this basic force of matter, except by letting opposing
forces act upon it. Now the resistance that it puts up to such forces is
disclosed to my feeling – if I apply this force myself – as a *repulsing,
repelling* force. In accordance with this feeling, I attribute to matter in
general a *repulsive* force, but the resistance it puts up to any force that
acts upon it I think of as *impenetrability,* and this not as *absolute,* but as
infinite (in degree).

The other *original* activity is *restrictive,* inherently negative, and in
this respect likewise *infinite.*

So the force which corresponds to it in the object must likewise be
negative in character, and inherently *restrictive.* Since it has reality only
in contrast to a *positive* force, it must in fact be opposed to the *repulsive*
force, i.e., be *attractive* force.

Moreover, the original activity of the human mind is wholly undetermined; it has no bounds, and thus no definite direction either – or
rather, it has *all* possible directions, which just cannot as yet be distinguished, so long as they are all equally *infinite.* But if the original activity
is restricted by the opposing one, these directions all become *finite,
determinate* directions, and the original activity now acts in all *possible
determinate directions.* This mode of the mind's action, taken generally,
yields the concept of *space,* which is extended in three dimensions.

As applied to the repulsive force, this yields the concept of a force
that *acts* in all possible directions, or – what comes to the same – endeavours to *fill up* space in three dimensions.

An inherently *negative* force has, as such, *no* direction *at all.* For
insofar as it is utterly *restrictive,* it resembles, in relation to space, *a
single* point. But insofar as it is thought of as in conflict with an oppos-

---

[2] for reflection . . . in intuition [added in 2nd Edn.].

ing positive activity, its direction is determined *by the latter*. But conversely, too, the positive activity can react upon the negative only in this one direction. And thus we have a line between a pair of points, which can equally well be drawn either forwards or backwards.

This line is also actually described by the human mind in the state of intuition. The same line in which its original activity was reflected, it again describes, in that it reacts upon the point of resistance. This mode of the human mind's action, taken generally, yields the concept of *time*, which is extended only in *one* dimension.

If we apply this to the attractive force of matter, it is thus a force that operates only in *one* dimension, or (to put it otherwise) a force that has only *one* direction for all possible lines of its activity. This direction gives the ideal point in which we would have to think all parts of matter united, if the force of attraction were *absolute*. If matter were all united into a single mathematical point, it would be matter no longer; space would cease to be occupied. To that extent we can even describe the attractive force, in contrast to that of repulsion (which endeavors to *fill* space), as a force that is trying to reduce space to *emptiness*. If the former is utterly resistant to all limits, the latter, on the contrary, is endeavouring to reduce everything to absolute limits (the mathematical point). The former, viewed in its boundlessness, would be space without time, a sphere without limits; the latter, equally boundless, would be time without space, limits without a sphere. Hence it comes about that space is *determinable* only through time, and that in undetermined absolute space nothing can be considered *successive*, and everything merely *simultaneous*. Hence, too, the fact that time is *determinable* only through space, that in an *absolute* time nothing can be thought of as *apart from* anything else, and has to be considered united (all in one point).

Space is nothing else but the undetermined sphere of my mental activity, and time gives it *limits*. Time, on the other hand, is that which is in itself mere *limits*, and only acquires *extension through my activity*.

Now since every object must be *finite* and determinable, it is self-evident that it can be neither limits without a sphere nor a sphere without limits. If it is an object of the understanding, then it is the repulsive force that provides it a *sphere*, and the attractive force that gives it *limits*. Both are therefore basic forces, i.e., forces of matter which precede all experience and all experiential determination, as necessary conditions of their possibility. *Every object of outer sense is as such necessarily matter*, that is, a space limited by attractive and occupied by repulsive forces.

We have now arrived at the point in our inquiries where the concept of matter becomes capable of being treated analytically, and where the basic laws of dynamics can be legitimately derived from this concept alone. But this task has been performed with such lucidity and completeness, in Kant's *Metaphysical Foundations of Natural Science*, that nothing further requires to be done at this point. Hence the following remarks are included here, partly – for the sake of continuity – as extracts from Kant, and partly as casual observations concerning the principles he has established.

Matter occupies a space, not through its mere *existence* (for to assume this is to cut off all further inquiry, once and for all), but through an inherently *moving force*, whereby the *mechanical* motion of matter first becomes possible.[3] Or rather, matter is itself nothing else but a moving force, and independently of this is at best something merely thinkable, and can no longer be anything real, the object of an intuition.

This inherently moving force is necessarily opposed to another force that is likewise inherently moving, and can be distinguished from the former only by its opposite direction. This is the force of attraction. For if matter possessed merely repulsive forces, it would disperse into the infinite, and a specific quantity of matter would nowhere be met with in any possible space. All spaces would therefore be empty, and there would simply be no matter there at all. Now since repulsive forces can be inherently limited neither by themselves (for they are entirely positive) nor by empty space (for although expansive force becomes weaker in inverse proportion to space, there is no degree of it that is actually the smallest possible – *quovis dabili minor*), nor by other matter (which we are not yet entitled to assume), we have therefore to postulate an inherent force of matter operating in a direction opposite to the repulsive, namely an attractive force, which attaches, not to any special kind of matter, but to matter *generally* and *as such*.[4]

It is now no longer a question as to why only these two basic forces of matter are necessary. The answer is, because a finite in general can only be the product of two opposing forces. But there is a question as to how attractive and repulsive forces are connected, and as to which of the two is the *primary* one.

We have already characterized the force of repulsion as *positive*, and the opposing force as *negative*. (Newton himself explained the force of attraction by the example of negative quantities in mathematics.) From this it is clear that since the negative as such, in a logical sense, is

---

[3] *Op. cit.,* p. 33 [English translation by James Ellington: *Metaphysical Foundations of Natural Science,* p. 41].

[4] *Ibid.,* p. 53 [Ellington, p. 56]. It is clear, therefore, that each of these two forces, considered in its boundlessness, leads to absolute negation (the void).

nothing in itself, but merely the denial of the positive (as with shadows, cold, etc.), the force of repulsion must *logically* precede the force of attraction. But the question is, Which of the two precedes the other in reality? And to that the answer is, neither; each one exists only insofar as its opposite does, i.e., in respect of one another they are themselves *reciprocally* positive and negative; each one necessarily restricts the action of the other, and only so do they become inherent forces of a matter.

For supposing that repulsive force precedes negative force in reality, repulsion can still only be thought of between two points. Repulsion is quite impossible to envisage without supposing a point from which it emanates, and which is to that extent its limit, and another point on which it acts, and which is likewise its limit. A boundless repulsion in all directions is simply no longer an object of possible presentation. This principle is very plainly evident in the applications which physics makes of it. The repulsive force of bodies, insofar as it has its *definite* degree, is called *elasticity*. But physics permits elasticity only between the two extremes (of infinite extension and infinite compression), neither of which it considers possible in reality. Of an elastic fluid, such as the air, for example, physics asserts the law that its elasticity stands in inverse relation to the space it occupies, or – what comes to the same – in direct relation to the compression it undergoes. So physics must also adopt the principle that the elasticity of air, for example, becomes *less* in inverse proportion to the space in which it is *extended*. On these assumptions rests the mechanism of the spring; for no pressure can be exerted on it, nor can it react against this, save in relation to the attraction that occurs between its individual parts (those that are nearest to the tip of the angle). Thus it is evident that the repulsive force itself presupposes the attractive; for it can only be envisaged as acting between points. But these (as limits to the repulsive force) presuppose an opposite attractive force. Could matter ever cease to cohere within itself, it would also cease to repel itself, and the repulsive force in its boundlessness would itself be abolished.

Owing to its negative character, we are far less inclined to maintain that the *attractive* force precedes the repulsive. Yet some not unreputed scientists, such as Buffon, have entertained the hope that it might well be possible, also, to reduce the repulsive force to the attractive. They seem, however, to have been deceived by the impossibility of conceiving repulsion without attraction; for they have not considered that attraction, conversely, is equally unthinkable without repulsion. They therefore quite wrongly transformed the relation of *reciprocal* subordination, which holds between these two forces, into a relation of *one-sided* subordination (of one to the other). For attraction, too, is conceivable only between points. Yet in virtue of mere attraction there are no *points*, but only an imaginary *point* (the absolute limit). So in order to be able even to envisage attraction, I must presuppose repulsion between two points.

Repulsive force without attractive force is *formless;* attractive force without repulsive force *has no object*. The one [repulsion] represents the original, *unconscious,* mental self-activity, which by nature is unrestricted; the other, the *conscious,* determinate activity, which first gives form, limit and outline to everything. But the object is never without its limit, or matter without its form. The two may be separated in reflection; to think of them as separated in reality is absurd. But because, by a common deception, the object seems to be present in perception earlier than its form (though it is never present without the latter, but merely wavers, in that state, between indefinite, uncertain outlines), the matter of perception, in virtue of this deception (very common amongst philosophers), takes on a certain primacy over the formal aspect of the object, although in reality neither is present without the other, and only through the other does the one exist.

Both forces, moreover, considered in their boundlessness, can still be envisaged only *negatively:* repulsive force as the negation of all *limits*, attractive force as the negation of all *magnitudes*. But because the negation of a negation is still something *positive,* the absolute *negation of all limits* at least leaves behind an indefinite idea of something positive as such, to which imagination lends a momentary reality. The absolute *negation of all magnitudes,* on the other hand – the attractive force absolutely considered, that is – leaves us not only with no concept of a *determinate* object, but with no concept of an object *whatsoever*. The notion that it leaves us is that of an ideal point, which we cannot even think of, as Kant would have us do,[5] as the direction-point of the attraction, without presupposing a second point outside it (i.e., repulsion between it and another). So when Kant says[6] that we should beware of considering the attractive force to be *contained* in the *concept of matter,* his point is merely that the attractive force is not simply a *logical* predicate of matter. For if we investigate the origin of this concept synthetically, attractive force necessarily belongs to its possibility (with regard to our power of cognition). No analysis whatsoever, though, is possible without synthesis, and thus it is easily possible, in fact, to derive the original force of attraction from the mere *concept* of matter, once the concept has first been synthetically produced. One should not, however, believe it possible to derive this force from a

---

[5] *Ibid.,* p. 56 [Ellington, p. 58].
[6] *Ibid.,* p. 54 [Ellington, p. 57].

merely *logical* concept of matter – I know not which – according to the principle of contradiction alone. For the concept of matter is itself, by origin, *synthetic;* a purely *logical* concept of matter is meaningless, and the real concept of matter itself first proceeds from the synthesis of those forces by the imagination.

So that which is *form, limit or determinacy* in matter we shall have to trace back to the force of attraction. That a matter is something *real at all,* we shall attribute to the force of repulsion; but that this real appears under these specific limits, in this particular form, must be explained by the laws of attraction. Hence we can also utilize the repulsive force, *in application,* no further than to make generally intelligible how a material world should be possible. But as soon as we want to explain how a *particular* system of the world should be possible – the repulsive force does not get us a step farther.

The structure of the heavens and the motions of celestial bodies can be simply and solely explained by laws of universal attraction. This is not to say that we could conceive a system of celestial bodies as such, without presupposing a repulsive force. In virtue of the foregoing, that is impossible. But the repulsive force is in fact only the *negative* condition (the *conditio sine qua non*) for a particular system of celestial bodies, not the *positive* condition under which alone just this *particular* system is possible. The laws of universal attraction can alone be considered a condition of that sort, since from these alone we must deduce everything that is *form* and *determinacy* in matter, or in a system (that rests on the basic forces of matter). Centrifugal force, applied to the motions of celestial bodies, is thus a mere expression of the *phenomenon,* which, if reduced to its principle, might ultimately be resolved once more into a relationship of the attractive force that inheres in bodies and makes them independent.[7]

So much concerning the use of dynamical philosophy in the large. Now for its application to individual concepts.

The basic forces of matter can in no way be represented in their boundlessness; beyond every degree of such a force, that is, a higher one must be possible, and an infinity of intermediate degrees between every possible degree and zero. The measure of a basic force is thus merely the degree of force that must be applied by an external agency, either to compress the body or to destroy the cohesion of its parts. "The expansive force of matter is also called elasticity.... All matter is, accordingly, originally elastic."[8] We must therefore distin-

---

[7] Centrifugal force is thus a mere expression of the *phenomenon*, which, if it is to be *explained,* can be accounted for only by the relationship of the attractive forces of the bodies to their distance from one another. [1st Edn.]

[8] Kant, *op. cit.,* p. 37 [Ellington, pp. 44–5].

guish between *absolute* and *relative* elasticity. The word "elasticity" is customarily used of the latter. But in this sense the elasticity of bodies cannot *by itself* yield the measure of their expansive force. For if one wishes to *compare* bodies with one another in this respect, volume and mass must also be taken into account, so that in regard to the quantity of expansive force, twice the volume with the same mass is equivalent to twice the mass with the same volume.

Moreover, since every body is *originally* endowed with elasticity, matter can be compressed *ad infinitum,* but never *penetrated,*[9] for that would presuppose a total *destruction* of the repulsive force.

If matter is allowed to *expand* to infinity, its repulsive force becomes infinitely *small,* for it behaves in inverse proportion to the spaces in which it acts; if we allow it to be infinitely *compressed* (= to a point), then for the same reason its repulsive force is infinitely large. But neither of the two can occur, if matter is to be possible. We therefore have to assume an infinite number of degrees between every state of compression and that of penetration, and likewise between every state of expansion and that of being infinitely extended.

Now by this assumption we avoid the necessity of postulating, with the atomists, ultimate particles for whose impenetrability there is otherwise no ground.[10] Nor would this lazy style of philosophizing ever have met with such great acceptance if it had not been assumed that the postulate of empty spaces was indispensably necessary, in order to explain the specific difference of materials.[11] So in that system compressibility can be admitted only in secondary bodies, but not in fundamental particles as well.

This necessity is now completely eliminated, in that *from the outset* matter is already allowed to arise only through the interaction of forces, so that (in accordance with the natural law of continuity) between every possible degree of these forces, down to the total disappearance of all intensity(= o), it is possible to have an infinite number of intermediate degrees (and thus an infinite compressibility of matter, no less than an infinite extensibility).

Moreover, since matter is nothing else but the product of an original synthesis (of opposite forces) in intuition, we thereby escape the sophisms concerning the infinite divisibility of matter, in that we no more need to maintain, with a self-misconceiving metaphysics, that matter is *made up* of infinitely many parts (which is absurd), than we require, with the atomists, to set limits to the freedom of the imagina-

9 *Ibid.,* p. 39 [Ellington, p. 46].
10 *Ibid.,* p. 41 [Ellington, p. 48].
11 *Ibid.,* p. 101 [Ellington, p. 94].

tion in the act of division. For if matter is originally nothing else but a product of my synthesis, I can also carry on this synthesis *ad infinitum* – can continue indefinitely to provide a substrate for my division of matter. If I claim, on the other hand, that matter is *made up* of an infinity of parts, I lend it an existence independent of my presentation, and thereby fall into the inevitable contradictions associated with the presupposition of matter as a thing-in-itself.[12] But nothing proves more plainly that matter cannot be a thing existing for itself than its infinite divisibility. For it may be divided as much as it pleases, without my ever finding any other substrate for it than that which my imagination lends it.

That matter is *made up* of parts, is a mere judgement of the understanding. It consists of parts, *if* and *for so long as* I wish to divide it. But that in itself it originally consists of parts is false, for originally – in productive intuition – it arises as a *whole* from opposing forces, and only through this *whole in intuition* do parts become possible for the *understanding*.

Lastly, the difficulty that is found in regarding the attractive force as a force that acts at a distance through empty space disappears as soon as we remember that matter is originally actual only through attractive forces, and that no body can be originally thought without already assuming another body outside it, by which it is attracted, and upon which it in turn directs its attractive forces.

Now it is upon these dynamical principles that the very possibility of a mechanics reposes, for it is clear that the movable would have no power of moving *through its movement* (through impact), if it did not possess originally moving forces,[13] and thus the mechanical physics is undermined in its foundations. For the latter is clearly a quite topsy-turvy mode of philosophizing, since it presupposes what it attempts to explain, or rather, what it thinks it can itself overturn with the aid of this presupposition.

[12] *Ibid.*, p. 47 [Ellington, p. 53].
[13] *Ibid.*, p. 106 [Ellington, p. 95].

Notes on the Foregoing Idealist Construction of Matter (Supplement to Chapter 5)

1. As has already been shown earlier (Supplement to the Introduction), relative idealism is but one aspect of absolute philosophy. It does indeed apprehend the absolute act of knowledge as an act of knowledge, but only from its ideal side, omitting the real aspect. In the absolute, both aspects are one, and one and the same absolute act of knowledge. For that very reason, they can never be one through a causal relation. The *in-itself* of the soul, or of knowing, produces the real in an ideal fashion, not *as if* there were nothing outside it, but because there really is nothing outside it. The real, as the other unity, falls outside it merely insofar as, in finite knowing, the ideal as relative-ideal becomes to it a form (of appearance), but not insofar as it is considered in itself. Idealism, too, as genuinely transcendental, does indeed integrate the ideal unity through the real, but only in the ideal; it knows the in-itself of the absolute knowledge-act, but only insofar as it is the in-itself of the ideal; nor, conversely, in the real, does it integrate the real unity through the ideal; it does not know the in-itself of the absolute knowledge-act as the same *in-itself of the real,* and so continues always to know it under a determination (of the ideal), and fails to arrive at the true absolute identity.

Now since that undivided act transmits what is grasped in it in the same fashion, and in the same forms, in both real and ideal – there only objectively, here subjectively – it follows that every possible construction of both real and ideal aspects is *in essence* one and the same; and since the ideal appearance of the absolute in-itself at least presumes that the latter is *here* appearing *as* ideal (not transformed into an other, a being), idealism accordingly, even when taken in its one-sidedness, as in the present work, still leads more directly to the *essence* of things than a realism bereft and robbed of all light of the ideal. Thus according to the system of transcendental idealism, only one step had to be taken in order to present the system of absolute philosophy in its entirety, upon the framework ideally projected therein.

2. It has already been recalled above (Supplement to Chapter 2)

that the two forces that were employed by Kant as factors of matter, in his otherwise purely analytical deduction, are merely *formal* factors, and that if both are to be thought of in any fashion as real factors, they must be thought of on the analogy of our two unities, so that one embraces and includes the other; which has also been hinted at, though very remotely, in the presentation of the preceding chapter, in what was said on p. 186 of the *mutual presupposing* of the one by the other, of the *reciprocal subordination* of each under the other, and of the impossibility of apprehending the one without the other.

3. More particularly, the preceding construction shares the defectiveness of the Kantian, in that the necessity of the *third* principle of the construction (itself to be found among its presuppositions) eludes it; that principle which, as gravity, has since been so admirably installed in its rights by Franz Baader, in his *The Pythagorean Square, or the Four Quarters of Nature*. That the attractive force is equated to gravity and conversely is merely a consequence of that first defect.

4. Of no less significance is the fact that all reality is located in the repulsive force, just as the whole basis of form is lodged in the attractive force. The first of these forces is as little of a real entity as the other. The only real is that which comes third, for appearance, but in itself is first, namely absolute indifference, the unity of the universal and particular, in and for itself; to the form belongs the particular and universal itself, the former so far as it is an expansion of identity into difference (which would have to be understood under repulsive force, in the sense described), the latter so far as it is a converting of difference into identity (and which could be thought to resemble the attractive force, in the sense laid down). Thus both would in this sense belong merely to the form.

6

Of Contingent Determinations of Matter – Gradual Transition into the Domain of Mere Experience

It is taken to be demonstrated that we are constrained to think of attractive and repulsive forces as *conditions* of our intuiting, which for that very reason must *precede all* intuition. A consequence of this is that absolute *necessity* attaches to them in respect of our knowledge. But the mind feels *necessity* only in contrast to *contingency;* it feels itself *constrained* only insofar as it feels itself in another respect to be *free.* So every presentation must unify the *necessary* and the *contingent* in itself.

It is clear from the start that attractive and repulsive forces only yield, in general, a *limited sphere.* Now in intuition the limit is *determined,* and that it is determined so and not otherwise appears to us as *contingent,* because this determination no longer belongs to the *conditions* of intuition as such. Nevertheless, the *object* and its *determination* are *never* separated in intuition; reflection alone is able to separate what reality always unites. It is clear, therefore, that already in the first intuition, necessary and contingent are most intimately united, so that our mind may distinguish the *necessary.*

Hence the *determinate limit,* the *size* of the object (its *quantity*), is contingent, and can only be known experientially. But in order, once it is known, to be able to *measure* this as well, we need other objects. From a variety of comparisons, taken together, the imagination first creates a *median* of sizes, as the measure of *all* sizes.

Now the cause whereby matter is confined to a specific limit we call cohesiveness, and since the force of cohesion is capable of varying degrees, this constitutes a specific difference of matter.

Now insofar as the size of a body, i.e., the sphere of cohesion of its parts, and also the degree of force with which these parts hang together, appears as *contingent,* it would be futile to insist upon making out anything *a priori* concerning cohesion or the specific difference of matter. It is better to distinguish at once the different kinds of cohesion. We must therefore distinguish between *original* and *derivative* cohesion.

Now how cohesion may *originally* be possible cannot be answered, so long as matter is taken to be present as something independent of all our presentations. For the force of cohesion cannot be derived analytically from the *concept* of matter. People therefore believe themselves obliged to attempt a *physical* explanation, i.e., to assume in fact that all cohesion is merely apparent. For if we explain the cohesiveness of bodies through the pressure exerted on them by the aether, or some kind of secondary fluid, that statement, too, is valid only of the *appearance* of our presentation; objectively speaking, it becomes a deception. But since cohesion holds of the smallest masses, as of the greatest, we would be obliged, insofar as it were merely apparent, to have matter consist ultimately of particles, for whose cohesion no further ground could be supplied.

Moreover, the degree of cohesion is in no way related to the surfaces of bodies, as it would actually have to be, if it were brought about mechanically through the pressure or impact of some kind of fluid. One would have, then, to take refuge in a new fiction, an original unchangeable difference in the *figure* of the primary bodily particles, whereby a different effect of impact, not proportional to the surfaces of bodies, would become intelligible. But for this purpose we would again have to suppose a matter of a quite special sort, which – as Councillor Kästner says – would permeate through all bodies, and at the same time exert pressure everywhere.

Now here there is an effort being made to explain something that neither philosophy nor natural science is able to explain. For we cannot even picture to ourselves any matter *as such*, but only a matter within specific limits, and having a specific degree of cohesiveness in its parts. Now these determinations are, and must be, *contingent* to us. So they also admit of no *a priori* demonstration. Moreover, they pertain so much to the possibility of a specific presentation of matter (they are, as has already been observed earlier, the *partes integrantes* of the presentation that must unite the *necessary* and the *contingent* within it) that it is equally impossible to give a physical explanation of them; for every physical explanation already presupposes them, as is evident from the above-mentioned attempt of the mechanical physics, which is ultimately obliged to assume particles whose cohesion it is not in a position to explain. So in regard to the original cohesion we are constrained, it seems, in natural science, to stop short at a mere statement of the phenomenon.[1]

---

[1] Kant, *op. cit.*, p. 89 [Ellington, p. 83], explains connection by *attraction, insofar as* it is thought of *merely* (exclusively) *as operative in contact.* But this explanation is nothing more nor less than a very precise expression of the phenomenon.

Derived cohesion I call that which does not pertain to the possibility of a matter as such.

To rectify the common conceptions, this may now be divided into *dynamical, mechanical, chemical* and *organic* cohesion.

Now so far as the first is concerned, it is merely *seeming* cohesion. That it operates in contact is not yet sufficient for regarding it as cohesion. For since it acts only in the common boundary of two spaces, this boundary can also be viewed as a space infinitely small, indeed, but yet *empty*. Here, therefore, there is *attraction*, i.e., an *effect at a distance (actio in distans)*; but this attraction, viewed as cohesion, is merely *seeming*. Cohesion, if it is not to be merely apparent, may not be thought of as acting between *different* bodies. For it is precisely that which makes a body a body (an individual). And hence only chemical and still more so organic cohesion is cohesion in the proper sense of the word.

For even mechanical cohesion can only very improperly be called *cohesion; adhesion* would be better. For the connection is here a mere consequence of the *figure* of the bodily particles, and rests entirely upon mutual friction. Yet there certainly are a few merely mechanical adhesions which yield the semblance of a cohesion. *Chemical* cohesion is normally also operative, in part at least. I take leave here to use the word "chemical" in the broadest sense, of *every* consequence connected with the passage of a body from one state to another. Now in the normal random aggregations of matter, that solidify in the course of centuries into cliffs and crags, the main contributing factor – to name only one – is water, which in conjunction with lime, for example, alters the state of the latter (whence at least the firmness of our mortar, our cement, etc.).

The cohesion effected by *chemical* means takes place wherever, from two bodies of differing mass and varying degrees of elasticity, a third body arises, as a *common product.* This cohesion is different from the merely dynamical or mechanical, in that (in a perfectly chemical process) a mutual *permeation* occurs. Or the cohesion is at least the result of a body's transition from one state to another, as from the fluid to the solid state. Since fire acts quite uniformly on bodies, they acquire, if the cooling-off is uniform (for otherwise the opposite occurs, as in the Rupert's drop, Bologna phial, etc.), an *absolutely* even degree of elasticity; this explains why such bodies, when broken, no longer show anywhere near the degree of attraction that they had from their solidification out of the fluid state;[2] it also explains why those very bodies

---

[2] Cf. *ibid.,* p. 88 [Ellington, p. 82].

which stick together most tenaciously are very often the most brittle,
since their cohesiveness, if it should merely be *altered,* is immediately
abolished.

This also accounts for the great cohesiveness among the particles of
fluid bodies. For since every liquid, so far as we know, is *chemically*
formed, it thereby acquires an utterly *uniform* degree of elasticity, the
connection of its parts being *continuous,* and this seems to be the case
in every *original* cohesion; while on the contrary, where cohesion
arises through mechanical accretion, the connection of the bodily particles is more or less *intermittent.* In the latter case we can determine the
figure of the bodily particles; in fluid bodies, at least, this is impossible, since the body is *one* mass. The more it approximates to this
continuity, the more fluid it is.

Organic cohesion cannot yet be dealt with at this point.

There are still questions that belong here, concerning the varying
shape of bodies. But I would prefer to expound this material in its full
context, at the point where the form of organized bodies falls to be
discussed.

As to the *specific difference* of matter – we shall talk of it later. For
now we merely remark that, since attractive and repulsive forces are
originally quite independent of one another, though every change in
the degree of the one is infallibly coupled with a changed relationship
of the other, infinitely many relationships of these basic forces are
possible. But the two uttermost extremes of bodies are – *fluid* and *solid.*
The question arises as to what the (mathematical) concept of *fluid*
bodies may be. They may be explained as bodies whose parts are
mutually capable of the most perfect contact, or – what comes to the
same – of which no part differs from another in respect of *figure.*

It might be objected that even in solid bodies, a perfect contact is at
least imaginable. This I do not deny; but the point is that the parts of a
fluid display a *natural endeavour,* peculiar to themselves, to take on the
shape (that of a sphere)[3] whereby they arrive at the most perfect
equilibrium, and thus at the greatest possible contact among themselves; solid bodies show nothing of this. It is thus a *property* of fluid
bodies, *as* such, that they are capable of the most perfect internal
contact, and only thereby are they fluid bodies, and become such.

Now from this it is apparent how the fluidity of bodies has come to
be explained by the minimal degree of cohesion among their parts.
There is no denying how easy it is to remove connection from among
the parts of a fluid substance; but this ease is itself a proof of how

---

[3] Presuming that no selective attraction takes place between the water and another
body. For this upsets the natural attraction of the fluid particles for one another.

closely they hang together. For since every single particle is equally attracted from all sides, it can be *shifted* without trouble, but never thrown out of contact.

From this ease of altering the internal connection of fluid particles, we may undoubtedly explain the great attraction that glass, for example, displays for water (whence the disproportionate ascent of the latter in capillary tubes, the depressed surface in a vessel not full, etc.). Kant, too, the first, so far as I know, to set aside the customary notions of fluidity,[4] has derived from this concept the main principle of hydrodynamics: ("The pressure exerted on a fluid particle is propagated in all directions with equal strength.")

Now with this, too, there is an automatic collapse of the false picture of fluids as an aggregate of single, separate, globular corpuscles (a relic of the older atomistic philosophy). For the nature of fluidity consists in the *continuity* of the mass, which cannot possibly occur in a mere aggregate.

But the new system of atomism claims as a major accomplishment the mechanistic explanation, which it professes to be alone able to give, of the properties of expansible fluids. Their elasticity, says M. le Sage, can only be explained in that the basic masses (molecules) of these fluids are moving with great rapidity in *different directions*.[5] Mathematically speaking, elasticity can indeed be explained as the *mobility of a static body, in opposite directions,* and the common explanation of elasticity ("the capacity of a body to regain its size or shape, when altered by pressure from without, as soon as the pressure ceases") is fully reducible to this. But M. le Sage applies this notion *physically,* and is therefore preoccupied with seeking out the *causes* of such a motion, in the constitution of the basic particles of fluids.

I merely point out that although M. Prévost speaks only of the elasticity of fluids, M. le Sage is in fact probably reducing all elasticity, including that of solids (which he undoubtedly regards as *derivative*) to the same causes.

Daniel Bernoulli, in his prize essay on the nature and properties of the magnet,[6] had already explained the expansibility of air by an internal motion of its basic particles. He takes the elasticity of air "to be sustained by a much more subtle fluid than is the air itself." Hence he believes it possible to derive the law that the elasticity of air increases in inverse proportion to the space in which it is extended. Moreover, this *internal motion,* he thinks, is the true *cause* of fluidity.

[4] Kant, *op. cit.,* p. 88 [Ellington, p. 82].
[5] Cf. M. Prévost, *op. cit.,* §34.
[6] Of 1746.

(Ordinary physics locates the *nature,* the *character* of fluidity in the *mobility* of individual particles *within* a [static] fluid mass): and on this internal motion Bernoulli bases a number of hydrodynamic principles. The principle of internal motion he ultimately conjectured to be *heat.* M. Prévost asks[7] why heat, then, should have this original motion. I fear that he will be asked a similar question.

Now in order to explain the internal motion of the basic masses of an elastic fluid as such, one might, with M. le Sage, suppose an *inequality* in the impacts of the weight-giving particles. Two opposite streams impinging on one and the same body, in one and the same *indivisible instant,* might not always, strictly speaking, be equal to one another. From this, therefore, arises the irregular motion or vibration of a second fluid, which M. le Sage calls *aether,* and which in general he will only allow to be set in motion by the primitive fluid (whose motion is as yet unexplained).

But this inequality of impacts is, after all, too indefinite a cause to suffice, by itself, in accounting for the phenomenon. M. le Sage wants a cause that is *inherent* in the primary basic particles, a cause that produces and reproduces the motion necessarily and at a moment's notice, and which satisfies all the conditions defined by the phenomena of expansibility.[8]

Now since matter is originally altogether uniform, and since we are talking of a purely mechanical motion (by impact), what else could this cause be, if not the outer form, or *figure,* of the basic particles of the aether?

Supposing an elementary body to be without concavity, then if equally struck upon from all sides, it could have no motion whatever. But if it is concave, then it will move in the direction opposite to the concavity, since the weight-giving particles which strike the latter make a stronger impact than their antagonists, which hit the convex surfaces. So the basic particles of the elementary fluid thereby have a source of motion *in itself,* which is wholly independent of the laws of gravity, although brought about by the weight-giving fluid.

All these basic particles together have their collective velocity, to which they approximate by successive acceleration. Since, moreover, they are always moved in the direction of the concavity, but their concavities may be turned to different sides, motion in opposite directions will thereby arise. But this motion occurs in every direction with the same (finite) velocity, whence the equal expansibility on all sides.

Furthermore, the *smaller* the basic particles, the swifter the motion

---

[7] Prévost, *op. cit., §35.*
[8] *Ibid.,* §§37, 38.

(of light and flame, for example, in comparison with the motion of the air), and the stronger the motion, the greater also the distance of one particle from another, and thus the less the density.

However much one may rejoice at the new and intelligent application which the age-old postulate of atomistic physics has received at the hands of M. le Sage, the following questions still remain unanswered. First of all, the weight-giving particles are a *primitive* fluid, according to M. le Sage. But whence, then, does the latter acquire the properties of an elastic fluid?

Moreover, this primitive fluid consists "of elementary, very hard and impenetrable corpuscles." Fluid materials (like the weight-giving fluid) are therefore a mere aggregate of solid bodies. Solidity is the primitive state of matter; fluidity, merely a special type of motion of solid corpuscles. But the mechanical physics also proceeds here as it usually does, in that it at once confers upon a purely mathematical concept a *physical* meaning as well. For the mobility of a *static* body in opposite directions does indeed yield a conception of elasticity in general, but not of the elasticity of expansible *fluids*. There is, in fact, no seeing how, by movement in opposite directions, however rapid we assume it to be, an aggregate of solid bodies can be supposed to yield the phenomenon of a fluid matter. For the *aggregate* can by nature be nothing else but what the individual parts are (it is quite otherwise with a *product* of diverse bodies).

That we picture the elementary bodies as small as possible is nothing to the purpose. Large or small, they are *solid* bodies. But an aggregate of solid bodies can never yield a fluid, if only for the admitted reason that friction occurs between solid bodies, which (if the laws of hydrodynamics and hydrostatics do not deceive us) is impossible with fluid ones.

This motion in opposite directions therefore explains only – as M. le Sage himself seems to say – the *expansibility* of elastic fluids. But with this their *fluidity* is not yet explained, as to which we are justly the more curious, since it seems exceedingly difficult to explain this at all on atomistic assumptions. The explanation would then have to extend to the *elastic* fluids (commonly not so-called), which M. le Sage seems not to have envisaged.

What lies at the bottom of all such abortive attempts is a common illusion, which we have already exposed above. Since, for example, the expansibility of a fluid can be separated in thought from the fluid itself, the latter is thereby accorded an existence independent of its expansibility. But only *through* its expansibility is it this particular fluid, or rather, it is itself nothing else but this particular expansibility of matter. If the fluid is something that exists for itself, and if this expansibility is *contingent* to it, we may *then* ask what has given it this expansibility; but not when we are talking of expansibility as a *general* property of fluids.

If, therefore, in regard to the specific difference of matter, we must altogether renounce the atomistic type of explanation, there is nothing else left for us, but to try the dynamical method. But now dynamics gives us nothing more than the general concept of a relation among basic forces *as such,* and this general concept alone is the necessary element on which we found all notions of external things.

But because, in consciousness, the necessary and the contingent must always be united, we are obliged, in order to be able to envisage this relation of basic forces itself as the necessary, to view it in another connection as contingent; and in order to be able to view it as contingent we have to presuppose as possible a *free play* of the two basic forces. But matter is inert, so this play of basic forces can only be effected by external causes. And this play is also to occur in Nature, and thus according to *natural laws.*

A free play of these forces only comes about, in that attractive and repulsive forces alternately gain the upper hand. But this must occur according to a *rule.* Hence we must presuppose causes which regularly produce this alternation.

These causes cannot simply be *thought of,* cannot be mere concepts, such as those of attractive and repulsive forces.

In relation to these two basic forces, they must actually be *contingent;* i.e., they must not belong to the conditions of the possibility of matter itself; matter could be real even without them.

For that very reason, they can absolutely not be known or deduced *a priori.* They are absolutely knowable only in *accordance with experience.*

They must announce themselves only through the senses. *Objectively* considered *in themselves,* they can thus be also something entirely different from what they *appear to be subjectively* – by their effect upon *feeling.*

This is precisely why they are by nature *qualitative,* and why there can be no other than a purely physical investigation of them.

These causes must relate both to attractive and repulsive force, since they are to bring about the free alternation of these forces.

But since attractive and repulsive forces pertain to the possibility of matter *as such,* these causes must be thought of as operative in a *narrower* sphere. They will therefore be thought of as causes of *partial* attractions and repulsions.

We must to that extent be able to consider their effects as *exceptions* to the laws of universal attraction and repulsion. They will thus be quite independent of *gravitational* laws.

These causes can be presented to us only through their qualities (in relation to sensation). They will thus be thought of as causes of qualitative attractions and repulsions.

Now the science which deals with the quality of matter is chemistry. So these causes will be principles of *chemistry,* and to *general* dynamics, as a science that is intrinsically *necessary,* there stands contrasted, under the name of *chemistry,* the *special dynamics,* which in its principles is utterly *contingent.*

Of the Form-Determinations
and Specific Difference
of Matter
(Supplement to Chapter 6)

According to the Kantian dynamics, no other reason is given for all the diversity of matter save the arithmetical ratio of the two forces, whereby different degrees of density, merely, are determined, and from which no other form of distinctiveness, such as cohesion, can be discerned. Under the guidance of this dynamics, in the preceding chapter, the contradiction was at all events bound to become insuperable, that cohesion was not apprehended empirically, by pressure or impact of a matter, nor was it grasped *a priori* either, and I am not ashamed of the limitation here imposed, since Kant, in so many passages of his *Metaphysical Foundations of Natural Science*, admits that he considers it quite impossible to understand the specific difference of matter from his construction of the latter.

Even on the assumption of a construction out of forces, yet another relation of them to space, besides the arithmetical, would have to be instituted – a relation that would contain the ground of their qualitative differences. But on the true construction, even the specific density or weight cannot be understood solely from a relative enhancement of one force or the other, or without taking cohesion as form into consideration as well. By what has been shown in the supplements to the two preceding chapters, *weight*, the *indifference of the two unities*, is in itself susceptible of no quantitative difference, for in it everything is one. Thus the specifics of weight can only lie in the thing as particular, though as *thing*, as *particular*, it is actually posited only through the form, and the specific weight therefore includes cohesion within itself, no less than does cohesion, in turn, comprehend the specific weight within itself, since it is of this form.

As to whether, on these assumptions, a true construction even of the specific differences of matter be possible, we may appeal to the demonstrations given on the subject in the various expositions of the *Journal for Speculative Physics* (especially vol. I, no. 2, and vol. II, no. 2; also the *New Journal*, vol. I, nos. 2 and 3, especially in the construction of the planetary system, and the discourse on the four noble metals).

Only the main outlines of this account can be presented here.

The very notion of *metamorphosis* in matter points us to the identity of form and substance as the common root of all metamorphosis, from which we therefore have to set out in our present construction as well.

The two kinds of cohesion correspond to the two unities of form, since in the absolute kind, identity in difference is posited, and in the relative kind, difference in identity.

Now the more perfectly we posit the indifference of these two unities, which correspond to the first two dimensions, the more perfectly is weight, which corresponds to the third, enabled to enter as well; for it is itself that indifference, considered in its essence. The central point of all metamorphosis is presented, accordingly, through the specifically heaviest things, which in their maximal indifference of form display most perfectly the character of metallicity, namely the noble metals.

But in virtue of the general law of dichotomy, the perfect indifference of general and special cohesion is itself again necessarily expressed in a dual fashion, either in special or general form.

In the *special case*, by the fact that in absolute as in relative cohesion, the factor of speciality is the dominant one (since the former is just as much a specialization of the general as the latter is a generalization of the special). This point is undoubtedly marked by the highest individualization.

In the *general case*, by the fact that in both unities the factor of generality is likewise dominant, with which is coupled annulment of individuality in the product, so far as it rests upon particularity.

These two points are marked out by two products, platinum and mercury.

Outside the points indicated, absolute and relative cohesion will still be able to be indifferent only in two possible ways, namely that the special be predominant in special cohesion in the same ratio as the general predominates in general cohesion; or conversely, that the general predominate in special cohesion in the same ratio as the special does in general cohesion. The former type of indifference is exhibited in gold, the latter in silver.

Outside this central region, we can no longer posit the absolute indifference-point, but only a relative one, *either* that of general *or* that of special cohesion. The decrease of specific weight is at the same time necessarily connected with this.

Here, too, the general tendency to objectivizing of the subject is carried to its extreme; matter, in its subjectivity and essentiality as absolute indifference of the general and particular, symbolizes itself through itself, in that by way of cohesion, according to one or both unities, it itself becomes form.

We first pursue the indifference-point of absolute cohesion, that in which the general is incorporated into the particular, up to the point of relative equilibrium. We take it that this point will be primarily represented by *iron*.

From this point on, two series are necessarily formed. Only where there is a certain degree of incorporation of the general into the particular does cohesion as such occur. For on the one side – to the extent that there is a total incorporation, so that the general is wholly objectified in the particular – the latter is abolished as particular, and resolved into identity. Here we have the state of expansion.

But on the other side, too, the smaller the degree of incorporation of identity into difference, the more the latter is necessarily predominant, as particularity; so from this we get contraction.

The former side may also be called the positive, the latter the negative side. The former is resolved, at the extreme, into the matter which the chemists have called nitrogen; the latter into what they they have called carbon.

Now in that the final degree of incorporation is produced towards the first side, in the total dissolution of the general into the particular, the indifference-point can only be produced wholly in the particular, that is, for *relative* cohesion. This is the case in *water*, as the identity-point corresponding to iron. The same can now be again potentiated, as indifference, in two directions, but without absolute or other than merely relative polarity, so that in the moment at which difference arises, the identity is also abolished, and one and the same substance is in fact presented under two different, though also spatially distinct, forms.

This is the final end of all earthly metamorphosis. These two corresponding points, from whose relationship we discern at the same time that of rigidity and fluidity as such, form, in the higher metamorphosis of the solar system, two distinct worlds, namely those of planets and comets.

Since the whole production of matter is directed to incorporation of the general into the particular, it follows that, seen from the one side, the fluid, as that in which the particular is the whole of the general, so that both are truly one, is the prototype of all matter. Now, depending on whether either this last indifference is produced or one of the two unities preponderates in the production, different relationships of the bodies are also set up towards the three dimensions; so that since these are reproduced only in the higher potency, in the three forms of the dynamic process, we may say that *all particular or specific determinations of matter have their ground in the differing relationships of bodies to magnetism, electricity and the chemical process.*[9]

[9] *Zeitschrift für spekulative Physik*, vol. I, no. 2: "Essay on the Dynamical Process," §47.

7

Philosophy of Chemistry
in General

We presuppose the most general concept of chemistry, as an empirical science which tells us how a free play of dynamical forces may be possible, in that Nature engenders new combinations and again abolishes those she has brought about.

The place which chemistry claims in the system of our knowledge has already been defined in part by the foregoing inquiries,[1] and is to be specified more accurately still hereafter. We have already established this much, that it is a consequence of general dynamics.

Its object, moreover, is to investigate the *qualitative* diversity of matter, for only to that extent is it necessary in the system of our knowledge.[2] It seeks to attain this object by effecting separations and combinations – artificially, to be sure, but by means that Nature herself provides. These separations and combinations must therefore relate to the *quality* of matter. For mechanical separations and combinations have to do merely with the quantity of matter; they are simply diminutions or accumulations of *mass*, without regard for any qualities it may possess.

So the subject-matter of chemistry is attractions and repulsions, combinations and separations, insofar as they depend upon qualitative properties of matter.

It therefore presupposes,[3] *firstly,* a principle of qualitative attraction. All attraction dependent on *qualities* of matter it traces to the *affinities* of certain basic substances, much as if some of them belonged to a *single* family, but all to a common *stem*. Thus the principle of chemical attractions has to be the *common factor* whereby one basic substance goes together with another, or the middle term which mediates the affinities of such substances for each other.

---

[1] The *necessity* of chemistry in the system of our knowledge has been set forth at the very outset (Chapter 1 [Book I]).

[2] Cf. the previous chapter.

[3] *Loc. cit.*

Now with this we at once assume a *non-uniformity* of matter, where previously it had been viewed as originally all alike. The system extends ever more widely; matter becomes more diverse.

But what the intermediary of chemical attractions may be can only be ascertained by experience. According to the inquiries of modern chemistry, it is a basic substance which Nature has entrusted to the universal medium in which we live, and which is equally necessary for the continuance of vegetable and animal life.

Every new combination that is effected by chemical means must be preceded by a chemical *separation,* or the basic particles of a chemically treated body must mutually repel each other, in order to be able to unite with foreign basic substances. Now in order to effect this separation, directly or indirectly, there must again be a *principle,* which in virtue of its qualitative properties is able to drag basic substances, which are mutually bound, away from equilibrium, and thereby make new combinations possible.

What this principle may be can again be decided only through experience. Chemistry finds it in *light* or (to indicate at once its connection with heat as well) in *fire.* Chemistry views this element in a wholly empirical fashion, and therefore regards it also as a special basic substance, which enters as such into the chemical process. The vehicles thereof are fluids, but especially that elastic fluid which contains, at the same time, the principle of all chemical attraction (vital air).

This is the account of the principles of chemistry, so far as it remains within the specific limits of mere experience. For there it has no other business than to let Nature act before our eyes, and to recount what is observed in doing so, as it strikes the senses; it does, however, have to reduce the scattered observations, as much as possible, to individual principles, though these are never allowed to go beyond the bounds of mere sensory knowledge. Thus it by no means undertakes to explain the possibility of these phenomena, but merely seeks to bring them into connection *among themselves.* Since, moreover, it takes everything as it strikes the senses, it also has the right, for purposes of the explanations that it gives, to appeal simply and solely to the *qualities* of these basic substances, for which it offers no further reason but merely endeavours to reduce these basic substances to as few as possible.

But *quality* is only that which is given to us in sensation. Now it is beyond doubt that what is given in sensation is capable, *as such,* of no further explanation – as for instance, the colours of bodies, taste-sensations, and so on. But anyone who takes up a science such as that of colours (called optics) must address himself to that question, notwithstanding that by explaining the *origin* of colours, he will never persuade himself of having also explained the *sensation* which colours evoke in us.

It is just the same with chemistry. It may reduce all the phenomena of its craft to qualities of basic substances, to affinities of these, and the like, just so long as it does not take on a scientific tone. But as soon as it does so, it must also permit one to remind it not to appeal henceforth to something that is valid only in regard to *sensation,* and can in no way be made (universally) intelligible by *concepts.* Thus light, for us, is originally nothing else but the cause of the two sensations that we express by the words "brightness" and "heat." But what then allows us to carry over these concepts of brightness, heat, etc., which have been fashioned, after all, from our sensations only, to light itself, and to suppose that light in itself might be hot, say, or bright? Thus it is with the concept of *affinity;* an appropriate image, to be sure, for designating the mere phenomenon, but one which, as soon as it is taken for a *cause* of the phenomenon, becomes nothing more nor less than an occult quality, which must be banned from any sound philosophy.

The mechanical physics, therefore, can truly count it a merit that alone until now it has undertaken to elevate a mere body of experimental lore into an empirical science, and to translate the pictorial language of chemistry and physics into generally intelligible, scientific terms. Nor has it ventured this attempt since yesterday merely, or the day before, but in this, as in all else, has remained, from Buffon to Morveau, almost wholly the same till now upon the main point.

That which *underlies* their explanations of chemical affinities, I can state no better than in Buffon's own words:

"The laws of affinity," he says,[4] "by which the constituent particles of these different substances separate from each other, in order to unite among themselves, and form homogeneous masses, are the same with that general law by which the celestial bodies act upon one another. Their exertions are mutual, and proportional to their masses and distances. Globules of water, of sand, or of metal act upon each other in the same manner as the earth acts upon the moon: and, if these laws of affinity have hitherto been regarded as different from those of gravity, it must be ascribed to the confined views we have taken of the subject. Figure, which, in the celestial bodies, has almost no effect upon their mutual action, because the distance is immense,

---

[4] *De la nature. Seconde vue.* (*Histoire naturelle des quadrupèdes*), vol. IV, pp. xxxii–xxxiv [*Natural History, General and Particular: The History of Man and Quadrupeds.* English translation by William Smellie, rev. edn. by William Wood (London 1812), vol. III, pp. 471ff.].

has great influence when the distance is very small. If the earth and moon, instead of a spherical figure, were both short cylinders, and equal throughout in their diameters, their reciprocal action would not be sensibly altered by this difference of figure, because the distance of all the parts of the moon from those of the earth would be very little changed. But, if these same globes were cylinders of great extent, and placed near each other, the law of their reciprocal action would appear to be very different; because the relative distances of their parts would be greatly varied. Hence, whenever figure becomes a principle in distance, the law seems to vary, though, in fact, it remains always the same.

"From this principle, the human intellect may advance one step farther, and penetrate deeper into the operations of Nature. We are ignorant of the figure of the constituent particles of bodies. Water, air, earth, metals, and all homogeneous substances, are unquestionably composed of elementary particles, which are similar among themselves, but whose figure is unknown. Posterity, by the aid of calculation, may disclose this new field of knowledge, and ascertain, with considerable precision, the figure of the elements of bodies. They will take the principle we have established as the basis of their reasoning: *all matter is attracted in the inverse ratio of the square of the distance; and this law seems to admit of no variation in particular attractions, but what arises from the figure of the constituent particles of each substance: because this figure enters as an element or principle into the distance.* Hence, when they discover, by reiterated experiments, the law of attraction in any particular substance, they may find, by calculation, the figure of its constituent particles. To make this matter more clear, let us suppose, that, by placing mercury on a perfectly polished surface, we find, by experiment, that this fluid metal is always attracted in the inverse ratio of the cube of the distance; we must investigate, by the rules of false position, what figure gives this expression; and this figure will be that of the constituent particles of mercury. If, from these experiments, it appeared that the attraction of mercury was in the inverse ratio of the square of the distance, it would be demonstrated that its constituent particles are spherical; because a sphere is the only figure which observes this law, and, at whatever distance globes are placed, the law of their attraction is always the same.

"Newton conjectured, that chemical affinities, which are nothing but the particular attractions we have mentioned, were produced by laws similar to those of gravitation. But he seems not to have perceived, that all these particular laws were only simple modifications of the general law, and that they appeared to be different, only because, at very small distances, the figure of atoms which attract each other has a greater influence upon the expression of this law, than the mass of matter."[5]

The prospect which this hypothesis opens for a scientific system of chemistry, and more especially the hope that it might very well succeed, as no other system could so easily do, in subjecting chemical attractions to actual calculation, is so pleasing that one is happy to entertain, for a time at least, a belief in the practicability of the enterprise, and to rejoice if the system itself acquires, by degrees anyway, a *hypothetical* certainty. For if the description of Nature only becomes *natural science* to the extent that mathematics can be employed in it,[6] we shall always prefer a system of chemistry which admittedly rests on false assumptions, but is nevertheless enabled, on such assumptions, to present this experimental doctrine in mathematical terms, for purposes of the scientific enterprise, to any other system, which admittedly has the merit of being based on true principles, but apart from these principles, must nevertheless forgo scientific precision (the mathematical construction of the phenomena that it enumerates).

So here we would have an example of a legitimate and very useful scientific *fiction*, whereby an otherwise merely experimental art might become a science, and achieve perfect cogency (only hypothetically, to be sure, but within its limits, cogency nonetheless).

The (till now, admittedly, very uncertain) hope that this idea might be capable of accomplishment has once more acquired some probability through the efforts of M. le Sage.

Unlike Buffon, M. le Sage does not believe that universal gravitation can perfectly account for the phenomena of affinity, although M. Prévost concedes that much which has been reckoned under affinity may be a consequence of universal attraction, since we do not know the *shape* and *position* of the interacting particles.[7] He therefore distinguishes the affinities properly so-called, which do *not* depend upon

---

[5] Even if this observation should find no application in the extended form that Buffon gives it, it may yet perhaps be applied to *some* phenomena, which till now have still to be satisfactorily explained. Among these, perhaps, are crystallizations. I am not sufficiently acquainted with the inquiries which M. Haüy has made on this subject, to know how far his own theory is based on a presupposition of this kind. In an earlier passage (Book I, Chapter 3), I regarded the regularity of raylike ice-crystals, etc., as an effect of heat (a uniformly operating force). But perhaps both are acting together, the impact of the departing heat, and the attraction that is determined by the *figure* of the particles. Since the latter are separated out from a *common* medium, under *like* circumstances, we can already find intelligible from that a similar shaping of their figure.

[6] Compare Kant's statements on this subject, and on the applicability of mathematics to chemistry, in the Preface to his oft-cited work, pp. viii–x [Ellington, pp. 6–8].

[7] §42 of the work often referred to.

either the *laws* or the universal *cause of gravity*, from the affinities improperly so-called, which are merely special cases of the great general phenomenon of attraction, or at least are subject to the same laws as the latter. (As was already observed above, this distinction is necessary in the context of our knowledge.)

Now how, by the laws of universal gravitation, *seeming* affinities may be possible M. le Sage has already sought to show, in his attempt at a mechanical chemistry. He reduces everything to differences of density and figure in the basic masses; if we suppose fluids, for example, whose basic masses are similar and equal, but of differing density, the homogeneous masses will endeavour to unite. (What does "homogeneous" mean here?) If it should refer to *equal* degrees of density, one would suppose that *heterogeneous* basic masses would in fact unite more easily. M. le Sage cannot be thinking of inner qualities, for the mechanical physics has no right to assume them.[8] So by homogeneity we would have to understand similarity and equality of figure, where again we would have reason, rather, to presuppose the opposite.

Moreover, since attraction takes place according to the ratio of the masses, a small mass can attract others equally small more strongly than the earth itself, if we suppose it to be much more dense.

Again, if the particles of one fluid be much smaller than the interstices of another, they will interpenetrate. Lastly, since the figure of the basic masses is different, they will have to endeavour, under otherwise equal circumstances, to unite among themselves with the largest possible surface, etc.[9]

More important for our purposes is M. le Sage's inquiry into the cause of affinities properly so-called (qualitative affinities). The universally pervasive cause of these is, for him, the *secondary* fluid, the *aether*, already alluded to above. The properties of the aether are as follows: It is in constant agitation. Its flows are often interrupted, but new ones again arise. Its elements differ appreciably from each other by mass, and since all these bodies are *elementary*, also by volume. Hence there is a coarser and a finer aether. Now immersed, as it were, in the aether, there are said to be numerous particles, as to which we abstract entirely from their relations to the weight-producing fluid. They can, on the other hand, be in equal or unequal relation to the aether. This unequal relationship is due to the differing sizes of their pores, which allow either completely free passage to the aether or a little passage, or none at all.

[8] Or if M. le Sage is referring to inner qualities of the basic masses, the mechanical physics has no right to assume them. [1st Edn., in which the sentence that follows is also lacking.]

[9] Prévost, *op. cit.*, §42.

In general, the (hypothetical) properties of the aether are now already by themselves sufficient to explain the phenomena of affinity.[10] M. le Sage gives its flows a very small extent, so that affinities, he says, which depend on the effects thereof, occur only on contact, or in very close proximity. The effect, too, must be proportional, not to the *mass* of the particles, but to the *surface*. Hence also the adherence which it produces in *contact* (where the surface is enlarged) is much stronger than that which it occasions at the smallest distance, and this in much greater measure than was supposed to follow from the general law.[11] Yet with all these assumptions, M. le Sage is still able to explain chemical affinities only in a very one-sided fashion; for from the differing relation of the pores of the particles to the coarser or finer aether, he derives the solitary principle, that *dissimilar* particles seek to unite with *lesser* force than *similar* ones.[12] To be sure, he explains the affinity of *dissimilar* particles (the main topic of chemistry), by allowing their figures to *become congruent* (as we know, he takes some of them to be concave, others convex). But this attraction he accounts for by laws of gravitation, and it takes place only on contact, and not at a distance as well.

M. Prévost himself admits, however, that there are cases in which we would have to postulate a greater affinity between *dissimilar* basic masses than between similar ones.[13] M. le Sage was thus obliged, at least for the affinities of expansible fluids, to assume an attraction of dissimilar basic masses, and also to seek out a special cause for this. Now here again, everything comes down to the figure of the basic masses, and these differences of figure proliferate, as needed, in a fashion that gradually grows more and more arbitrary. Some particles are concavo-concave, others convexo-convex, others concavo-convex, others again are cylinders with one end hollowed out to a certain depth, others actually kinds of cages, "whose wires themselves, augmented in thought by the diameter of the weight-producing particles, are so small in comparison with the mutual distances of the parallel wires of the same cage, that the earth cannot even capture a ten-thousandth part of the particles that present themselves, in order to pass through it," etc.[14] Now all these particles oscillate, strike or are struck, fit to one another or do not fit, attract or repel each other – all this, however wonderful it may sound, by mere inferences drawn from simple observations, and not even themselves entirely cogent.

[10] *Ibid.*, §43.
[11] *Ibid.*, §46.
[12] *Ibid.*, §45.
[13] *Ibid.*, §§48ff.
[14] De Luc's *Idèes sur la météorologie*, German translation, p. 120.

Now this finding, that till now there has been no success in elevating the mechanical chemistry to full credibility, must necessarily very much dampen the hope expressed above. Yet it is now time, without any regard for what may be congenial in such a science, to go back to its foundations. Thus the whole system stands or falls by the atomistic presuppositions, which in individual parts of the theory of Nature may perhaps be hypothetically applied to some advantage, but can nevermore be accepted by the *philosophy* of Nature, which is supposed to rest upon assured principles. Since our concern is now with such a philosophy, it is also incumbent on us to examine the claims which this part of the theory of Nature makes to a scientific approach, and to see how large might be the utility or otherwise that would accrue from the possibility or impossibility of such an approach – an undertaking from which, in any case, we may at least expect to profit in a negative sense.

Everything that pertains to the quality of bodies is present merely in our *sensation,* and what is sensed can never be made intelligible objectively (through concepts), but only by appeal to universal feeling. This is not, however, to eliminate the possibility that what is in one respect an object of sensation may in another become an object also for the *understanding.* If we now seek to force what is valid merely of sensation, as a concept upon the understanding as well, then we limit the latter unduly in regard to empirical investigation, for as to that which is *sensed,* as such, no further inquiry is possible. Or else we see that the *sensed,* as such, can never be transformed into generally intelligible *concepts,* and accordingly reject the very possibility of finding expressions for qualitative properties, which are also valid for the understanding.

Here, therefore, is a conflict whose basis lies, not in the subject-matter itself, but merely in the viewpoint from which we look at it; for it is a question of whether we consider the object simply with reference to sensation or bring it before the tribunal of the understanding; and if the former (very naturally) is incapable of bringing *sensation* to concepts, the understanding, conversely, is likewise unwilling to apply also to concepts expressions (such as quality) which are valid only of sensations.

It therefore seems necessary to investigate more closely the origin of our concepts of *quality* as such. If I also revert here, once more, to philosophical principles, this will seem useless only to such readers as have got into the habit of groping about *blindly* among empirical concepts, but not to those who are accustomed to seek connection and necessity everywhere in human knowledge.

That which is *necessary* in our conceptions of external things is simply their materiality as such. Now this rests upon the conflict of attractive and repulsive forces, and so nothing more pertains to the possibility of an object *as such* than a concurrence of dynamic forces, which reciprocally limit each other, and so make possible by their interaction a *finite* as such – a hitherto quite undetermined object. But with this we also have no more than the mere concept of a material object as such, and even the forces that produce it are as yet something merely thought.

Thus the understanding spontaneously projects a general schema – the outline, as it were, of an object as such, and it is this schema, in its generality, which is thought of as necessary in all our conceptions, and in contrast to which that which does not belong to the *possibility* of the object *as such* first appears as *contingent*. Since this schema is supposed to be *general* – because it is meant to be the generalized image of an object as such – the understanding thinks of it, so to speak, as a mean,[15] to which all individual objects approximate, but no one of them, for that very reason, entirely corresponds; whence the understanding inserts it, beneath all ideas of particular objects, as a *common image,* in relation to which they first appear as *individual, specific* objects.

Now this outline of an object as such yields nothing more than the concept of a *quantity* as such, i.e., of a something within undetermined limits. Only through deviation from the *generality* of this outline do *individuality* and *specificity* gradually arise, and we may say that a particular object is absolutely conceivable only insofar as we are able (unwittingly, through a marvellously rapid act of the imagination) to estimate its deviation from the common image of an object in general, or at least from the common image of the species to which it belongs.

This peculiarity of our power of conception lies so deep in the nature of our mind that we transfer it, involuntarily, and by a wellnigh universal agreement, to Nature herself (that ideal being, wherein we think of ideation and production, concept and act, as identical). Just as we think of Nature as a purposive creatrix, so we also picture her as having brought forth all the multiplicity of species, types and individuals in the world by gradual deviation from a common archetype (which she has projected in accordance with a concept). And Plato has already observed that all man's artistic faculty rests on the capacity to project a general picture of the object, in accordance with which even the mere craftsman (who must forgo the name of artist) is able, with the most various deviations from *universality* – and retaining only the *necessary* – to bring forth the individual object in his design.

---

[15] [1st Edn. has *Medium,* changed to *Mittel* in 2nd.] Kant says that the schema as such *mediates between* concept (the universal) and intuition (the individual). It is thus something that hovers, as it were, in the *middle* between determinacy and indeterminacy, between universality and individuality.

I resume the thread. That undetermined something, the necessary in all our conceptions of individual things, is a mere object of pure imagination – a sphere, a quantity, something in general that is merely thinkable or constructible.

Our consciousness is to that extent merely *formal*. But the object is to become *real*, and our consciousness to become *material* – filled up, as it were. Now this is possible no otherwise than by the idea forsaking the generality in which it had hitherto preserved itself. Only in that the mind departs from that mean, in which only the formal idea of a something was in any way possible, does the object, and with it the consciousness, acquire *reality*. But reality is only *felt*, is only present in *sensation*. Yet what is *felt* is called quality. Thus only in that it departs from the generality of the *concept* does the object first acquire *quality*, and cease to be mere *quantity*.

Only now does the mind relate the real in sensation (as the contingent) to an object as such (as the necessary), and *vice versa*. But by the contingent the mind feels itself absolutely determined, and its consciousness is no longer a *general* (formal) consciousness, but a *determinate* (material) one. But even this *determinacy* must again seem contingent to it, i.e., the real in sensation must be able to increase, or diminish, indefinitely; it must, that is, have a *specific degree*, though one that can equally well be thought of as infinitely greater, or as infinitely smaller; or, to put it otherwise, between which and the negation of all degree (= o) an infinite sequence of intermediate grades can be imagined.

And that is how it is. We feel merely the *more* or *less* of elasticity, heat, brightness and so on, not elasticity, heat, etc., themselves. Only now is ideation completed. The creative power of imagination projected, from the original and reflected activity, a common sphere. This sphere is now the necessary, on which our understanding founds every conception of an object. But what the original real in the object is, what corresponds to the passivity in myself, is a *contingent* (*accidens*) in regard to this sphere. So we attempt in vain to derive it *a priori*, or to reduce it to concepts. For the real itself exists only insofar as I am affected. Yet for me there is absolutely no concept of an *object*, but only a consciousness of the state of passivity that I am in. Only a spontaneous power in me relates what I sense to an object *in general*, and only thereby does the object acquire *determinacy*, and the sensation *duration*. It is clear from this that quantity and quality are necessarily connected. The former first acquires determinacy through the latter, and it is through the former that the latter first acquires limits and degree. But to transform what is actually sensed into *concepts* is to rob it of its reality. For it has reality only at the moment of its effect upon myself. If I elevate it into a concept, it becomes a work of thought; as soon as I myself give it *necessity,* I also take from it everything that made it into an object of sensation.

These general principles of quality as such can now be very easily carried over to the quality of bodies as such.

The necessary, which the understanding sets at the foundation of all its conceptions of individual things, is a manifold present in time and space as such. In dynamical terms, this is to say that what the understanding posits, as the necessary, to found our (dynamical) conceptions of matter, and to which the contingency of the latter is first related, is an undetermined product of attractive and repulsive forces as such, which the imagination registers quite generally, and which for now is a mere object of the understanding, a quantity as such, without any qualitative features. We can think of this product of imagination as a mean of all the possible relationships which might hold between attractive and repulsive forces. Force is certainly present, but only in our concept; force *as such,* not *specific* force. Force is simply that which *affects* us. What affects us we call *real,* and what is real exists only in sensation; force is therefore that which alone corresponds to our concept of quality. But every quality, insofar as it is to affect us, must have a *degree,* and that a *specific* degree, a degree which *could* have been higher or lower, but is now (at *this moment*) precisely of this *particular* degree.

Thus force as such can affect us only insofar as it has a particular degree. But so long as we think of these dynamical forces quite generally—in a wholly indeterminate relationship—neither one of them has a particular degree. We can picture this relationship as an absolute *equilibrium* of these forces, in which the one always cancels out the other, and neither allows the other to grow up to a particular degree. So if *matter* as such is to acquire *qualitative* properties, its forces will have to have a particular degree; i.e., they will have to depart from the generality of the relationship in which the mere understanding thinks of them—or more plainly—they will have to deviate from the equilibrium in which they are originally and necessarily conceived.

Only now is matter something determinate for us. Understanding gives the sphere as such, sensation the boundaries; the former gives the necessary, the latter the contingent; the former the general, the latter the particular; the former the merely formal, the latter the material element of presentation.

This, therefore, is the result of the foregoing investigations. *All quality of matter rests wholly and solely on the intensity of its basic forces,* and since chemistry is properly concerned only with the qualities of matter, we have thereby at once elucidated and confirmed the concept of chemistry set forth above (as a science which teaches how a free play of dynamical forces may be possible).

It appeared above that only insofar as it *is* such a science does chemistry have *necessity* in the context of our knowledge. Here we have arrived at the same concept in a quite different way, by having inquired, that is, how far *quality* appertains to matter as such.

Before we now proceed to the *scientific* application of these principles, I consider it advisable to test their reality by reference to such topics as have hitherto still been among the problem areas of this science.

Is Chemistry as a
Science Possible?
(Supplement to Chapter 7)

It has been shown in the preceding supplement that a scientific insight is possible into the ground for the specific differences of matter; that a like insight is possible into the phenomena conditioned by those differences of matter which we call chemical might be sufficiently inferred already from the previous claim.

But from that it would not yet follow that chemistry, *as such,* can be a science, since all those inquiries belong in a much higher and more general domain, that of general physics, which treats of no natural phenomenon in isolation, but must rather depict everything in connection and absolute identity. So if chemistry, *as such,* were to be a special branch of knowledge, this would be possible only insofar as it confined itself merely to experimentation, and not insofar as it might have the pretension to be a theory.

Only an age that was capable of putting chemistry itself in the place of physics could consider it, in this its scientific nakedness and bareness, to be a self-sufficient science, and take its report of observed facts, disfigured by meaningless concepts, for theory itself. It needs only the simple reflection, that whatever may be the cause or ground of the chemical process cannot itself, in turn, be the object of chemical investigation, in order to perceive the contradictory nature of a theory of chemical phenomena discovered by chemistry itself, and the futility of exalting it above physics.

But as for the reasons which might be advanced against a genuine *physics* of chemistry, the foremost of them would undoubtedly be drawn from that universal and deeply rooted conception of the specific in Nature, which pursues unending differentiations down into the essence of matter itself, proclaims absolute qualitative differences, and under the name of a false, merely outward affinity, entirely does away with the true inner affinity and identity of matter. It is typical of this mode of conception to imagine entities of a peculiar kind in order to account for qualities, and since we are unable either to determine with certainty the number of these entities or to discover all their vagaries by experience, an exhaustive physics and true science of their appearances is therefore as impossible as a physics, say, of the spirits of the air, or of other intangible entities.

The absolute identity and truly internal likeness of all matter, under every possible difference of form, is the one true core and centre of all material phenomena, whence they emanate as from their common root, and into which they strive to return. The chemical motions of bodies are the breakthrough of the essence, the endeavour to return from external and particular life into the internal and universal, into identity.

Other reasons against the possibility of knowing the *causes* of chemical phenomena could be drawn from the presuppositions whereby the indwelling principles of motion and life are themselves given material form.

In this case they are either themselves made subject to chemical relationships, so that they, too, are capable of disassembly, composition, affinity, etc.; with this the question as to the ground of all chemical phenomena, and of that which we call affinity, binding, etc., in themselves, reverts merely into the higher case; or else these material principles are allowed to produce chemical phenomena in an external and mechanical fashion, so that with this explanation the whole nature, as such, of these very phenomena – namely as dynamical – is abolished; in this case, since the enduring ground of these phenomena can then be sought solely in the figure of the smallest parts, which is inaccessible to all experience, any prospect whatever of a science of chemistry is totally eliminated.

The other condition of the possibility of such a science, apart from the inner and essential unity of matter, is, therefore, that the activities of heat, magnetism, electricity, etc., shall be activities immanent and inherent in the substance of the body itself, just as the form as such, even in regard to dead matter, is one with and inseparable from the essence. But it has been sufficiently demonstrated by the dynamical physics, that all these activities have a relationship to the substance just as immediate as the three dimensions of form itself, and that changes other than of the relationships of body to the three dimensions, including chemical changes, do not.

Finally, for the ultimate task of a physics of chemistry, which also has to depict in these phenomena the totality alone, it is necessary to grasp their symbolic character and connection with higher relationships, since every body of individual nature is again, in its idea anyway, a universe. Only if we seek among chemical phenomena, no longer for laws that are peculiar to them as such, but for the general harmony and regularity of the universe, will they come under the higher relationships of mathematics; to which end some steps have been taken, through the acuity of a German author, whose discoveries, of which we would here cite by way of example only those of the constant *arithmetical* progression of the alkalis, in relation to every acid, and of the *geometrical* progression of the acids to every alkali, are a pointer, in fact, to the deepest secrets of Nature.

8

Application of These Principles to Particular Topics of Chemistry

It seems to be an advantage of the mechanical chemistry that it is able, with little trouble, to render intelligible the greatest specific difference of matter. But if we look at the thing more closely, a principle that is ultimately obliged to reduce everything to differences of *density* is actually a very impoverished principle, inasmuch as we have to consider matter as *originally* uniform, and all individual bodies as mere aggregates of atoms. The dynamical chemistry, on the other hand, admits no *original* matter whatever – no matter, that is, from which everything else would have arisen by composition. On the contrary, since it considers all matter originally as a product of opposing forces, the greatest possible diversity of matter is still nothing else but a diversity in the relationship of these forces. But forces are in themselves already infinite; i.e., for every possible force an infinite number of degrees can be supposed, of which no one is the highest or the lowest, and since all quality rests solely on degrees, it is possible, from this assumption alone, already to derive and comprehend the infinite diversity of matter in regard to its qualities (as they are known to us from experience). But if we suppose in addition a conflict of opposing forces, such that each is originally independent of the other, the multiplicity of possible relationships between the two again runs into the infinite. For not only is the individual force susceptible of infinite degrees, but one and the same degree can also be quite differently modified by the opposing force, which may grow *ad infinitum* while the other is infinitely diminished, or *vice versa*. So obviously the principle of dynamical chemistry (that all quality of matter rests upon relationships of degree among its basic forces) is already in itself far richer than that of the chemistry of atomism.

Now this principle assigns to chemistry its proper position, and divides it sharply and distinctly from both general dynamics and mechanics. The former is a science that can be established independently of all experience. But chemistry, though a consequence of dynamics, is nevertheless wholly contingent in relation to that science, and can demonstrate its reality simply and solely through experience. But a science which rests wholly upon experience, and whose subject-matter is chemical operations, will have to be dependent, not upon a single basic force, such as that of attraction, but rather upon the *empirical relationship of the two basic forces.* Now this relationship of the basic forces is left wholly undetermined by dynamics. So chemistry is not a science which has *necessarily* resulted from dynamics, as is true, say, of the theory of universal gravitation. Rather, it is itself nothing else but *applied* dynamics, or *dynamics considered in its contingency.*

So chemistry, since it is *parallel* with dynamics, must be independent of all the laws that are *subordinate* to those of dynamics. Thus chemical operations are independent of the laws of *gravity,* for these rest upon the mere attractive power of matter, and presuppose that the dynamical forces in matter have already come to rest. But chemistry presents these forces in motion, for its appearances are all nothing else but phenomena of an *interaction* of the basic forces of matter.

Bergman, the celebrated chemist, asks: How great, surely, must have been the astonishment of those who first saw how a metal was dissolved into a bright transparent liquid, how the heavy opaque body totally vanished, and suddenly, after another material had been mixed in, again reappeared as a solid body out of the whole seemingly uniform fluid. The chief ground of astonishment would surely have lain, from the very beginning, in the fact that the observer here saw *matter arise* and come to be, as it were, before his eyes; anyone who gave the subject further thought could doubtless soon have seen that *one* experience of this kind was enough to yield conclusions on the *nature* of matter itself. For the evidence was plain that here it was not compounded from parts, or resolved into parts, but that the fluid into which the solid body vanished would be a common product of the *degrees* of elasticity of both bodies – and thus that matter as such would no doubt be originally nothing else but a phenomenon of degree relationships – an *expression,* as it were, of these relationships for the senses.

Chemistry, moreover, is independent of *mechanics,* for this, too, is subordinate to dynamics. It presupposes a determinate, unaltered relationship of the dynamic forces, and relates to bodies, i.e., to matter within determinate limits, whose moving forces await an impact from without, if the body is to move. Chemistry, on the other hand, considers matter in its *becoming,* and has as its object a free play – and thus also a free motion – of the dynamic forces *among themselves,* without impact from outside.

Within its customary limits, chemistry may be allowed to multiply the elements of bodies according to need. It therefore assumes certain *permanent,* unchangeable basic substances, which differ from one another in virtue of inner qualities. But *quality* as such is something that is present only in sensation. So something that is merely sensed is carried over to the object itself – by what right, one may ask. For the body in itself, i.e., without reference to our sensation, considered simply as object of the understanding, has no inner quality; *to that extent,* all quality rests merely on relationships of degree among the basic forces. But then we can no longer think of these substances as *permanent* and unchangeable; they are themselves nothing else but a specific dynamical relationship, and as soon as this changes, they themselves take on another nature – and likewise another relationship to our sensation.

This has also been assumed, apparently, in many theories, at least so far as finer matter is concerned. Thus there has very often been talk of *latent* light, *latent* heat, etc. There is no denying the fact, if we merely take into account the heating of bodies by light, which is all the greater, the more invisible the light becomes, etc. Yet if light differs from other matters by *inner* qualitative properties, if its existence does not depend merely on relationships of degree, there is no seeing how, by mere contact with other bodies, it so alters its nature that it now ceases to affect the eye.

This is the point at which to assess the customary ways of picturing light, heat, etc. It has often been asked, of late, whether light is a special matter. (I ask in reply, What in the world, then, is *special* matter?) I would say that everything we call matter is simply a modification of one and the same matter, which admittedly, in its absolute state of equilibrium, we do not know by sense, and which must enter into special relationships to be knowable for us in this way.[1]

Again, if the attempt is made to consider light as a *force,* and to interpolate philosophical principles into physics, I ask in return, What, of everything that seems to act upon us, is not *force,* and what, in general, can act upon us except *force?* And if it be said that *light-matter,* as such, is a mere product of our imagination, I ask in return, What matter is not such a product, and what matter is, *as* such, really existent outside us, independently of our presentations?

But the question arises, whether an element such as light, which stands, if it is matter, at the boundary of all matter, could also become a chemical component,[2] and enter as a chemical substance into the chemical process. But this doubt is already proof that we have very

---

[1] Everything we call matter is simply a modification of matter as such – if only matter *as such* were a mere thought [1st Edn.].

[2] Whether a matter so subtle as light could also become a chemical component [1st Edn.].

dim notions of light and of matter as such. Light is itself nothing else but a particular relationship of degree among dynamic forces (if you will, the highest degree known to us of the expansive force). So if matter forsakes this particular relationship, it is no longer light, and now takes on other *qualitative* properties, and has undergone a chemical change.

This becomes very clear, as soon as we consider the successive levels encompassed by light itself. The light of the sun seems infinitely brighter and purer to us than the ordinary light that we are able to produce. And sunlight is also far more brilliant when it encounters less resistance on its way to us. But that can only diminish its elasticity, and this diminished elasticity is also associated with a lesser effect upon the eye. So the *quality* of light is altered, as soon as its elasticity is changed.[3]

The light that we obtain by decomposition of vital air is much purer and more vivid than the light from atmospheric air. Many modern chemists[4] therefore consider the former as the sole source of light. It was already noted by Lavoisier that light must absolutely play a part in the formation of vital air. And the great influence of light on the regeneration of burnt bodies is also relevant here. But it demonstrates no more and no less than this, that vital air in a state of decomposition comes closest to that relationship of forces in all substances, with which light-phenomena are associated.[5] For otherwise, as Buffon already says, *every matter could become light,* were it not that there this transition has to pass through many more intermediate degrees than is the case with vital air, which begins to glow as soon as its elasticity is increased, in that it loses *one* part of its mass (the oxygen).

Now this can also apply in reverse, in that the plus of elasticity which is peculiar to light has the most capacity for the minus of elasticity which belongs to oxygen.

Atmospheric air is capable of *glowing* only to the extent that it approaches the specific degree of elasticity that is peculiar to vital air.[6] Indeed even the light that we obtain from the decomposition of atmo-

---

[3] It is therefore of the utmost importance for natural science to distinguish the different *kinds* of light.

[4] For example, Fourcroy, in his oft-cited work.

[5] Among all the kinds of air we know, vital air comes closest to the degree of elasticity that is peculiar to light matter. [1st Edn.] False, therefore, is the conjecture put forward above (p. 63), that light is a common component of *all* elastic fluids, and with this the question (pp. 70–71) is answered, why in other decompositions no light becomes visible. In general, all the above-proposed hypotheses about light first receive here their rectification from principles.

[6] This also explains why the combustible body refracts light out of proportion to its density, evolution of oxygen from plants.

spheric air is more or less pure, depending on the constitution of the air from which it is produced.

Nature has marked very clearly the two extremes between which light-production is possible at all. The less elastic kinds of air (the mephitic non-inflammable) are of as little use for the purpose as the most elastic (the mephitic inflammable). Midway between the two lies the source of light, vital air.

Infallibly, also, a great difference appears in regard to the velocity with which light is propagated, in proportion to its greater or lesser purity.

The most evident proof that light also alters its quality with the degree of its elasticity is the phenomenon of colours. For obviously the seven major colours are nothing else but a sequence of stages in the intensity of light, from the degree that is highest and most sensible to our eyes, down to total disappearance. Even the mechanical splitting of the light-ray in the prism is dependent on the fact that the elasticity of the ray is diminished in stages.

The phenomenon of shadow, or of total darkness, as soon as the illuminated body is removed from the light, proves that light, in touching the body, entirely changes its nature. For why does the body not continue to shine when removed from the light, if no change occurred when the removal took place? But no further change goes on in it, beyond a lessening of its elasticity.

What has raised the most doubt within the material view of light is the extraordinary subtlety of this matter. Man has by nature a propensity for the large. The greatest, though it may surpass his imagination, finds acceptance with him, for he feels himself exalted thereby. But he is resistant to the small, regardless of the fact that Nature no more acknowledges limits in the one than in the other.

Here is perhaps the place to say something more about the modern hypotheses concerning phlogiston.

A number of well-known chemists (Richter, Gren, *et al.*) take light to consist of matter of fire and heat. As to the assumption itself, we may ask: What, then, will matter of fire and heat consist of? But if the proof of this assumption is drawn from the fact that in combustion a double elective attraction occurs – that there will therefore have to be a component of the body which has become liberated in combustion, and joins forces with the matter of heat in the air, and produces light – then for this there is no one decisive proof. And since light, in any case, differs from every other matter only in the degree of its elasticity, any matter can really be regarded as *light-stuff*, i.e., any matter can become light, and acquire an elasticity equal to that of light. But we are talking, not of what *may* be, but of what *is*. Now in its normal state, body does not possess this elasticity. Indeed light, when it touches a body, loses its elasticity and thereby ceases to be light. So the question arises, whether the basic material of body only takes on the properties of light during combustion. And if this could be demonstrated, which is actually impossible, nothing would have been gained thereby, and nothing lost. Of everything that can become of a matter nobody can say, but what is *now becoming* of it, in this *particular* process, we must be able to say, for *experience* teaches it, and the latter obviously says that vital air alone takes on relations of elasticity in this process, which yield the phenomenon of light.[7]

Macquer had already maintained that phlogiston has no weight. Herr Gren has lately claimed (as Dr Black did earlier) that it has negative weight. M. Pictet also gives fire a direction contrary to gravity. With equal justice one might give to every body such a countergravitational tendency, namely in the principle of extension, and thus here also permit the occurrence of mere differences of degree, so that light would merely represent an approximation to the pure form of expansion, and hence any relation to heaviness[8] in it would be unknowable for all media.

With *matter of heat*, things are quite otherwise than with light. Light itself *appears* as matter of a specific quality, whereas heat is itself *no* matter, but mere quality – mere modification of *every* matter (regardless of which?). Heat is a particular degree of expansion. This state of expansion is not merely peculiar to one particular matter, but can attach to every possible matter. It will be objected, perhaps, that bodies are warm only to the extent that the heat-fluid accumulates in their interstices. But even supposing that such an accumulation occurs, we still do not understand how *bodies* themselves become heated by this. And if heat is only a particular degree of elasticity, then as soon as it touches the body, it must either lose this elasticity or put the body itself into a similar state. At least we have to say that the heat-fluid *permeates* bodies. But no permeation of a body occurs without the latter changing its state.

This is not to deny that solid bodies, for example, become heated by means of the fluid that surrounds them (the air). But this fluid is itself not heat-matter, but merely fluid of a more definite degree of expansion, whereby it becomes capable of producing in our organ a feeling

---

[7] is capable of a degree of elasticity that yields the phenomenon of light [1st Edn.].

[8] By the same token one could also deny heaviness to inflammable air. Without proof from experience, such a statement cannot be maintained, and if it is sought to prove it from particular cases, we confuse, without thinking about it, *heaviness* and (specific) *weight*. But there is evidence enough to prove that light must have weight [1st Edn.].

of warmth. Nor is it the mere approach of this fluid to the body which heats it; it is the effect which it exerts upon the basic forces of the body itself. Only now, once the degree-relationship of its basic forces has been altered, can the body itself be called heated; where not, its heating is merely *apparent,* and belongs only to the fluid located in its interstices.

So here the situation is very different from that of light. For till now we know of only one matter as such (vital air, and some others that approximate to it), which can take on the degree of elasticity that is accompanied by the phenomenon of light. We are therefore entitled to speak of a light-substance. But *every* matter can be *heated* directly in itself (through friction), and this not by the *advent* of an unknown fluid alone, but by a simultaneous change that takes place in the body itself.

If we now take it, in addition, that in very many *undoubted* cases, heat arises by mere change of capacity, we shall be inclined to regard heat in general as a mere *phenomenon of the transition* of a matter from the more elastic to a less elastic state (as from steamy to liquid). It will be objected that heat, after all, was required, for example, to produce the steam. But what, then, was this heat? A special fluid, say, that combined with the water to form steam? But all that experience shows in the evaporation of water from a heated body is that through interaction and equilibration with this body, which is notably enhanced in its expansive force, the water took on a degree of expansion which converts it into the form of steam.[9]

Now it is furthermore established, by Crawford's experiments, that *heat* is an altogether *relative* concept, that different bodies are quite differently warmed by equal amounts of heat. For this varying constitution of bodies, Crawford has invented the term capacity, which was very well chosen, since it designated the phenomenon completely – but also not more than that. In any case, however, it follows from this that it is not, say, a *particular* absolute degree of expansive force that yields the phenomenon of heat, but that every body has its own specific degree of expansion, at which it appears warmed or heated.

There is thus no *absolute* heat, and heat in general is merely the phenomenon of a *state* in which the body happens to be. Heat is no *absolute* quality – everywhere the same – but a quality dependent on contingent circumstances. If, among the empirically unknown elastic and originally expansive fluids, we ourselves posit one, which has the

---

[9] But why do we call this fluid heat-matter? Because it has a specific degree of expansive force – hence it is always this degree-relation alone which produces heat. The fluid is not heat itself (and far less still is it heat-stuff), but is now – in this particular case – the vehicle of heat [1st Edn., replacing the sentence above].

foremost ability to heat bodies, then the *nature* of it is, of course, matter, like all the rest, and it is only the property of a relatively greater force of expansion that distinguishes it from the others. But this property attaches also to the solid body that conveys heat to another. If a fluid, as such, is by *nature* a cause of heat, from whence, then, does this fluid get its ability to communicate heat? To postulate a heat-matter as the cause of heat is not to explain the situation, but to pay oneself with words.

But, it will be objected, it has been proved that heat-stuff enters into chemical combinations, that it is the cause of fluidity, for example, and is therefore the basic material of every fluid body. But what, then, is the concept of a fluid anyway? Crawford says: "A fluid body has more capacity than a solid one, and hence it is that in passing from the solid to the fluid state, it takes up so much heat which does not raise its temperature at all." But for the term capacity a more general expression may very easily be found. And then Crawford's statement can be reversed: Because, one might say, the ice is furnished with far more heat than it can take up in the state it was in, it changes this state; so it is not because it now has more capacity that it absorbs more heat; rather, because and insofar as it has absorbed more heat, it henceforth has greater capacity. Thus the capacity of a fluid body is itself a plus or minus of heat that it has taken up. The more heat it had to absorb, in order to get into this particular state, the more must be applied in order to get it to pass into a still more elastic state.[10] So if heat, for example, is a cause of the fluidity of ice, this merely means that heat (i.e., a higher degree of expansibility), which some matter (e.g., water heated to a certain degree) communicates to the ice (in that it tries to reach equilibrium with the latter, and diminish its expansion in relation thereto), gives the previously solid body a higher degree of expansibility, so that it takes on the attributes of a fluid one. Thus it is not the *heat,* or a special heat-stuff, that enters into chemical combination with the ice; it is the very matter referred to, e.g., water, employed in the experiment, which engages with the other matter in a dynamic process, and the fluid obtained is a common product of the thermal plus and minus of the heated and frozen water, just as, when we blend fluid matters of different density, the fluid obtained is the product of the densities of both. Nobody will suppose a special stuff which has combined with the matter that has become more fluid. Since the water in the above process *loses* its heat, we might with equal right assume a

---

[10] [1st Edn. here adds the following]: So capacity, more generally expressed, is a particular *state* of a body, a particular degree of expansibility, or however else one may want to put it. And hence every fluidity is nothing else but a particular degree of expansibility, or, what comes to the same, a particular degree of capacity.

cold-making stuff, which the ice gives up to the water in exchange for the heat-stuff.

A perceptive student of Nature has made the following objections to Crawford's account of the genesis of fluid bodies: "A question arises," he says, "which is of great importance for Crawford's theory: Does the absorption (of heat by melting ice) proceed merely from an increased capacity, or does the heat-stuff here undergo a sort of chemical combination with the body, and thereby produce fluidity? If this absorption of heat is attributed merely to an increased capacity, and if the capacities of ice and water should be in the proportion of 9 to 10, then at first sight, indeed, everything hangs nicely together; the water is nothing else but an ice of greater capacity. But it then goes unnoticed that in this kind of reasoning one of the greatest phenomena in Nature remains entirely without explanation. If, by a considerable accession of heat, ice becomes water that is no warmer than this ice, then the first question is surely: Has not this heat been partly employed in giving fluidity to the ice? And only when this has been established is it possible to inquire what sort of capacity the resultant fluid may have. It must first be explained how fluidity arises, before we trouble about its capacity, for the greater capacity cannot, after all, be the cause of the greater capacity. I can very well *imagine* a fluid whose capacity was in no way greater than that of the solid body it has arisen from, and which would nevertheless have absorbed a large amount of heat in its genesis. It seems, rather, that to make water from ice, the heat enters into combination with the ice, forms a new body thereby, and owing to this combination loses all power to warm, and is thus no longer free, and hence cannot be reckoned as part of that heat on which capacity depends."[11]

As to these objections, let me remark as follows:

That heat-stuff combines chemically with the ice – even if we admitted it – could still not *explain* how the latter becomes fluid, unless we were to revert once more to a particular concept of *chemical combination,* whereby we eventually return to the point that water is a product of the plus and minus of expansibility (for reasons of brevity, I shall always express myself in this fashion) of the heat-material and the ice. But that plus of expansibility which produces fluidity can likewise be only a modification of the fluid employed in the process, and in this fluid, e.g., water, we are not *compelled* to suppose a second fluid, whereby the water has itself first become *warm.*

But so far as the concept of capacity is concerned, this notion is far too narrow in the theory of Crawford, though it admits of enlarge-

[11] Lichtenberg, *Comments on Erxleben,* p. 444.

ment, and there is then an end to the objection that "the genesis of fluidity must first be explained, before we trouble about its capacity." For this fluidity and this particular capacity (i.e., this particular degree of expansibility) are one and the same. Only insofar as water is this *particular* fluid does it also have this particular *capacity,* and conversely, only insofar as it has this particular capacity is it this particular fluid. If its capacity changes, then the degree of its fluidity also changes,[12] and conversely, if we presuppose another fluidity, we also presuppose another capacity.

There exists no fluidity *as such,* so how fluidity arises as such, and what fluids may be *possible*—we do not need to go into. But this *one* particular fluid absorbs in its genesis this particular amount of heat, and just for that reason, and only *to that extent,* is it this particular fluid and this particular degree of capacity.

A distinction has very properly been drawn between aeriform fluids that are destructible by cold and those that are not. The former, if they are destroyed by pressure or cold, yield up a large amount of heat; the question is, To what is this difference due? We note that in the first case the substance, namely water, merely changes its outer state, as atmospheric air also does when rarefied under the air-pump—it does not thereby become inflammable air; in the other case, however, the inner dynamical relation is altered, and the aeriform fluids which can only be destroyed by decomposition no longer behave like the vapour of what is still water, despite its different state, but are substances of a peculiar kind, and one that differs from others.[13]

It seems to me that there is no such great difference as is commonly supposed between Crawford's theory of heat (leaving aside the hypotheses of the older chemistry that are mingled with it, but have no bearing on the issue) and the theory of modern chemists. The whole difference is ultimately one of language. The language employed, for preference, by the chemists is more *popular,* and better adapted to

----

[12] We may lay down the general law: The degree of capacity is the degree of non-excitability through heat.

[13] [In 1st Edn., this passage runs]: The former, if they are destroyed by pressure or cold, yield up a large amount of heat; it may be asked, In what way has this heat been combined with them? Undoubtedly it was simply the heated air, made more elastic by heat, which penetrated into certain interstices between the particles of water, and so produced an expansion thereof, which was capable of keeping it in the form of steam. But aeriform fluidities, which are destructible only by chemical decomposition, are *constant* and uniformly elastic fluids; the heat-matter and the basis of the fluid are not separate, but both, reduced to a *single* degree of elasticity, now present only one common mass. And hence the chemists were right to depict the heat in this case as *bound.*

customary ideas; that of Crawford is more philosophical. But even the theory of combustion must eventually be expressed in this language, as soon as we cease to be content with the terms of popular chemistry – affinity and so on. And the *extended* theory of Crawford – in and for itself already the work of a truly philosophic mind – will sooner or later become the theory of all *philosophical* students of Nature; though so far as the experimentalists are concerned, it is preferable for them to stay with their briefer and more generally understandable vocabulary.

But now what is the true reason for the interest that scientists take in the hypothesis of a special heat-stuff? They have undoubtedly feared that if heat were to be regarded as a mere phenomenon – a mere modification of matter as such – an assumption of this kind would confer all too much freedom upon the imagination, and would thus hamper the progress of research. This fear is not ungrounded. Since heat is originally known to us only through sensation, we are able to imagine entirely as we please what it might be, independently of our sensation; for a specific matter leaves less freedom to the imagination, whereas mere modifications of matter we can conceive of in infinite numbers, and yet not one of them *distinctly,* if they are not *given* to us in intuition.

Yet we do, after all, know how to remove topics that are in themselves problematic from the arbitrariness of speculation, in that we subject their appearances to specific laws, and seek to determine the *causes* thereof; for in this way our findings acquire connection and necessity, and the caprice of imagination is checked.

Now the former has been undertaken by the acutest scientists of our day. To facilitate their inquiries, they may certainly presuppose the existence of a special heat-stuff. But once the laws obeyed by the phenomena of heat are discovered in their full *generality,* it will become very easy to translate them into the more philosophical idiom.

But if heat-stuff is to designate nothing more or less than the *cause* of heat, then all the students of Nature who otherwise still think so differently will be agreed upon the necessity of assuming a heat-stuff, provided that this cause be not again something purely hypothetical. For it is a very convenient philosophy to suppose modifications of matter without introducing a specific *cause* that produces these modifications, and so long as we cannot supply this, our whole philosophy is idle. But if a cause is provided, which itself in turn is merely problematical (like heat-stuff), then no bounds to speculation are set.

Now regardless of the means which Nature employs to diminish the capacity of bodies, a major cause of heat that belongs here is *light,* a claim in which I am supported by the verdict of common sense, as well as by the testimony of experience.[14] Now light is something that is not merely given in sensation, but is also determined objectively by laws, and whose motions can likewise be measured as intensity. A perfected *science of light*, in which I would particularly include photometry, will also beat, in part at least, a sure path for investigations on the phenomena of heat.

But we have no right to suppose that light warms in itself. In fact I have already shown above that light warms precisely in that degree to which it ceases to be *light*. To the findings adduced in proof of this, a number of others could be added, if exact tests were to be made on the differential heating of the same bodies by the different rays of the prism.[15]

And very much may yet be accomplished by investigation of the varying influence of light on different types of air, and on different materials of all kinds whatsoever. The way in which the colours of bodies are connected with the degree of their oxidation must draw attention to this.

But if we propose light as the cause of heat, we must never forget that in Nature nothing is one-sided, so that heat, conversely, can also be regarded as a source of light; for just as light can pass from its more elastic state into the less elastic state of heat, so heat, conversely, can also revert from the latter state to the former. Hence it comes about that a number of investigators have considered light as a *modification* of heat, a view that seems erroneous for this reason, that not *every* heat can become light, or *every* light become heat.

So much concerning the more refined sorts of matter. I now pass on to the coarser substances.

The endeavour of ordinary chemistry, to reduce substances as much as possible to basic elements, already betrays that (in idea at least) it has a principle of *unity* in view, which it constantly seeks to approach, so far as it may. But if there is such a principle, it provides no reason for halting anywhere in the effort to unify our knowledge; on the contrary, we must at least assume it possible that continued investigation, and a deeper grasp of the inner side of Nature, will discover substances which now seem totally heterogeneous to be modifications of a common principle.

But if, as is then necessary, we ask what that ultimately may be, of which all qualities are modifications, there is nothing else left to us for the purpose but *matter as such*. So the regulative principle of a scientifi-

---

[14] Cf. Book I, Chapter 2.
[15] Senebier has done this, in part, but subject to considerations which too greatly restricted his investigations.

cally progressive chemistry will always be the idea of regarding *all* qualities as merely different modifications and relationships of the basic forces. For these are the one thing that empirical science may *postulate*, they are the data of every possible explanation, and in that research sets these limits for itself, it simultaneously assumes the responsibility of considering everything that lies within these limits as subject to its explanations. Chemistry, from a principle of this sort, has very much indeed to gain.

For *firstly*, it serves, at the least, as a hypothesis which can legitimately be opposed to the assaults of a semi-philosophical scepticism, to which a merely empirical chemistry is all too readily exposed. The qualities of bodies, such a sceptic might say, can only be called qualities, after all, with respect to your sensation; so what right do you have to transfer something that is merely valid for your sensation to the objects themselves?

Such an objection can be totally ignored, so long as we confine ourselves to ordinary practical chemistry. But the theoretical, scientific tone which chemistry has lately adopted is incompatible with a total indifference to first principles, to which we must eventually return, once we have experimented long enough, and now wish to assign to our own science also its place in the context of all knowledge.

A chemistry which assumes one basic substance after another, without even knowing by what right it does so, or how far the validity of such an assumption extends, does not deserve to be called a theoretical chemistry.

For a mass of basic substances, all differing from one another by special qualities, are so many barriers to further research, so long, at least, as there has not yet been any inquiry as to what, in the end, *all* qualities wholly and solely rest upon. But once it has been found that *quality*, as such, is something that can also be validly expressed for the understanding – in terms available to all – one may unhesitatingly postulate as many different qualities of matter – and hence as many basic substances – as are needed for purposes of empirical scientific research.

For *basic substance*, in chemistry, ought surely to mean no less than a substance beyond which we cannot get in our experiments. But the only thing that can legitimately elude all empirical studies of Nature is the relationship of the basic forces of matter. For since this itself first makes possible a *determinate* matter (nor is there any other), we cannot in turn explain it on a physical basis, i.e., one that *presupposes* matter. So with this presupposition (that all quality in matter rests on relationships of its *basic forces*), we have provided the warrant for subjecting empirical research to certain limits, which it is not permitted to overstep. And with this we have secured the right to express every particular *quality* of matter, if only it be a definite and permanent quality, by means of basic substances, which may be regarded as limits to distinguish the field of an experiential study of Nature, resting upon *facts*, from the domain of a purely *philosophical* natural science, or from the broad and uncertain terrain of mere imagination and speculation.

Hence the concept of a *basic substance* in chemistry is this: *the unknown cause of a specific quality of matter.* So by *basic substance* we are to understand, not matter itself, but only the cause of its quality. Moreover, where this cause can be stated and presented, we have no right to take refuge in basic substances.

This being presupposed – a few backward glances at light and heat! It is an almost intolerable confusion of concepts when we hear talk of *light-stuff,* by which the majority in fact understand nothing else but *light* itself. But that this matter we call light has these particular qualities may indeed be derived – by the right in question, that is – from a basic substance, like the qualities of other kinds of matter; yet precisely here there is next to nothing gained, since light stands in any case at the limits of all matter known to us, and to that extent seems itself to be pure quality.[16]

But we are far less entitled still to speak of a *heat-stuff,* if by this be meant an unknown cause, whereby matter can be so modified that it displays the phenomena of heat. For such a cause is nothing unknown, seeing that *light* cannot be called *heat-stuff* for this very reason, that it is a matter whose laws we know; and so it is also with the causes whereby the capacity of bodies is diminished, and heat accordingly produced.

Moreover, the name "basic substance" can be given only to the cause of a *quality,* but of a quality such that it attaches neither to matter *as such* nor to a *particular* matter, in a merely contingent fashion. To that extent, admittedly, the assumption of basic substances has very broad limits. Thus modern chemistry speaks of scent-stuff, sweet-stuff – perhaps we shall soon get a general taste-stuff. That sort of thing is defensible. But a heat-stuff does not exist, for heat is a quality that can pertain to *all* matter, is contingent and relative, and has to do only with the state of the body; by its presence or absence the body neither gains nor loses a single absolute quality. And if, finally, we were to hear or have heard anyone speak of a *hard-* or *soft-stuff,* or of a *light-* or *heavy-stuff,* we should not know what we were supposed to make of it.

Now so far as the main substances of modern chemistry are con-

---

[16] [Last words added in 2nd Edn.]

cerned, not one of them can be presented *for* itself, and only to that extent, too, can they be called basic substances.

But if we advert to the idea which, in regulative fashion, must underlie all inquiries as to the different qualities of matter, we are obliged to assume that the whole distinction among these basic substances will rest merely on differences of degree. Thus if, of several substances, none attracts the others, but all together attract a third, we can assume that this third has the median relationship to all the rest. But if the latter are distinguished from one another only by their greater or lesser deviation from that common mean, they are to that extent all *homogeneous to themselves* through their common relationship to this mean, but *heterogeneous* to that basic substance which they all collectively attract (for only between heterogeneous materials does qualitative attraction occur).

This idea is itself not without utility for the progress of empirical research.

For it arouses the hope of eventually being able to reduce all difference among basic substances to just one single opposition. Nature thereby becomes simpler. The cycle in which she operates is more intelligible to us.

I give a few examples. The basic substance of vegetable bodies is said to be *carbon;* now if we go back to the growth of plants, the sole source of their nourishment is soil and air. But what they chiefly attract to themselves from both is water. One constituent of the latter is oxygen, the basic substance which, heterogeneous to all others, is for that very reason attracted by them all. The other constituent is the totally problematic hydrogen of modern chemistry. The question is, what changes are these basic substances capable of? Since the difference of all together is only a difference *of degree,* we may answer: *all* possible changes; for Nature can apply a multitude of chemical means that are simply not in our power, and the growth-mechanism of all organic products leaves us in no doubt that their organs are instruments in the hand of Nature, whereby she effects modifications of matter, which with all our chemical art we strive to produce in vain. Thus we do not even need to assume that Nature provides plants (in which the mechanism of assimilation is not so striking as it is in animals) with nutrient juices already fully prepared. The plant is what it is, not through its component parts (we know the components of most plants, yet can produce none); its whole existence depends on a continuing process of assimilation.

This being assumed, we know that plants exhale the one component of water as vital air. So the main material of all vegetable bodies, namely carbon, might well be nothing else but a modification of the inflamma-

ble substance in water – the hydrogen of modern chemistry – and by
this already we should have discovered a unity of principle between two
basic substances, which otherwise subsist in isolation.

More important is the question, By what means is Nature able to
replace the constant loss of pure vital air to which the atmosphere is
subject? The existence of an element so important for life cannot be
exclusively due to the production of this type of air from plants (which
depends on time and circumstances). Now we can certainly think of
many other possibilities, e.g., that water might yield up its inflammable substance to other bodies, and turn into vital air, that this constituent of pure air might be released by constant restitutions (deoxida-
tions) of formerly burnt bodies in and on the surface of the earth, etc.
But all these possibilities leave all too much to chance for us to be able
to rest content with them. So Nature must certainly have means of
continually renewing this element of vital air, of effecting modifications which it is absolutely impossible for us to bring about. And *this*
ought now to be the great object of the endeavours of the chemists
and students of Nature, to trace out on the large scale the manner of
Nature's working (which they have hitherto sought with such happy
results to imitate on the *small* scale), to investigate by what means, and
by what unalterable laws, Nature gives stability and continuance to the
eternal cycle in which she persists – not in detail but as a whole, not to
the individual but to the system.

It is also worth noting in this connection the internal mixing of two
quite heterogeneous kinds of air in the atmosphere, and the well-nigh
always similar and never-disturbed relation between them, so finely
calculated for the continuance of animal and vegetable life. To this it
should be added that the origin of one of these kinds of air (the azotic)
is till now still totally unknown to us. For that the basis of this type of
air is the fundamental substance of saltpetre serves only as a hint for
assuming a common mode of origin for both. In virtue of this uncertainty, I thought that in the chapter on types of air[17] I might even
recommend a hitherto still quite problematic experiment to the more
exact investigation of the chemists, as a means of approaching closer
to the question.

Since the conjunction of the two kinds of air in the atmosphere
must be a sort of chemical combination, the conjecture very readily
arises that both might well have been already combined in their original development. Their source would thus have been a common one,
and of such a kind that by the means which Nature employs for their
development, only the two together could be evolved from it. Yet we

[17] Cf. above, p. 90.

are all the less constrained to such an assumption, in that so far as we know at present, and if new discoveries do not teach us otherwise, there is a far smaller expenditure of azotic gas in Nature than of vital air.

But the student of Nature must bear in mind that in her major chemical processes, Nature is able to employ means which we first have to discover, and hence, too, that our own inability to modify a given body or basic substance in a particular way is no proof that Nature is subject to the same inability. Thus water, for example, is a body whose constituents, it seems (and as actual experiments show), are capable of various quantitative relationships, and of which the two that are designated as oxygen and hydrogen are themselves only two possible kinds.[18] Since this fluid is the middle term between elastic liquids and solid bodies, we may conjecture in advance that it is not wholly idle in the major processes of Nature, in the formation of basic substances and solid bodies, and perhaps even in the production, on the large scale, of types of air.

These examples, I think, are sufficient to show what profit to the enlargement of our knowledge might accrue from the idea that all basic substances in bodies ultimately differ from one another only by relationships of degree, as soon as this notion is implanted, as a regulative idea, at the foundation of empirical research.

The purpose of this whole inquiry was to establish a general, comprehensible and objectively applicable concept, in place of the merely subjective concept of quality (which loses its sense and meaning when objectively employed).

The purpose could not have been that of explaining the nature of our *sensation*. If it is said, for example, that "light is the highest degree of elasticity – heat an already diminished degree of the same," we have not thereby explained the sensations of light and heat, and nor (if we know what we are doing) are we even *wanting* to explain them. In regard to many a reader, this remark is perhaps not altogether superfluous.

Chemistry itself is a science which advances securely upon the beaten path of experience, even when it does not turn back to first principles. But a science which in itself is so rich, and which has lately made such great progress towards *system*, surely deserves to be led back to such principles.

But so long as chemistry adheres solely to experience (as from now on it will always do), even the negative advantage which such a reversion to principles might have (in the avoidance of idle hypotheses) is not so evident as it would have to be in the opposite case. Happy if (as

[18] [Last words added in 2nd Edn.]

the only one of the empirical sciences to base *everything* on experiment) she is never in need of philosophical discipline.

And chemistry itself, within its empirical boundaries, can continue to adhere to the language which it has spoken hitherto. For a more philosophical idiom is indeed better suited to the understanding, but an empirical science requires that the concepts and laws on which it rests should be *intuitable*. Whether this be the case, and can be, with the proposed principles of chemistry, I shall answer in the chapter that follows. Should the answer perhaps turn out negative, we see from the outset that, instead of forcing upon ordinary chemistry an abstract language and philosophical concepts which cannot be construed, it is preferable, rather, to leave her with her pictorial concepts and the sensory language which, if it does not satisfy the understanding, is at least far better suited to the imagination (which in empirical sciences never gives up its right).

Appendix to the
Previous Section
[Literary Notices]

It is extremely advantageous for the experimental sciences to know their *boundaries* exactly, so that they do not, say, dabble in inquiries that belong before an altogether different tribunal, and are thus themselves embroiled in contradictions and contentions that have no end whatever, because mere experience is no longer capable of deciding about them. Conversely, however, if we lay down principles, in order, by limiting its pretensions, to free the experimental doctrine from doubts and difficulties which it has needlessly imposed upon itself, it may easily happen that the empiric himself thereafter disowns that difficulty, and even makes out that it was first concocted for the benefit of the new theory.

Since questions about the *principles* of chemistry do not, in my opinion, belong before the tribunal of merely *experimentalist* chemistry, I am happy, before the conclusion of this part, to encounter a knowledgeable author, himself already with a reputation in empirical chemistry, who has likewise had the aim in his endeavours of banishing from his science unnecessary inquiries, which lie beyond its frontiers.[19]

The following essays of this author have particularly engaged my attention: (1) "On the Identity of Light and Heat,"[20] (2) "On the Chemical Relationships of Both,"[21] and (3) "On the Immateriality of Heat-stuff and Light-stuff."[22]

When the author speaks of the identity of the matters of light and heat, he cannot mean the *absolute* identity of both. It would thus have been profitable to define in advance what is required for two matters to be regarded as one and the same. If all difference of matter rests merely on the differing relationships of its basic forces, we shall have as many different matters as we are acquainted with qualities. But

[19] I refer to Herr Scherer's supplements to his *Grundzüge der neuern chemischen Theorie,* Jena, 1796.

[20] *Op. cit.,* pp. 18–120.

[21] *Ibid.,* pp. 121–56.

[22] *Ibid.,* pp. 157–85.

quality is valid as such only in respect of sensation. So differing sensations also entitle us to assume different qualities, and thus different matters.

Yet notwithstanding this general identity of matter (for all matter differs from any other only by relationships of degree), there can still be reasons for postulating an immediate identity between different matters, A and B, in the case, that is, where the one, B, can be regarded merely as a *special state* of the other. Now this seems to be the case with heat and light. Heat is a modification of bodies which can be brought about by light, or heat is the next state into which light passes, as soon as it ceases to be light (or – what comes to the same, for how else do we know light but through our sensation? – as soon as it ceases to affect the eye).

But here a difficulty emerges, which does not allow us to assert forthwith an *identity* of light-matter and heat-matter. For if they were identical, light would conversely have to be capable of being regarded, also, as a mere modification of heat; but this, as I conceive, is utterly impossible.

For firstly, we thereby lend heat an absolute existence, which it simply does not possess (in the way that light does). For according to Crawford's discoveries, there is no absolute heat, it being purely a relative thing; not only is it, as such, a *mere* modification of other matter – it is also a modification for which there is no absolute measure (hence the concept of capacity in bodies). I am very well aware that without this concept of heat, the notion of regarding light and heat as reciprocal modifications is a very natural one, and I myself, earlier on (p. 70, since I was not yet presupposing this concept), have declared it to be wholly indifferent whether we regard light as free heat, or heat as bound light.

But we do not in fact have a single demonstrative proof that heat – I will not say in general, and according to rule, but even in the mere individual case – becomes *light,* in the way that light *always* and regularly becomes *heat,* when it acts upon bodies.

The only possible proof of this claim is the light which is engendered from vital air. For, as someone might say, that which constitutes the universal component of all kinds of air is heat-stuff, and in *this* case at least, therefore, the heat-stuff of vital air takes on, by decomposition, properties of light. But here the following has been overlooked, namely that according to the statements of the leading chemists of our day, *light* is absolutely requisite for the formation of vital air. Now I am very happy to concede that light, as soon as it enters into combination with other substances, becomes *heat,* or *heat-stuff,* and hence that even the light which forms vital air has taken on the properties and mode of action of heat-stuff; and from this it is intelligible why vital air in particular should also, *in reverse,* again display phenomena of light.[23] But the case at hand is a case of a *special* kind, from which we cannot at once draw the general conclusion: Hence heat *as such* can take on the properties of light.

It is therefore very consistent, at least, for Herr Scherer to deny that vital air *alone* is a source of light. But by this statement, so far as I can see, we are claiming only this much, namely, that vital air has *till now been known to us* as the only matter which yields the phenomenon of luminescence. So until we discover another matter of this kind, say a gas whose decomposition is associated with the production of light, we have no right to claim that heat-stuff *as such* (which after all is the common component of *all* elastic fluids) is identical with the matter of light.

But now we are also compelled to ask: By what, then, do light and heat differ, as modifications of a common matter? What is the cause of the same matter acting now as light and now as heat, in the one case on the eye, and in the other on feeling?

Now that *light*, in the combinations that it enters into with bodies, becomes or produces *heat* is attested by experience,[24] and where experience decides, there is no further need to grope around blindly among possibilities.

But how heat, on the other hand, is so modified as to exhibit phenomena of light, there is no experience to tell us, and *hence* in fact we get the indefinite explanations on the subject, which are to be found even among acute students of Nature: e.g., on p. 106 of a work by Professor Link: "Whether a body glows or warms, or does both together in a precise ratio or not, depends solely on the differing rapidity with which the parts of heat-stuff are evolved. If they all fall into a

[23] The question why, for example, in the decomposition of vital air by nitrogen, no light is observed, is unanswerable as soon as light is considered as a *stuff,* and not, as on our view, as a *matter,* which is capable of the most varied modifications, and whose properties depend wholly and solely on these modifications.

[24] Cf. above, pp. 68–70. Herr Scherer thinks it possible to regard the phenomenon of cold in the upper regions of the atmosphere as a result of the *mechanical expansion* of the air, "which is in constant motion" – (but in the upper regions the atmosphere is in a constant state of rest) – "by which (motion) elastic fluids attract or absorb heat, whereas on their mechanical condensation the heat-stuff is again squeezed out of them, which happens in that the air in the lower regions is compressed by the columns of air lying upon it." – I think that another explanation is possible, cf. above, pp. 69, 70. – On [his] p. 110 the author also adduces Pictet's experiment, referred to on [my] p. 69 above, as a very *important* finding. I am therefore all the more ready to believe that I may count on his approving the conclusion that I have drawn from it.

slower motion, it will merely warm; if they all fall into the *swiftest* motion, it will merely glow; and, as easily follows from this, the more parts move swiftly, the more it will glow, and in the opposite case, warm. Whether one or the other occurs, moreover, will depend solely on the manner in which the heat-stuff is precipitated." (Herr Scherer praises the *facility* of this explanation. But this very facility makes it suspicious, since we cannot refrain from asking: *How* swiftly, then, must the heat-stuff move in order to glow? Physics is wary of all *more* or *less,* for which there is no longer any weight or measure.) Or on p. 114: "It may be assumed that in accordance with the different mode of *motion* of the heat-stuff, our senses, too, can be very differently affected, and that *light,* accordingly, is observed when it propagates with *exceeding swiftness* in straight lines – (these, surely, have nothing to do with the matter) – while heat, on the contrary, is felt only when the heat-stuff moves *more slowly* and in all directions – (does not light do the same?) – within bodies."[25]

So much as to the relationships of light and heat *to one another.* Now for their relationship to other kinds of matter.

The author flatly denies that heat-stuff enters into *chemical* combination with any single body. I have refuted this assumption in the foregoing, on the presumption that no special heat-stuff exists. Herr Scherer's arguments tell against the chemical combination of heat-stuff itself, assuming this fancied element to be real. "Heat-stuff," he says,[26] "does not just warm certain bodies, to which it has *elective attraction;* it produces in all the modification which arouses in us the sensation of heat. It does not just expand *some* substances, but exerts this effect upon *all.* But is this not wholly at variance with *chemical* effects? For is not the result of the chemical combinations of oxygen in every case an acid, and indeed *one and the same* acid; does it not produce, with hydrogen, only water; with metals, only metallic calces; with the various acid radicals, also *various* acids? What a variety of differing products is not brought

---

[25] Far more definite and observationally grounded is another statement of the same author, put forward on p. 116: "Light produces heat only in such bodies as oppose some resistance to its passage; it warms up opaque, dark-coloured bodies the most, transparent ones less so, and completely transparent ones, if such were to be met with, perhaps not at all. The explanation of this phenomenon is easiest and simplest if we abide by what immediately struck the physicists who first observed these appearances. The light in fact loses its rapid motion, takes on a slower one, and is manifested as perceptible warmth, perhaps also loses its motion entirely and becomes latent heat." I would like to say that *these phenomena do more to serve as proofs in favour of the agreement of light and heat than against it,* notwithstanding that they have led to the majority of hypotheses concerning the components of light- or heat-stuff.

[26] *Op. cit.,* pp. 127–8.

about by combination of the various acids with the equally various salifiable substances (alkalis, earths and metals)! And heat-stuff is supposed in *all* bodies to engender *only* heating and expansion? And if, moreover, we also go on to suppose specific, bound or latent heat-stuff, what, then, is brought about by that? Nothing whatever! But how, as a chemically active body, can it have entered into chemical combination with another body, without having altered the nature of the latter or brought about any new product at all? Is it not wholly otherwise with all other substances? Is not metal very strikingly altered, when it unites with heat-stuff? But what happens when metal takes up heat-stuff? Does it not remain metal, even when it becomes liquid? So how could a latent heat-stuff have been so hastily assumed, where no heat is felt?"

I cannot forbear adding to these remarks the observations of another philosophical student of Nature. It has gone so far that philosophical arguments advanced in such matters are rejected as illegitimate, on the pretext *that* they are philosophical. But philosophy has the office of deciding what in our knowledge is *objective,* and what is mere sensation. It is therefore profitable to demonstrate that even the empirical researcher (for it is now thought that philosophy can be of no use to experience) must go back to philosophical principles, if he does not wish to abandon himself blindly to the fictions of a merely empirical doctrine of Nature.

"The force of attraction," says Herr Link,[27] "which bodies exert upon heat-stuff, has no likeness whatever to chemical affinity. Here a body snatches its component from the other either wholly, or in large part; there a body abstracts from the other only so much heat-stuff as to equalize the absolute elasticity of the heat-stuff in both bodies. Equally little can it be maintained that this attraction is on a par with universal attraction. The latter acts at a distance, falls off as the square of the distance increases, and is proportionate to the quantities of matter which exert their pull from both sides. Of all that we see nothing here; we do not see that denser bodies attract the heat-stuff more strongly than those less dense, nor that the distribution of heat-stuff is adjusted to their densities, as we would have to expect if mere universal attraction were in operation here.

"It would be a misuse of accurately defined terms, to wish to maintain that the heat-stuff which makes up the bulk of the specific heat in any body, is chemically bound therein. This heat-stuff flows from the warmer into the colder body, and likewise returns to the first, as soon as it again becomes the colder. In chemical combinations we observe nothing of all this. Thus no component separates from the rest be-

---

[27] I borrow these passages from Herr Scherer, *op. cit.,* pp. 138–40.

cause it is present there in larger quantity, nor does it ever return to the previous body, if the latter is suffering a shortage thereof. The chemical separations and combinations are more definitely evinced – they are consequences of a selective attraction, and can be ordered according to tables of affinity; but heat-stuff, in this case at least, is not subject to any such rules. But supposing there were a heat-stuff so firmly bound to the body that it could not be abstracted or diminished by a colder body, the term 'chemically bound' could still be incorrect, since numerous sequences are possible in the unification of bodies, which differ greatly among themselves, but might be quite distinct from chemical affinity."

I have, I believe, sufficiently explained my views in the foregoing on the question already often raised of late: Is light actually a matter? Since I have now become acquainted with Herr Scherer's investigations "on the *immateriality* of heat- and light-stuff," I append here a few reasons which still strike me as possible to advance on behalf of the materiality of light.[28]

The reasons that the author adduces for his opinion are actually valid only against the hypothesis of a *light-stuff*, not against that of a *light-matter*. This distinction (which is not without significance in the present inquiry) I have, I think, made clear in the foregoing. I have shown that *basic stuffs in general*, not just this or that particular stuff, are a thing entirely *imaginary*. This claim proves itself, as soon as we just know the chemical basic substances; for not one of them has so far been presented in intuition. Nor should we ever hope to present them. And what is intuited is no longer called *basic substance*, but matter. It is therefore self-evident, from the outset, that light-stuff, too (i.e., not *light-matter*, but the imaginary *cause* of the *properties* of this matter), belongs just as much as, but also no more than, any other basic substance of chemistry to the class of chemical fictions (which, within certain limits, I consider to be themselves unavoidable).

I hope, furthermore, that if philosophical principles count for more, hereafter, than they formerly did in the empirical sciences, the presumption of matters which are supposed to differ from one another by inner (and to that extent occult) qualities will totally disappear from our theories. According to these principles, *every* individual matter is now actually a mere modification of matter as such, and all qualities of matter, however different they may be, are nothing else but different relationships of its basic forces. So this is actually something that holds good, not of light only, but of *every* matter, and if anyone wanted to prove the immateriality of light from the proposi-

---

[28] which continue to require me to stand by the *materiality* of light [1st Edn.].

tion, say, that "light is a mere *modification* of matter," we could by the same token demonstrate the immateriality of all matters – for where have we ever seen matter as such, and not mere modifications of matter?

The inquiries that are undertaken, in the work under discussion, as to the materiality or immateriality of light, are therefore, perhaps, in need only of philosophical amplification, in order to agree entirely with the results of philosophy. I infer this from the fact that the author himself, in order to demonstrate his theory of heat, makes appeal to the basic propositions of philosophical dynamics. "If it is proved," he says,[29] "that the possibility of matter – as the moveable in space – depends on the two basic forces of attraction and repulsion; and if, finally, the infinitely possible specific difference of matters is explicable through mere difference in the combination of these original forces, what, then, still obliges us to derive the various forms of bodies from a corporeal relationship between heat-stuff and substances? Cannot the form of aggregation then depend merely on the reciprocal influences of the basic forces, and their respective intensity?

"The most important objection that might be levelled at such a proposition is undeniably this: that, after all, the different form that we produce by the heating of solid bodies would seem to be the result of a combination of the body whose form is altered with the cause of the heat. I admit that, at first sight anyway, this fact seems to make all further argument superfluous, in that here there is no mistaking the most palpable evidence. Yet I venture to maintain that this evidence has been planted; it is founded merely on the one-sided arguments of the atomistic philosophy, whereby any and every phenomenon is supposed to have its basis solely in the conjunction or combination of the variously shaped basic parts (atoms) of the bodies juxtaposed, as if without this assumption no simpler explanation, or one more suitable to Nature, could be imagined.

"It strikes me as very probable, that by heating of a body nothing is added to it, but only the mutual relationship of the basic forces is so altered, that the repulsive gains a preponderance over the attractive. How is this actually brought about? *By the impact*, I believe, *of the ponderable parts of the air,* which becomes capable of doing this by heating (i.e., through the *basic forces* that are put into action). I locate this power, during the heating of bodies in air, solely in the ponderable parts of the air, because this influence, after all, can only hold good of matter – i.e., something ponderable that moves in space. Heat, therefore, is merely the phenomenon that is coupled on each

[29] *Op. cit.,* pp. 164–6.

occasion with this exercise of force. The impact operates, in my opinion, insofar as it brings about a *removal of the equilibrium between the forces,* just as we assuredly find ourselves obliged to attribute to this such universal phenomena as motion, and the like. As will readily be observed, I am here approaching the ideas of a le Sage, which I also cheerfully concede, save that I think that the domain of the mechanical will here have to be exactly separated from the chemical field; that the laws of dynamics must certainly not be lost sight of. For at present we are not yet permitted to abolish entirely the distinction between chemical and mechanical forces, as has, indeed, already been attempted here and there."

I have cited this passage to show that the inquiries so currently contentious in chemistry are at last being themselves *compelled* to go back to philosophical principles, concerning the nature of matter and the ground of its qualities—not that I would wholly agree with the statements of the author (who seems, strangely enough, to want to combine the dynamical and the mechanical physics). For when, for example, he derives the heating of solid bodies from an impact of the ponderable parts of the air, the question is, What, then, has produced this impact itself? (Undoubtedly heat again; but this was the very thing to be explained.) It is also a question, how by (mechanical) impact "the *relationship of the basic forces* (which is purely dynamic) can be so altered, that the repulsive gains a preponderance over the attractive." For an *impact* can itself in turn only act *mechanically,* and so on.

What was very much of an obstacle to previous inquiries on these subjects, is the perfectly equal treatment of light and heat, notwithstanding that it had sufficiently long ago been proved of the latter that it is nothing whatever in itself—nothing absolute—but simply a modification of bodies, and a wholly relative thing into the bargain. Now light, to be sure, is also a mere modification—but one of which not *every* matter is capable; it is a *peculiar* modification—something that itself *has* qualities, and not merely *is* a quality, like heat.

But precisely for that reason, if the origin of light is to be explained, we cannot rest content, either, with the general philosophical explanation that "it is a modification of the matter of the activated basic forces as such," etc. Fortunately, we are here met halfway by experience, which does not leave us in ignorance of the true source of light.

Many celebrated students of Nature (the name of Bacon can stand here for all the rest) have denied the substantiality of fire, and regarded the whole phenomenon as merely a peculiar motion into which bodies are thrown. But it is clear that this motion could not be thought of as actuated in a merely *mechanical* fashion. It had to be explained *chemically,* i.e., by an influence on the relationship of the *basic forces* in the body. It was just that experience had not yet provided enough data to make such a chemical motion intelligible. Empirical chemistry has by now made such advances that we no longer have to fear of such an undertaking that it cannot be carried out.

What Herr Scherer has attempted in this connection, I communicate from the work cited, and refrain from any further annotations on it, since the author himself would wish to have his explanation regarded as a first – and to that extent also most imperfect – attempt.

"The properties of bodies," he says on p. 286, "are to be considered a result of the activated basic forces of bodies.

"Through the activated basic forces, a motion of bodies is brought about, whereby they obtain the opportunity to act upon one another.

"Every chemical permeation is preceded by mere mechanical contact; this explains the necessity of form-change, to bring about the manifestations of affinity.

"The different forms of aggregations in bodies depend on the relationships of the basic forces to one another. According to whether the *repulsive* or *attractive* force comes to predominate during the disturbance of their reciprocal equilibrium, a *more fluid* or *more solid* form will also be produced.

"Through manifestations of affinity, the forms are changed about, and largely from a more fluid into a more solid state, whereby heat, light or flame is commonly observed. Simple dissolutions or mechanical combinations (mixtures) are normally accompanied by an exchange of the more solid form for the more fluid; hence only cold arises in the process.

"Oxygen and oxidizable substances are active here during the production of fire – and fire seems therefore to have its basis merely in the *motion* into which the uniting substances enter, through removal of the *equilibrium of their basic forces*. If the *attractive* force gains the preponderance here, heat, etc. result; if the repulsive force predominates, on the contrary, these phenomena are either not noticed at all, or are observed only to a very small degree."

I note further that Herr Scherer has communicated some very interesting remarks about heat and light, insofar as both are produced by *friction*. From what is said of this subject on p. 274, it is hard to believe that the source of it is to be looked for in the bodies themselves. I point this out, because it strikes me as important for the theory of electricity propounded above.

Still more important in this connection is a statement by Lavoisier, reported on p. 492, from vol. III, p. 270 of his physico-chemical writings: "I think some day," he says, "of giving an account of the reasons which impel me to believe that the electrical phenomena which we perceive are only the consequence of a decomposition of the air," – (The main reason, it seems to me, is surely the *division of the two electrical matters* between the bodies rubbed; for it occurs in accordance with the nearer or remoter affinity to *oxygen*.) – *"that electricity is only a kind of combustion, in which the air delivers up the electric matter, just as, in my view, it delivers up the matter of fire and light in ordinary combustion.* It will be astonishing to see how applicable this new doctrine is to the explanation of the most diverse phenomena."

Herr Scherer agrees with this conjecture. "For a long time now," he says,[30] "I have been busy with the idea that a very great analogy exists between the phenomena of fire and electricity. The calcination of the amalgam, during friction of the glass of the electrifying machine upon it, made me still more attentive to this agreement. In the end I could find nothing more probable than that electricity is a kind of fire, whose production might depend, perhaps, on the very same grounds as those of ordinary fire. This surmise acquired for me the highest degree of probability, partly through the view of the subject which Lavoisier propounds, in the cited passage of his writings, and partly through the findings of a van Marum, which set the agreement of electrical phenomena with those of heat in an even clearer light.

"It is extremely probable[31] that in all the manipulations whereby we excite the so-called electric matter, we are producing nothing else but a decomposition of the atmospheric air. This type of decomposition is admittedly strikingly different from that accomplished by burning and calcination; it very probably occurs much more slowly, but the result of it is for that reason all the more striking." I think I have shown that this decomposition of the air takes place *mechanically*, but that this mechanism (of friction) could well produce phenomena of heat or fire, yet not those of electricity, without the concurrent effect of the *heterogeneity* of the bodies employed for the purpose.

From a letter of the chemist van Mons, Herr Scherer finally, on p. 199, reports the conjecture that the electric fluid could be due to a *condensation* of the air. Without doubt, he says, the *two kinds of gas* which make up the atmospheric air are thereby separated and again combined. But the calcination of metals by electricity he likewise attributes to the presence of oxygen.

I have deliberately brought together everything that has become known, hitherto, in favour of the proposed hypothesis, because I would like to be able to occasion, by whatever means it may be, a testing of this hypothesis through the performance of experiments.

[30] *Ibid.*, pp. 493–4.
[31] *Ibid.*, p. 496.

I also have great pleasure in mentioning here an excellent academic work, which deserves to become better known than such writings normally are, in which the author has been the first that I know of to attempt, in a truly philosophic spirit, to apply the principles of dynamics, as set forth by Kant, to the empirical theory of Nature, and above all to chemistry.[32]

[32] *Principia quaedam disciplinae naturali, in primis Chemiae ex Metaphysica naturae substernenda.* Auctore C. A. Eschenmayer. Tubingae, 1796. [Principles to be taken from the Metaphysic of Nature as the Foundation of Certain Natural Sciences, especially Chemistry.]
To confirm the above judgment, we subjoin some of the author's main propositions:
[In place of Eschenmayer's Latin, as quoted *in extenso* by Schelling, we give an English version, kindly supplied by Dr A. H. Coxon. – Trans.].
The quality of matter follows the mutual ratio of forces of attraction and repulsion.
Every variety of matter, on this view, is brought about by the uniquely differing proportion of the same forces, and so reduces to a distinction of degrees.
Since matter fills space, not through existence alone, but through forces, and the uniquely varying proportion of the same forces imports a distinction of degree only, all diversities of matter reduce ultimately to a diversity of degrees. The qualities of matter are therefore relations of degree.
Chemical operations are concerned with changes in the degree-relations of matter.
Chemical motion depends on the victory of either an attractive or a repulsive force, chemical rest upon peace between them.
There has to be accepted a maximum and minimum in relations of degree, between which the remaining degrees are inserted as intermediate.
The metaphysic of Nature attaches to the force of attraction the notion of infinitely small, to the force of repulsion that of infinitely large. Let the force of attraction be signified by the letter A, that of repulsion by the letter B, and A will be $= \frac{1}{\infty}$, B ∞. Since therefore $\frac{1}{\infty} \times \infty = 1$, so A $\times$ B together give something finite. But since matter is formed by the marriage of a repulsive with an attractive force, A $\times$ B will $=$ M, if we put M for matter.
The force of repulsion produces for our empirical intuition a positive character, since it fills a space, the force of attraction a negative character, since it introduces a limitation of the filling.
According to the predominance of the positive or negative element, the scale of substances can be classified into two orders; the median point of it, which is occupied by the power of either element when made completely equal, should be expressed as brought to a potency $= 0$.
The chemical solution of two substances takes place by a dynamical distribution of the two degrees; whence must proceed the characters of homogeneity and neutrality.
If an eminent degree of the positive order is admitted in the nature of phlogiston, and on the other hand a conspicuous degree of the negative order in the basis of air, the phenomena of combustion are easily explained from the proposed principles, and the way is simultaneously opened for a reconciliation of the Phlogistics and the Antiphlogistics.

On the Substances in Chemistry
(Supplement to Chapter 8)

How absolutely one and the same matter gives birth to the multiplicity of forms has been sufficiently discoursed upon in the foregoing. Just as, in the individual, its unity forms into difference only in the shape of magnetism, so it also does in the whole. The inner and essential identity is not thereby abolished, and remains the same under all the forms or potencies that it takes on in the metamorphosis. Just as the leaves, blossoms and collective organs of the plant are related to the identity of the plant, so the collective differences of bodies are related to the one substance, from which they proceed by graduated change. If we designate the factors of form generally as potencies, it is necessary for the greatest preponderance of one potency over the others to fall at the extreme of that magnetic line, and since (by the Supplement to Chapter 6) we have to assume a double indifference-point, matter, too, must terminate in poles on four different sides, as four quarters of the world, so that on each side the identity of matter remains, but the indifference of the form is more and more taken away.

The poles of absolute cohesion will present themselves on the one side by a maximum of expansion, and on the other by a maximum of concentration. Since, in their indifference-point, cohesion itself appears dissolved, the poles of relative cohesion will present themselves only in the expanded state, yet in such a way that, within this, the one again appears as the contracted, and the other as the expanded pole.

From these extremes of matter, where the form-determinations appear in the greatest diversity, chemical empiricism now takes over its substances. If we ask what concept guides it in so doing, it is that of the composite character of matter generally, and of the non-presentable character of a special matter, as such. All its so-called substances, so it says, are compounded with some other one, e.g., heat-stuff, and in such a way that, if they are ejected from any given combination, they pass over at once into another one. Inasmuch as these substances do not appear *per se,* they are plainly fictitious entities, for empiricism has no right to go beyond appearance; to this it is replied that they can, after all, be presented through weight, and that this non-presentability occurs only in relation to the means we are able to employ, and so is more contingent than necessary. But now if we suppose an actually occurring and successful presentation, what was previously substance would then enter into the sequence of matters, and the true principle of quality, which had been sought in this matter, would retreat further still. The character of non-presentability is thus at the same time a character *essential* to the concept of substance, and yet a totally contingent one in the individual case. An essential character, because a substance, as soon as it is presentable quite separately *for* itself, becomes a matter, which we can now in turn think of as further compounded; a contingent character, since the non-presentability of substance has to be supposed contingent, in order not to go beyond experience in assuming that it exists.

To be sure, the highest instance in such a beginning is *weight,* and the sole reality, that which falls to be weighed; but nor, on that account, is a chemical process grasped in its essence therein. What is here *at work* cannot be laid upon the scales. It is that of which individual things, and all bodies, are the mere organs and members. So although this kind if chemistry has labelled itself the pneumatic, it is still for that reason neither spiritual nor spirited, but earthbound and blind to the nature of the case.

9

Projected Outline of the First Principles of Chemistry

Now that we have subjected the first principles of chemistry to our critique, it still remains for us to inquire whether these principles are even capable of a scientific *presentation*.

But the indispensable condition for such a presentation is the possibility of constructing such concepts mathematically. "So long, then," says Kant,[1] "as there is for the chemical actions of matters on one another no concept which admits of being constructed, . . . chemistry can become nothing more than a systematic art or experimental doctrine, but never science proper; for the principles of chemistry are merely empirical and admit of no presentation *a priori* in intuition. Consequently, the principles of chemical phenomena cannot make the possibility of such phenomena in the least conceivable, inasmuch as they are incapable of the application of mathematics." Should the result of this outline turn out adversely, the preceding investigations at least have the *negative* virtue of having directed chemistry back within its appointed limits (of mere experience).

Principle
All quality in bodies rests on the quantitative (gradual) relationship of their basic forces.

For quality exists only in relation to sensation. But only what has a degree can be sensed: Now in matter no degree is conceivable save that of the forces, and even of these only in their relation to one another. So all quality rests on forces insofar as they have a specific quantity (degree), and, since matter presupposes for its possibility *opposing* forces, on the *relationship* of these forces according to their degree.

Explanations
    1. Those substances are said to be *homogeneous* in which the quantitative relationship of the basic forces is the same.

[1] *Op. cit.*, Preface, p. x [Ellington, p. 7].

For homogeneity designates like qualities. Now all quality rests on the quantitative relationship of the basic forces, hence, etc.

We perceive at once that an *absolute* homogeneity would be an *identity* of qualities. But the term "homogeneous" is still needed in a wider sense, in which it denotes a mere approximation to identity.

2. Two substances are said to be *heterogeneous* if the quantitative relationship of the basic forces in one is the inverse of that relationship in the other.

So basic substances can still be called homogeneous, even though the quantitative relationship of their basic forces is *different,* just so long as it is not *opposite.* It is self-evident from this that there must be far more homogeneous than heterogeneous basic substances. It is clear, moreover, that there are also graduated approximations to *absolute* heterogeneity, which is perhaps nowhere to be met with in Nature.

Basic Laws

I. General Conditions of a Chemical Process

1. No chemical process is anything else but an interaction of the basic forces in two bodies.

For no chemical process takes place without qualitative attraction occurring between two bodies. It is thus an interaction of qualities. Now quality is nothing else but, etc.

2. Between *homogeneous* basic substances, *no* chemical process occurs.

For the quantitative relationship of the basic forces is more or less the same in both, so no change in these relationships can occur, nor can there be a chemical process between the two.

3. Between *heterogeneous* basic substances alone does a chemical process occur.

For only between these is an interaction of basic forces possible. But since there are graduated approximations to absolute heterogeneity, there will also be a difference among chemical processes in regard to the *facility* with which they are brought about.

4. Only if the quantitative relationship of basic forces in one body is the inverse of the same relationship in the other, is a chemical process possible between two bodies.

(The measure of repulsive force is *elasticity,* that of attractive force, *mass.* So the statement can also be expressed as follows: Only if mass and elasticity in one body have an inverse relation to mass and elasticity in the other, does a chemical process take place.)

For only in this case is a change of basic forces – an *adjustment* of elasticities and masses – possible.

Upon these basic laws depends the art of bringing about a chemical process. For since there exists no absolute heterogeneity in Nature, and since there are also differences in regard to the *facility* of chemical processes, it is an object of the chemical art to *bring about* processes that would otherwise not be possible, and to *facilitate* others, that would otherwise result only with great difficulty. This includes, for example, the raising of temperature, which serves no other purpose than to produce in both bodies that relationship of the basic forces which is requisite for the chemical process.

Every chemical motion is an *endeavour towards equilibrium,* so in order to give rise to such a motion, the *equilibrium* of the forces in the two bodies must be disturbed.

Hence the old principle of chemistry: *Chemica non agunt nisi soluta* – between two *solid* bodies no chemical combination is possible. Even where no chemical combination in the narrower sense of the word is supposed to go on, similar bodies, too, must be thrown into flux before they combine with one another. But where combination is to be effected between bodies that are not similar, either one of them must be originally fluid, or one, if not both, must be thrown into the fluid state by fire. We might also express the law as follows: Only between extremes is a chemical process possible. At least Nature, for the benefit of most chemical processes, has set up extremes, namely fluid and solid bodies.

Since a chemical process is nothing else but a restoration of the disturbed equilibrium of the forces, we may lay down the general basic law:

5. If a chemical process is to arise between two bodies, the force with which they mutually cohere must be smaller in both than the force with which they endeavour to enter into equilibrium one with the other.

From this there follows a major law, to which we shall return later on. No chemical process takes anything but a continuous course. The bodies must go through a number of stages, up to the point where the process itself actually begins. Thus metals, to be dissolved in acids, must first be *calcined* (oxidized). Only after this has happened does the dissolution begin. And if, say, the right amount of acid has not been employed, the process halts at the mere calcination.

Now there will be as many different ways of effecting a chemical process as there are means of altering the equilibrium of forces in a body, or – what comes to the same – of weakening the cohesive force of the bodies. But the main means consists of fluids which, in accordance with their affinity for solid bodies, combine with the latter and thereby change the mutual interconnection of their particles. To these may be added the aeriform fluids, sometimes as vehicles of *heat*, sometimes as vehicles of that basic substance to which all other basic substances display affinity. By fire, solid bodies are transformed into fluid ones. This transformation itself is already commonly regarded as a chemical process, and to that extent is called *dissolution, and, indeed, dissolution by the dry way*. Another means of altering the composition of bodies is calcination, which also occurs in the dry way, by fire, being itself a chemical process and, at the same time, the means for promoting total dissolution.

Also to be included here are the *liquids*, which as vehicles of oxygen serve first to *calcine* solid bodies, such as the metals, and then to *dissolve* them. If the latter occurs, such a dissolution is called *dissolution by the wet way*.

6. Bodies in which the equilibrium of the basic forces cannot be removed are incapable of any chemical treatment.

It will be obvious that such an impossibility is *merely relative*, having regard, that is, to the chemical means available.

II. Outcome of a Chemical Process
1. The result of the chemical process is the product of an interaction of the basic forces, which, having been artificially set into activity, return to equilibrium.
2. The chemical product, regarded in its quality, is the median dynamical relationship of the basic forces that were set into activity in the process.

For the basic forces reciprocally confine one another until an *identity of degree* is present. The product of an elastically fluid and a solid body, for example, may be expressed by the median relationship between the mass of the solid and the elasticity of the fluid, and *vice versa*.

3. The chemical product is totally different, in its qualitative properties, from the constituent parts out of which it was composed.

It can be regarded as the median quality between the two extremes from which it has arisen.

4. In the chemical product, identity of degree or quality must occur.

It is obvious that, since a *perfect* chemical process is an *Idea*, this law permits of qualifications in experience.

    5. The term "chemical" applies only to that action of a body upon another, whereby *qualities arise* or are *annihilated*, but not when merely the *state* of the one body is altered.

Chemical annihilation of one quality by the other is called *bonding*. Thus hydrogen and oxygen are bound together in water – acid and alkali in the neutral salt, etc. Concept of *neutralization*.

    6. All chemical processes can be reduced to chemical combination.

For even chemical separation occurs only by means of the selective attraction of a third body for the constituent of the chemical product.

    7. Between *solid* bodies, no chemical combination is possible, unless they have previously been dissolved.

This occurs either through *liquids* (acids), and the bodies are said to be *dissolved* (in the narrower sense of the word), or by the *power of fire*, and then we are said to *liquefy* the bodies. So here, in the first case at least, the chemical process is doubled. For as to the liquefaction of bodies, it is a mere *one-sided* change in the relationship of their basic forces. The question also arises, whether the common dissolution of two bodies, or their melting together, can be called a *chemical* process. Strictly speaking, a process can only be called *chemical* if its product is different in quality from its constituent parts. But this does not happen if totally homogeneous bodies are combined. So the only case to belong here is the melting together of heterogeneous bodies, which is very often possible only through the mediation of a third.

    8. Between *fluid* and *solid* bodies, no perfectly chemical process occurs, unless both are brought to a common degree of elasticity, such that the solid body gains in elasticity what the fluid loses of it.

Thus here we have the concept of dissolution in the narrower sense. According to the notions of the atomists, dissolution is always merely partial; i.e., it extends only to the smallest particles of solid bodies, which are dispersed in the solvent at infinitely small distances from one another. But this assumption can be made intelligible only by help of the hypothesis that all bodies are aggregates of particles which it is physically impossible to divide any further. For otherwise there is no seeing why the power of the solvent (assuming that its quantitative relation to the body to be dissolved is perfectly observed) should have any limit, or the dissolution stop at any point.

This theory also betrays itself already as unnatural by the fact that, in order to explain dissolution, it has to take refuge in incomprehensibilities, e.g., that a solvent penetrates into the inmost pores of even the densest bodies (which still leaves unexplained how this penetration should have so great a power as is needed to tear solid bodies apart), or even that the little particles of menstruum act as tiny arrows, to drive the solid parts of the body away from each other, etc.

Nor, indeed, is it any easier to see how some recent authors, following Kant's example,[2] can suppose a *permeation* (of the solid body by the fluid one), without simultaneously assuming that the chemical process is a *change in the dynamic forces* themselves. For a body in which the dynamic forces are in *equilibrium* can only act *en masse* by means of mechanically repellent (impactive) forces. So if dissolution is not an *interaction of forces,* the solvent would have to penetrate the solid body mechanically; i.e., it would have to reduce its repulsive force to zero, which is absurd.

So in order to explain the possibility of a dissolution, we are compelled to assume that in the chemical process (in the narrower sense of the word), the dynamic forces themselves get out of equilibrium, and thereby take on a quite different mode of action from that which pertains to them in the resting or equilibrial state.[3]

And since we can conceive of the origin of matter itself only through a collision of dynamic forces, we have to picture every such process to ourselves as the *becoming* of a matter, and chemistry is for this reason an *elementary science,* because by means of it, that which in dynamics is only an object of the *understanding* becomes an object of *intuition.* For chemistry is nothing else but sensory dynamics (dynamics made intuitable), and so retroactively confirms, in turn, the very principles on which it depends.

This *erroneous* way of picturing a permeation of the solid body by the fluid one also presupposes that false conception of a solvent which many students of Nature have already justly censured,[4] as though in the process of dissolution the solvent alone were active, and the solid body entirely passive.

The idea of a perfect dissolution already implies, moreover, that it

---

[2] Cf. the oft cited work, p. 96 [Ellington, pp. 87–8].

[3] Kant (in the work cited) has nowhere expressly declared himself concerning his conception of chemistry, but this utterance (as to the necessity of assuming a chemical permeation) obviously presupposes the notion that chemical operations are possible only through *dynamic forces, insofar as they are thought of in motion.* For a mutual permeation of two matters is absolutely unthinkable, unless it be that by interaction (reciprocal limitation) of the basic forces, one matter is engendered from both.

[4] E.g., Professor Gren, in his *Systematische Handbuch der gesammten Chemie,* Part I, Halle, 1794, p. 55.

cannot be demonstrated by any observation. For that in a solution, even under the greatest possible magnification, no single particle of the solid body can any longer be discerned is still very far from proving that the dissolution (in the sense given) is *perfect;* on the contrary, that the dissolution should be thought of as infinite is proved by the fact that it is *possible as such,* since it is not explicable mechanically, and so must be accounted for dynamically, by a *movement* of dynamic forces.

But then we are no longer talking about *parts* of matter, for here the matter is not given through its parts (as in mechanical compounding), but on the contrary, the parts are given through the matter, and for that reason the dissolution is called *infinite.* For if I proceed from parts of matter to the whole, the *synthesis* is *finite.* But if I proceed, on the contrary, from the whole to parts, the *analysis* is *infinite.* Thus in every dissolution I have given to me a chemical *whole* which is totally *homogeneous,* and precisely for that reason, like every other, is infinitely divisible, and nowhere obliges me to halt in the division, because I continue, *ad infinitum,* to encounter particles that are homogeneous, and thus always still equally divisible.

So the basic forces of matters that are dissolved by one another are now common forces. Because mass and elasticity are common to them, they occupy, as Kant says, one and the same space, and not a part can be found which would not have been compounded out of the solvent and the body to be dissolved.

Precisely because such a dissolution is not immediately demonstrable by any observation, it can never be claimed that the individual dissolution is totally adequate to the *Idea* of a perfect dissolution: This refers, however, not to the *concept* of dissolution, but to the means we have employed, or are able to employ at all.

If we consider what great power fluids exert over metals, how a few drops of acid transform metals instantly into powder or powdery calx, we find ourselves utterly deserted by the ordinary concepts of matter, and are compelled to admit that matter is quite a different thing for the understanding from what it is for the senses. The same difficulty, in making shift with the ordinary concepts of matter, is also apparent elsewhere. Kant reminds us, in this connection, that one can suppose a seemingly free passage of certain matters (e.g., of magnetic matter) through others in such a fashion (as *permeation*), without preparing open channels and interstices for it in all matters, even the densest. In fact, if we consider the hypotheses of a Descartes, a Euler or others, on the subject of magnetic matter, we perceive very clearly what paltry notions we must be led to by the maxim of subjecting everything in Nature to mechanical laws.

Far more fruitful and conducive to the necessary enlargement of our thoughts is the law of *equilibrium* in Nature, whereby the greatest things are governed, as well as the smallest, and which first, in general, makes a Nature possible. Only where higher forces are at rest is there any effect from impact, pressure and whatever else may be reckoned as mechanical causes. Where those forces are activated, we there find internal motion in matter, change and the first stages of formation; for therein lie the genesis and change, not of forms alone (which can also be impressed upon matter from without), but of qualities and properties that no merely external force is able to destroy. What is it, after all, which gives the ore that we call magnet its constant alignment to the terrestrial pole, if it is not the endeavour towards equilibrium? That a prevailing difference in our hemispheres should act upon so inconsiderable a metal strikes us as wonderful, but as unintelligible only if restricted notions of Nature cause us to forget that she herself is nothing else but this eternal equilibrium, which itself finds its continuance in the interplay of conflicting forces.

But I return to the point from which I set out. There are different kinds of dissolution. The distinction between dissolution in the dry way and the wet is already presupposed here. The distinction of *mechanical* dissolutions (improperly so-called) from *chemical* ones is of more importance. It is not denied that even purely mechanical dissolutions are possible, of such matters as actually contain empty spaces and are but weakly cohesive, so that if a fluid penetrates into them they fall to pieces. Such dissolutions are justly called *superficial (superficiales)*, for they can certainly contain a matter separated into similar particles, and distributed everywhere in a fluid of sufficient quantity; but the effect which such dissolutions exert on these particles extends merely to their surfaces, and the division, too, can very often be effected by purely mechanical means.

A dissolution, properly so-called, occurs only where there is a resultant change in the *degree* of elasticity, expansibility or capacity of the solvent and the body to be dissolved, of such a kind that both are brought back to a *common* degree. Hence the majority of chemical dissolutions are associated with *effervescence,* and with the production of *heat* and *kinds of gas.*

Meànwhile, a further distinction can also be made among chemical dissolutions. They are chemical, in some cases, merely in relation to the *means* that have been employed in them, without a *chemical* combination, in the strict sense of the word, or a separation of *heterogeneous* constituents, having occurred in the process. Examples thereof are homogeneous metals that are smelted together through the power of fire (a chemical means). Here, too, must be included the dissolution of salts, e.g., of saltpetre in water, which is soluble in cold water only with great difficulty, but in *warmer* water is very easily dissolved. But by this chemically active means, no chemical combination of water and salt is effected; the latter, dissolved by heat, seems merely to have been uniformly dispersed in the water. It is for this reason that a number of salts, without water having been withdrawn from them, already crystallize, merely by an often very minute withdrawal of heat-stuff.

For a perfect chemical permeation, it is also requisite that no part of the solution contain less dissolved matter than it could, i.e., that both bodies be *saturated* by one another.[5] But if we admit the *possibility* of a mechanical dissolution, it is obvious that this, too, has its limits, and in that case this feature is not one that would be *peculiar* to chemical dissolution.

Now the major principle for all dissolutions (in the strict sense of the word) is as follows:

  9. Every dissolution of a solid and a fluid body by one another yields the median degree-relationship between the elasticity of the one and the mass of the other.
  10. Combination between similar *fluid* bodies is called *mixture*.[6]
  11. The density of the fluids in the mixture is equal to the median relationship between the densities of both before the mixture.
  12. As a rule, the space occupied by a chemical mixture will observe the median relationship of the spaces which the two fluids occupied before the dissolution.

Not every mixture (even of heterogeneous fluids) is *chemical*. Only that mixture can be called chemical in which both ingredients of the mixture lose properties, or take on new ones.

The surest indicator of this is a lessening or increase of capacity, so that heat is thereby absorbed or liberated. Thus the mixture of spirits of wine with water, and still more that of inflammable fluids with acids, of oil, for example, with nitric acid, etc., are chemical in nature.

---

[5] One has to express it thus, as soon as it is assumed that the menstruum is not solely active in the dissolution.

[6] [In the 1st Edn. no. 11, since it was preceded by the following]: 10. The space which the bodies occupy in solution will normally be the mean between the two spaces they occupied before solution.

This is necessary as soon as the solution is *perfect*. Where the law does not apply, this is not the case. But perfect chemical solution requires that a perfect interpenetration of both bodies (in the above-defined sense) should occur, so that no part of the solution could contain more dissolved matter than it actually contains (i.e., that both bodies are saturated by each other).

So normally the space occupied by the solution is *larger* than the space occupied by either body *alone*, but *smaller* than the *sum* of the spaces occupied by *both*, prior to solution.

Types of air, on the other hand, which in themselves are totally heterogeneous, such as vital air and nitrogen, can be mixed with one another, without either one or the other changing its properties. Only the specific weight of the mixture is equal to the sum of the specific weights of both before the mixture.

Many fluid bodies do not mix with each other at all, without the mediation of a third; thus water and oil mix only by the mediation of salts or soap (the latter acts in virtue of its origin from oils and potash). The mediating body (as also between solid bodies) is called the *means of adaptation.*

Fluid bodies differ from one another only by the degree of their fluidity, and not also by the structure of their parts, difference of surfaces, or of the empty spaces they contain, etc.; for this reason they are the easiest to use for experiments on communication of *heat.*

The degree of heat which a fluid can take up without altering its state (in the narrower sense of the word) determines its *heat-capacity.* The difference of degree which various bodies of equal mass are able to take up is equal to the difference of their specific capacity.

The rule for mixtures of similar but differently heated fluids is the well-known rule of Richmann, that the heat of the mixture is the arithmetic mean between the heats of the two fluids.

But the general law for mixtures of dissimilar fluids is this: In order to bring two dissimilar fluids to an equal degree of heat, *either the quantitative relationship of the fluids,* or the relationship of the *quantity* of heat that is transmitted to both, must be equal to the difference of their capacities. The latter, however, must be found by experiment. Moreover, we here find an application for what was observed earlier, namely, that no mixture is called *chemical* in which qualities are neither lost nor engendered. *Heat,* however, is not a permanent quality, but merely a contingent property of bodies.

13. Combination between liquid and aeriform fluids is commonly called *dissolution.*

As is well known, this proposition has lately been very shrewdly contested. Granted even that meteorology could expect no advantage from it (which has yet to be proved), still, there is no denying the fact that at least *seeming* dissolutions of liquids by the air do take place.

But I admit that, notwithstanding the many discussions of this subject, I have hitherto been unable to find anywhere a determinate conception of this type of dissolution.

Taking the word in its ordinary sense, the air cannot dissolve water without the latter itself receiving a relatively higher degree of elasticity. But where does it obtain this? It does not disperse of *its own accord,*

as do strong-smelling and, in general, all spirituous substances, owing
to the original centrifugal force of its parts. Is heat perhaps responsi-
ble? Then it is no longer the air, but heat, which has dissolved the
water. But then the question arises: What has the water become?
Vapour or air? I see nothing absurd in holding to the former. For at
least a number of observations tell in its favour. Thus carbonic acid
gas, whose production is always undoubtedly coupled with that of
aqueous parts as well, contains water in solution (the Dutch scientists
have precipitated it by means of the electric spark). The great volume
to which water expands, in the shape of vapour or steam, makes it
intelligible that it should disperse freely and permeate the denser air.
Now it may further be assumed that the greater elasticity of vapours
(which must be presupposed if they are to rise in the air) is gradually
nullified by the lesser elasticity of the air, and that if air and water
occupy the space of the atmosphere in proportionate quantities, both
may gradually revert to the same degree of elasticity. A disproportionate increase in the elasticity of the air could then occasion the reverse
process, and the water be precipitated again in liquid form. For that
water is precipitated out of the air through a rapid chilling thereof is
by everyday experience not very probable; for although we may derive the warmth that precedes rainfall from a liberation of heat out of
the air, that still does nothing at all to explain this liberation itself. The
most natural thing is still to suppose a rapid increase in the elasticity of
the *air*, which, like many processes of this kind, may be long in prepa-
ration, but now follows suddenly and at once, whereby the vapours,
now no longer equal in elasticity to the air, and so no longer supported by it either, are then precipitated in the shape of clouds, and
eventually fall in liquid form.

    14. The reverse process to the foregoing, where aeriform fluids
    combine with liquid ones, is called *absorption*.

Here the *chemical* combination becomes very dubious. The atmospheric air cannot be adduced as an example of this proposition in so
straightforward a fashion as it normally is. For air is only absorbed by
water when a strong movement of both has preceded. (Priestley noticed very early on that when air and water are shaken together in a
sealed vessel, the former becomes vitiated. He concluded from this
already that water must contain phlogiston.) A more reliable example
is the absorption of carbonic acid gas by water.

    15. The combination of light with various fluids is a truly chemical
    combination.

For everything occurs in this case which occurs in every chemical
combination. The light, a peculiar matter, *loses as much* elasticity as the

other body *gains*. In that it evolves vital air from plants, from oxidized bodies, etc., it ceases to *shine*, and loses a quality that it previously displayed, just as, conversely, a decomposition of the water must also go on in plants, in order for it to combine with light. So here everything is occurring which occurs in every chemical process.

It will not do, therefore, to consider light merely as a modification of matter *as such*, since it actually shows itself plainly enough as a specific modification, and to that extent as a *specific* matter.

There cannot, on the other hand, be a chemical combination of *heat* with any other matter, for heat is a mere modification of matter *as such*. Thus one matter can certainly *communicate* heat to the other, i.e., effect this modification in another, according to the familiar law: One body communicates heat to another, up to the point where the heat in both is in equilibrium. But by this there arises a merely contingent change of *state*, not a *product* marked out by new qualities. Thus water, on heating, becomes *steam;* that is, it changes its state, but not its qualities. But if I allow water to pass over red-hot iron, it changes not only its state but also its qualities. The type of gas that is produced is the result of a chemical attraction, and what is *chemical* in this process occurs merely between the water and the metal, not between the water and the heat.

Of chemical combinations between *originally* elastic matters (as I call light, etc.), we know nothing reliable, for the combination which many have supposed, in combustion, of the combustible matter in the bodies and the heat-stuff of vital air, is still doubtful. The sole examples of this kind are the electrical phenomena which are produced by the separation of two electrical matters, and which cease as soon as they mutually annihilate their respective elasticities. But this example does not belong here, since these matters, so far as we can see, are not *originally heterogeneous*, but are set at variance only by artificial means.

16. The reverse process to chemical combination (the chemical proof-test, as it were) is chemical *separation*.
17. A perfect chemical combination would have to make all separation impossible (it is thus a mere Idea, to which reality approximates more or less).

For if a chemical combination of two bodies were perfect, an *identity of degree and quality* would have to occur between the two. If this were so, then in relation to a third body the chemical product would have to have a wholly *equal* relationship; i.e., it could never be chemically separated.

That we are here erecting *Ideas* of chemical combination, dissolution, etc., cannot alienate anyone who recalls that in empirical sciences as such, only approximations to universal principles are possible.

The means required for separating combined basic substances are the same as those whereby their combination is effected (see above).

The force with which the combined substances cohere has to be weakened, the equilibrium of the two removed. The latter cannot happen without a third factor, whereby it is disturbed. This third factor is either a third body, which displays attraction for one of the combined basic substances, or the universally dissolving medium, fire.

18. Bodies with an absolute identity of degree and quality are called indecomposable bodies.

Normally simple, such as light, etc. Of no body can it be reliably claimed that it is indecomposable, although of many, e.g., of light, it is highly probable. Depending on the greater or lesser degree of probability of being able to decompose bodies, they were formerly called undecomposed or simple – better, undecomposed or indecomposable bodies. The word "element" – also to be used only of the latter – is contrary to the original meaning of the term. Taking it in its oldest sense, there is no *element,* for according to our philosophy there is no original matter.

19. Solid bodies are separated from solids through fire and selective attraction.

What selective attraction may mean, we presuppose as familiar. Likewise what chemical attraction may be *as such,* and on what it depends (for the above-established laws are also valid here). Selective attraction occurs only if, between two bodies especially (rather than one or more others), the equilibrium of forces is removed. The endeavour to restore this equilibrium is called attraction, and in this case, selective attraction.

What simple and double selective attraction may be is likewise well known, and the above-established laws apply to the latter twice over.

An example of simple selective attraction also occurs, so far as we see at present, in the *combustion* of bodies.

20. The result of the separation of solid and fluid bodies is *crystallization; coagulation,* the *increase* or *decrease* of the latter.

Which of these two occurs depends on the relationship of the specific weight of the dissolved body to that of the menstruum.

If the dissolution were perfect, no decrease could result. It occurs only when the dissolution is not *perfectly saturated* (for what is ordinarily called saturation is such only more or less). Either it is the endeavour of the *menstruum* to dissolve the superadded body, or it is the attraction that the *dissolved* body displays towards the superadded one, which occasions the separation. But neither the one nor the other would take place, if the reciprocal permeation (the saturation) were perfect.

21. Even fluid bodies can be divided by fire or elective affinity, if they are capable of a different relationship to heat, or to some third body.

Fluid bodies provide examples of perfect mixing, since in general they are by nature more capable of an identity of degree than other bodies.

Whether, for example, the separation of water out of the air (in rain) can be called a precipitation comes down to concepts, about which I have already explained my views above.

Originally elastic fluids, such as light, we can so far separate from their combination only through simple selective attraction.

III. Construction of Chemical Motions

It is self-evident that the universal law of gravitation also applies to chemical motions.

22. No chemical motion results without solicitation from outside, and

23. In every chemical motion, action and reaction are equal to each other.

The discussion of these laws, insofar as they belong to mechanics, is here presupposed.[7]

But so far as their application to chemistry is concerned, the laws established above are already nothing else but applications of this universal law to chemical interaction.

24. Chemical motion, as such, cannot be constructed in a purely phoronomic fashion, for *as such* it is not an extensive, but simply an intensive, magnitude.

This is the major principle that has to be demonstrated, and from which all other propositions concerning the construction of chemical motion can be readily derived.

Every chemical motion is merely a change of degree-relationships. It consists in mere *changes of degree,* where one body loses *by degrees* what the other gains, and *vice versa.*

Chemical motion, as such, can therefore be constructed only as intensive magnitude, according to laws of continuity.

---

[7] It is important to know what meaning they have been given by Kant. Cf. in the work cited the 3rd section, "Mechanics."

But as intensive magnitude it can be represented only as a continuous approximation of degree, from both sides, towards the common product. So the approximations of both bodies to the common product can indeed be constructed, insofar as they are in general continuous, but not insofar as they progress *by degrees* at every individual moment, for *degrees,* as such, are incapable of any *a priori* representation.

It is a question, however, whether a law of this continuous approximation can be found. An example of this is the law of acceleration: *The acceleration of chemical motion increases, ad infinitum, as the sum of the surfaces.* This law is followed, at least, by practical chemistry, in the dissolutions of solid bodies, in that it seeks to enlarge as much as possible the surface of the body to be dissolved. It is self-evident that, since we are compelled to represent the sum of the surfaces of a body-to-be-dissolved as increasing *ad infinitum,* the acceleration, too, increases indefinitely, which (since the dissolution still takes place within a finite time) can be represented no otherwise than according to the law of continuity (since no possible instant is the smallest possible).

But for that very reason, this law, since it applies to nothing less than an infinite division of matter, is of absolutely no *constitutive* use; it serves simply and solely for purposes of a possible representation, which can be opposed to the pretensions of atomism, whereby the dissolution of solid bodies into fluid ones is seen as an argument for having matter to consist of ultimate parts. It is meant, therefore, to serve no other purpose than that of preserving the freedom of inquiry. For if matter does consist of ultimate parts, these are limits which research into Nature does not recognize. So if we wanted to use this principle *constitutively,* we should thereby ourselves be lapsing into the presuppositions of atomism. It is thus a purely theoretical maxim, to recognize nothing in the dissolution of a body which would count as an ultimate part, without, however, claiming that, since the dissolution is perfect, a division *ad infinitum* has *actually taken place.* On the contrary, rather, if the dissolution is perfect the whole cannot be given to us by its parts (for otherwise the dissolution would be *finite*); it is actually the other way round, and the parts will have to be given to us by the *whole.*

As for the *quantity of chemical motion as such,* it cannot, like the quantity of mechanical motion, be measured by the compound relationship of the amount of matter and its velocity; for *chemical* motion, *as such,* must be related to a specific *quality,* as *product* of this motion. It is therefore a magnitude that does indeed grow continuously, but is still only an intensive magnitude.

In mechanical motion, the body is regarded insofar as it moves *en masse.* In that it moves in relation to other bodies, *it is at rest relative to itself* (the motion, in relation to its parts, is *absolute* motion). Thus it is now matter within specific limits, and (given equal velocity) can be compared in quantity of motion with every other. With chemical motion, *as such,* the situation is quite different. For there the matter does not exist within specific limits, the body is in process of *becoming,* and only the *result* of the chemical motion itself is a specific *occupied space.*

Moreover, every motion can be conceived only relatively, and to that extent is also (on phoronomic principles) constructible. If we ask whether chemical motion, *as such,* can be constructed, this is equivalent to asking whether chemical motions reciprocally related to *one another* (and not, say, to a body that is not involved in the chemical process) can be constructed. If the question is so expressed, we see at once that it must be answered in the negative – for chemical motions, as such, determine no material space to which I could relate them. This material space is itself only a result of the chemical motion; i.e., it is not *phoronomically described,* but dynamically *produced* (by interaction of *forces*).

But now *concepts* relating to *degrees* in general, such as quality, force, etc., cannot be presented *a priori* in any intuition whatever.

Only insofar as the forces set into interaction have a *degree,* are they objects of a *synthesis* – albeit only in relation to *inner sense.* But everything that corresponds to *sensation* is apprehended only as a *unity;* the whole does not arise through *composition* of the parts, but on the contrary, *parts,* or better, *multiplicity,* can be conceived in it only by approximation to zero. But every construction presupposes a production of quantity through parts, and hence *no construction whatever of chemical motion is possible;* it can in general be apprehended only by the law of *continuity,* as a production of *intensive* (not extensive) quantity.[8]

[8] [There followed at this point, in the 1st Edn., as "Conclusion and Transition to a Further Part"]: We began with the origin of matter from the nature of our intuition. We have shown, from *a priori* principles, that matter is a product of opposing forces, and that only through their interaction do these forces occupy space. From these fundamental axioms, *dynamics* evolved. On *a posteriori* principles we proved the same proposition by findings that are explicable only by an interaction of basic forces. These findings are the concern of *chemistry,* or *applied* dynamics. Only now can we consider matter as a *whole,* which, insofar as its basic forces are at rest, obeys laws of quantitative attraction (heaviness) or *mechanical* influences. These laws are the subject-matter of *statics* and *mechanics,* two sciences to which we now proceed.

Construction of the
Chemical Process
(Supplement to Chapter 9)

The chemical process must everywhere be viewed only in connection with the other forms of the dynamical process. For if the magnetic defines for us the line, or first dimension, and the electric appends the second dimension, the chemical completes the triangle, in that it unifies the difference posited in the electric process by means of a third, which is at the same time intrinsically one.

For these reasons, the original schema of the chemical process, conceived in its purity, is a whole compounded, in the simplest construction, from two different rigid bodies and a third fluid one. For since the two former posit in themselves reciprocal and relative changes of cohesion, such that the one is enhanced in the same way that the other is diminished, and both together behave as a totality, and like the magnet, of which each pole can posit only its opposite outside itself, so, within this reciprocity the third component, which in itself is indifferent, will be simultaneously potentiated or polarized on two sides, yet because as the fluid body it is only the indifference-point of relative cohesion, in such a way that, at the moment of incipient difference, the identity of both poles is also abolished, and both are presented by different matters, which then appears to ordinary observation as a decomposition of the fluid.

Now since everything that can be called decomposition and chemical process reduces everywhere to an interaction of fluid and solid, where each changes its state, it is obvious that the relationship we have supposed is the simplest under which chemical process can take place at all.

It is sufficiently well known, and now taken for granted, that the case where the third term is an animal organ is merely a special instance of this general case, in that here actually two processes are taking place at once – the wholly general and as it were inorganic process, in which the animal term enters only in the general capacity of a fluid, and the special process which is manifested herein as contraction, and which though not indeed different from the first in its conditions, is determined in its mode of operation by the special organic nature that it has.

So just as every form of the dynamic process is solely determined by the fact that general, particular and that wherein both are one are posited as different and external to one another, this can also take place either under the form of magnetism, where the three factors lie as three points in one and the same line; or under the form of electricity, where the two bodies denote the opposing factors, and their point of contact the indifference; or finally under that of the chemical process, where each of them is expressed by a special product.

So since this triplicity of general, particular and the indifference of both is, when expressed as identity, magnetism, when expressed as difference, electricity, and when expressed as totality, chemical process, these three forms are therefore but one form, and the chemical process itself is a mere shifting of the three points of magnetism into the triangle of the chemical process.

It cannot seem strange, therefore, to encounter, in the more perfect form of the chemical process, the totality of all forms of the dynamic, so that it is possible to apprehend the so-called galvanism in the voltaic pile, wholly as magnetism, wholly as electricity, and wholly as chemical process. This merely depends on which moment of the whole we wish to fixate. The process in this whole is to be apprehended according to the determinations we have given of the magnetic line (*Zeitschrift für spekulative Physik*, vol. II, no. 2, §46, supplement). Through the whole, the *same* is posited, namely the indifference which, as such, is polarized on two sides. What is true of the whole is again true of each part, so that each term is for itself positive, negative and indifferent. The whole is divisible *ad infinitum*, and everything within it merely relatively determinable, so that the same term which in one connection is indifferent, can be thought of in the others as positive or negative, or that which in a certain context is negative, can be thought of in the others as positive, and *vice versa*.

But precisely as the schema of magnetism is repeated in the voltaic whole, so the process thereof can likewise be viewed as electricity, as was done by Volta, and in such a way that this electricity is independent of the chemical process, and is not mediated by that process, in that it is actually the mediatrix thereof, and the form through which the latter necessarily passes.

If we view the process at a later moment, and want at the same time to state it in its totality, we must designate it as chemical process, in that in our view the electrical process is in no way excluded thereby, and is in fact expressly posited. I observe here that my contention, that so-called galvanism is the chemical process itself, has been totally misunderstood by some, in that they took it to mean that I regarded the electricity therein as an electricity engendered by the chemical process as such, which runs altogether counter to the tenor of my construction (which puts electricity ahead of the chemical process), just as it is also strikingly contradicted by experience. For oxidation is so little of a conditioning factor to electricity that the phenomena of the latter stand, rather, in a kind of inverted relationship towards it, as is necessary if the electrical process precedes the chemical, and is dissipated therein.

But if we wanted to ask, as some have done, why water is required for the electrical phenomena in the voltaic whole, when in my view the electricity is sufficiently transmitted, in and for itself, by the contact of rigid and different bodies, and would also have to be enhanced by repeated addition of this relationship to itself, my reply is that two rigid and different bodies are by contact immediately put, for themselves, into an equilibrium that could only be destroyed once more by removal of the contact; that the same thing would happen between a series of different members, consisting merely of rigid bodies; and that in order to keep the process alive and in continuing activity, a constantly mutable intermediary, such as water, is needed, and even the free access of oxygen, in order to maintain this process in a state of persistent mutability.

After these explanations, we turn back to consideration of the course of events in the chemical process as such.

What we have said of the possibility of reducing the chemical triangle to the magnetic line already sufficiently persuades us that what is transformed in the chemical process is not the substance of the matter in itself, but the mere potencies of form or cohesion, so that in the empiricists' sense, there is no more a true chemical composition than there is a true disintegration. All composition consists in a reciprocal abolition of opposite potencies by one another, so that the most perfect composition is a state of total depotentiation. All decomposition, on the other hand, as presentation of one and the same substance under different forms, is potentiation in various directions.

All matter is therefore in itself simple, for every possible division within it is always posited only by the advent of another body. Acid, for example, as a body that is determined by the potency of the negative factor of relative cohesion, is to that extent simple, and only the adventitious body, the metal, posits in it the division into solid and fluid, so that the acid, in that it seeks to restore itself from its expansion, diminishes the adventitious body in its cohesion, and determines it to pass from absolute into relative cohesion. With the lesser degree of oxidation there is posited, in general, a disintegration of the body;

with the next, a total dissolution of it, just as, at the highest degree, which is only attained, however, by combustion, the highest degree of *relative* cohesion is posited.

The combustion process has already been dealt with above (Supplement to Chapter 1 of Book I).

Concluding Note and
Transition to the
Following Part[1]

The final goal of all consideration and science of Nature can only be knowledge of the absolute unity which embraces the whole, and which allows itself to be known in Nature only from its one side. Nature, as it were, is its instrument, whereby, in an eternal manner, it brings to execution and reality what is prefigured in the absolute understanding. In Nature, therefore, the whole absolute is knowable, although appearing Nature produces only successively, and in (for us) endless development, what in true Nature exists all at once and in an eternal fashion.

The root and essence of Nature is that which combines the infinite possibility of all things with the reality of the particular, and hence is

[1] [The planned third book was to cover the theory of organic Nature, and to culminate in a scientific physiology, but it never appeared. Cf. editorial notes at the end of 1st Edn. Preface, and at end of Chapter 9 above; also the postscript to the 1st Edn. Preface to *On the World-Soul* (1810). The latter runs as follows]:
This work is not to be regarded as a continuation of my *Ideas for a Philosophy of Nature*. I shall never continue it, until I find myself able to conclude the whole with a *scientific physiology*, which alone can give it completeness. At first I thought it a service simply to *venture* something in this science, so that at least the acumen of others might be exercised in the discovery and refutation of error. Yet I would wish that readers and critics of the present essay were acquainted with the ideas that are put forward in that work. The authority for assuming all positive principles of Nature to be originally homogeneous can only be derived philosophically. Without this assumption (I presume it is known what an *assumption for purposes of a possible construction* may be), it is impossible to construct the primary concepts of physics, e.g., of the theory of heat. Idealism, which philosophy is gradually introducing into all the sciences (in mathematics, primarily since Leibniz and Newton, it has long since become *dominant*), still seems intelligible to few. The concept, for example, of *action at a distance*, which to many is still a stumbling-block, rests entirely on the idealist conception of space; for by this, two bodies at the greatest distance from each other can be regarded as touching, and conversely, bodies which (on the common notion) are actually touching can be seen as acting on each other from a distance. It is very true that a body only *acts where it is,* but it is equally true that it only *is where it acts,* and with this principle the last bastion of the atomistic philosophy is surmounted. I must abstain from adducing still further examples here.

the eternal urge and primal ground of all creation. So if, of this most perfect of all organic beings, which is at once the possibility and actuality of all things, we have hitherto contemplated only the separate sides into which it resolves itself for appearance, namely light and matter, there now stands open to us, in the disclosures of organic Nature, that path into the true interior whereby we penetrate at last to the most perfect knowledge of the divine Nature, in *reason*, as the indifference wherein all things lie in equal weight and measure as one, and this veil in which the act of eternal producing is clothed, itself appears dissolved in the essence of absolute ideality.

It is the highest pleasure of the soul to have penetrated, through science, to contemplation of this most perfect, all-satisfying and all-comprehending harmony, the knowledge of which is as far superior to any other as the whole is more excellent than the part, the essence better than the individual, and the ground of knowledge more splendid than knowledge itself.

Appendix: Checklist of
Scientific Authors

ACHARD, Franz Karl (1753–1821). German-born, of French parents, he taught physics at the Berlin Academy, and wrote on thermometry, electricity and galvanism. In later life he was best known for his development of a successful process for the manufacture of beet-sugar.

AEPINUS, Franz Ulrich Theodosius (1724–1802). After teaching mathematics at Rostock, he became (1755) director of the Berlin Observatory, whence he moved, two years later, to St. Petersburg, and remained there for forty years as observatory director and professor of physics. A study of the thermo-electric properties of tourmaline suggested to him the analogy between electricity and magnetism. Following Franklin, he adopted a one-fluid theory of both, set forth in his *Tentamen theoriae electricitatis et magnetismi* (1759). This work, though scarce, was long esteemed as the first mathematically coherent account of electrical phenomena, based on the conception of action at a distance.

ARGAND, François-Pierre Ami [Aimé] (1755–1803). A Geneva physician and chemist, he was influenced by Lavoisier, and collaborated with the Montgolfier brothers in aeronautics and the later invention of a hydraulic ram. He is chiefly remembered, however, as designer (1784) of the Argand burner, or lamp, the first scientifically constructed device of its kind, widely used in Europe and America during the late eighteenth and early nineteenth century.

BECCARIA, Giambatista (1716–81). Professor of physics at Turin from 1748 onwards, he was an energetic champion of Franklin's electrical theory, and wrote a number of works on atmospheric electricity, phosphorescence, etc. He also invented the electrical thermometer. His *Dell' elettrismo artificiale e naturale* (1753) was translated into English in 1776.

BERGMAN, Torbern Olof (1735–84). Professor of chemistry at Uppsala (1758), he was a follower of Franklin and Aepinus on electrical questions, but worked mainly on the chemical analysis of minerals, mineral waters and metallic ores, publishing tables of chemical affinity (after Macquer) and studies of crystals, chemical nomenclature, etc. Though a believer in the phlogiston theory, Bergman was one of the best-informed chemists of his day, and several of his works were translated, e.g., his *Physical and Chemical Essays* (1784), *Usefulness of Chemistry* (1784) and *Dissertation on Elective Attractions* (1785).

275

BERNOULLI, Daniel (1700–82). A scion of the celebrated Swiss mathematical family, he spent seven years with Euler in St. Petersburg, as a mathematical professor, before returning to Basle, where from 1733 onwards he occupied chairs in a variety of scientific fields. He won, or shared, no fewer than ten Paris Academy prizes, including two for papers on magnetism (1743, 1746), and also wrote prolifically on hydrodynamics, probability, mechanics and physiology, to say nothing of an immense volume of contributions in pure mathematics and mathematical physics.

BLACK, Joseph (1728–99). After a medical education in Belfast, Glasgow and Edinburgh, he taught for ten years at Glasgow, before succeeding his mentor, William Cullen, in the Edinburgh chair of chemistry (1766). The founder of modern quantitative chemistry, he showed, in 1756, that the causticity of lime is due to the absence of "fixed air" (carbon dioxide), but did not pursue this result, and is thus remembered chiefly for his later work on latent and specific heat. For long a believer in phlogiston, he was eventually converted to the views of Lavoisier. A reluctant author, who published little, Black's *Essays and Observations* appeared in 1756, and his *Lectures on the Elements of Chemistry*, compiled by his old pupils, in 1803.

BONNET, Charles (1720–93). A Geneva-born naturalist of French origin, he was the first to observe parthenogenesis in aphids, and the regenerative abilities of worms. His *Traité d'insectologie* (1745) was followed by *Recherches sur l'usage des feuilles dans les plantes* (1754), which advanced the study of plant respiration and photosynthesis. In later life, failing eyesight led him to turn to philosophical theorizing, in which he was an advocate of preformation and palingenesis, and upheld a catastrophist theory of evolution.

BRANDIS, Joachim Dieterich (1762–1846). A health official at Hildesheim, and a spa physician at Driburg, he later became professor of medicine at Kiel (1803), and royal physician in Copenhagen (1810). His *Versuche über die Lebenskraft* was published at Hanover in 1795.

BUFFON, Georges-Louis Leclerc, Comte de (1707–88). French naturalist, of independent means, he was appointed, in 1739, director of the Jardin du Roi, and there compiled his forty-four volume *Histoire naturelle,* an exhaustive repository of information on all aspects of the natural world. A mechanistically minded disciple of Newton and Locke, Buffon held life to be a property of matter, believed in the reality of species, and was in some respects a forerunner of the theory of evolution. Despite its size, the popularity of his work was such as to ensure many editions, and translations or adaptations of it into many languages, including English.

CANTON, John (1718–72). A London schoolmaster and self-taught physicist, he confirmed Franklin's experiments on lightning, investigated electrostatic induction, invented the pithball electroscope, demonstrated the compressibility of water, and was the first to make strong artificial magnets. His paper on the subject procured his election to the Royal Society in 1749.

CAVALLO, Tiberius (1749–1809). Italian-born physicist who settled in England (1771), he carried on the work of Franklin and Canton in atmospheric electricity, and as a designer of electrical instruments. His *Complete Treatise on Electricity* (1777) went through several editions, and he also published *A Treatise on Magnetism* (1787) and *Elements of Natural Philosophy* (1803). He became FRS in 1779.

CAVENDISH, Henry (1731–1810). A wealthy, reclusive, eccentric aristocrat who seldom published his results, he was nevertheless among the ablest physicists and chemists of his day. He identified hydrogen and discovered the composition of water and nitric acid; rediscovered latent and specific heat; did pioneer work on electrical conduction and capacitance, in which he anticipated the findings of Coulomb and others; and, in a famous experiment (1798), first estimated the density of the earth. He was elected to the Royal Society in 1760, and found there almost his only social outlet. His papers on electricity were published by Clerk Maxwell in 1879.

COULOMB, Charles Augustin de (1736–1806). A military engineer turned scientist, he worked initially on friction, and in 1777 invented the torsion balance. In electricity he held to a two-fluid theory, after the manner of Du Fay and Symmer, but was able, in 1785, to prove Priestley's conjecture that the electrical attraction or repulsion between bodies varies in accordance with the inverse square law – a discovery also made, but not published, by Cavendish. His other reseaches included work on cohesion, elasticity and the theory of machines.

CRAWFORD, Adair (1749–95). A doctor at St. Thomas's hospital, and later professor of chemistry at Woolwich, he followed Black in a first attempt to measure the specific heat of gases. In 1779 he published a phlogistical theory of animal heat, arguing that arterial blood has more heat-capacity than venous, and can absorb heat in the lungs – a precursor, in essentials, of Lavoisier's later view.

DELUC, Jean André (1727–1817). A native of Geneva, he emigrated to England in 1773, and became reader to Queen Charlotte and an FRS. A prolix author in several fields, he sought unsuccessfully to reconcile science with Genesis, and was an opponent of both Hutton's geology and Lavoisier's chemistry. His best work was in meteorology and the theory of heat; he also designed improved thermometers, an electrical dry pile, and a hygrometer, and was the first to measure the heights of mountains accurately with a barometer.

DUFAY, Charles-François de Cisternay (1698–1739). A soldier turned physicist and chemist, he became director of the Jardin du Roi, and was an early investigator of magnetism, phosphorescence and double refraction. About 1733 he drew attention to the difference between vitreous (= positive) and resinous (= negative) electricity, which he took to be separate "fluids." He also studied the properties of insulators and conductors, and experimented on electrostatic repulsion.

ESCHENMAYER, Karl August (1768–1852). Originally a doctor, he became (1811) professor of philosophy and medicine at Tübingen, and later held the chair of practical philosophy. He was at first a disciple of both Jacobi and Schelling, but departed from the latter in denying any rational knowledge of the absolute, and expounding a mystical philosophy of belief. His later writings, though they include an interest in nature-philosophy and animal magnetism, are centred upon religion and the supernatural.

EULER, Leonhard (1707–83).   Swiss mathematician, a pupil of the elder Bernoullis, and friend of the younger, he followed the family to St. Petersburg, where he became professor of physics (1730) and mathematics (1733). In 1741 he moved to Berlin for fifteen years, but then returned to St. Petersburg, where he continued, in spite of the onset of blindness, to contribute prolifically to many branches of mathematics and physics, from number theory and calculus to astronomy, hydrodynamics and optics. His *Lettres à une princesse d'Allemagne* (1768–72) gives a more popular account of his scientific interests and views.

FOURCROY, Antoine-François de (1755–1809).   A French physician who took to chemistry, and in 1784 succeeded Macquer as professor at the Jardin du Roi. After conversion to the antiphlogistical party, he collaborated with Lavoisier, whom he later tried to save from the guillotine. Fourcroy worked mainly on the analysis of mineral waters and the separation of metallic ores. His eleven-volume *System of Chemistry* was translated into English.

FRANKLIN, Benjamin (1706–90).   Printer, publisher, diplomat, statesman and the first internationally known American man of science. His electrical experiments (from 1745) led him to the law of charge conservation, an explanation of the Leyden jar, and a basically correct theory of electricity, as a single, positive or negative, weightless "fluid." The famous kite experiment proved the identity of atmospheric and laboratory electricity, and resulted in the invention of the lightning-rod. Franklin held a wave theory of light, and an elastic-fluid theory of heat. He also made commendable studies of the Gulf Stream, atmospheric convection and population trends. His *Experiments and Observations on Electricity* was published, in two parts, 1751–53.

GIRTANNER, Christoph (1760–1800).   Of Swiss origin, he worked at Lausanne and Göttingen, before becoming privy councillor to the Duke of Saxe-Coburg. A Brunonian in medicine, he wrote on both Brown and Erasmus Darwin, was an early convert to the views of Lavoisier, and published in 1792 his *Anfangsgründe der antiphlogistische Chemie*.

GREN, Friedrich Albrecht Karl (1760–98).   The German-born son of Swedish immigrants, he began as a pharmacist, attended Helmstedt and Halle universities, and founded the journal which later evolved into the *Annalen der Physik*. An adherent of the phlogiston theory, he was defeated (1793) in controversy with the followers of Lavoisier, and adopted the compromise theory of Richter. His *Principles of Modern Chemistry* was translated into English in 1800.

HALES, Stephen (1677–1761).   A Fellow of Corpus Christi College, Cambridge, and later perpetual curate of Teddington, he became FRS in 1718. His pioneer studies of sap-pressure and transpiration in plants, and of blood-pressure in animals, are recorded in his *Vegetable Staticks* (1727) and *Haemastaticks* (1733). His invention of the pneumatic trough led him to investigations of the composition of air which paved the way for Black, Cavendish and Priestley.

HAÜY, René-Just (1743–1822).   A priest who became professor of mineralogy at the Sorbonne, he elucidated the geometry of crystal structure, and worked on mineral classification. In electricity and magnetism he was a follower and popularizer of Aepinus. During the French Revolution, he helped to introduce the metric system, and was one of those who tried to prevent the execution of Lavoisier.

HENLEY (or HENLY), William (d. ca. 1779). Said to have been a linen-draper, he was an associate of Cavallo, published papers in the *Philosophical Transactions,* and became FRS in 1773. His achievements included an experiment to confirm Ingen-Housz's theory of the electrophore, an investigation of the relative value of blunt and pointed lightning-rods, and the invention of a (not wholly successful) perpetual-motion machine.

HERSCHEL, Frederick William (1738–1822). A German-born oboist and bandmaster, he emigrated to England in 1757, and there took up astronomy and telescope-making. In 1781 he discovered Uranus, which brought him many honours, and the post of private astronomer to George III. Besides much systematic observation and cataloguing of celestial objects, his later accomplishments included the discovery of double stars, the first sighting of two moons of Saturn, and an early determination of the shape of the Milky Way. He also discovered infra-red radiation. He was elected FRS in 1781, and was knighted in 1816.

HUMBOLDT, Friedrich Wilhelm Heinrich Alexander, Baron von (1769–1859). After education at Berlin, Göttingen and elsewhere, he entered the Prussian mining service. His early writings were on the chemistry of life, but his reputation as a geographer, geologist and traveller was made by an extended tour of South America and Mexico (1799–1804), and the subsequent publication of his journals. His later life was spent largely as a diplomat, in Paris and Berlin, though he visited Central Asia in 1829. His *Cosmos* (1845–62) is a survey of virtually all that was then known of the natural universe.

INGEN-HOUSZ, Jan (1730–99). A Dutch physician, he emigrated in 1764 to England, where he made the acquaintance of Priestley and Franklin. His early advocacy of smallpox-vaccination later gained him an appointment as court physician in Vienna. His *Experiments upon Vegetables* (1779) clarified the chemistry of plant and animal respiration, and the nature of photosynthesis. He was a pioneer of oxygen-therapy, explained the mechanism of Volta's electrophore, and was perhaps the first to observe Brownian motion.

JÄGER, Karl Christoph Friedrich (1773–1828). A Stuttgart medical man who served (1798–1817) as curator of the royal natural history collections. He wrote on chemistry (with A. N. Scherer), on electrometry, on electroscopic forces in the voltaic pile, and on the reactions of vegetables to metals.

KÄSTNER, Abraham Gotthelf (1719–1800). Mathematical teacher in Leipzig, and later Göttingen, where he became professor in 1756. His *Mathematische Anfangsgründe* appeared in four parts, from 1757 to 1800, and he also published a large history of mathematics. His work on the parallel postulate influenced Lambert, Gauss and other pioneers of non-Euclidean geometry. He also wrote on hydrostatics, crystallography and astronomy.

KNIGHT, Gowin (1713–72).   A London doctor who became FRS and held a position as librarian at the British Museum. He wrote on attraction and repulsion, magnetism, and the effects of lightning on the compass.

KRATZENSTEIN, Christian Gottlieb (1723–95).   A teacher at Halle, he spent five years (1748–53) at the St. Petersburg Academy, and was later professor of medicine and physics at Copenhagen. He wrote on physical forces, celestial mechanics, meterorology and electricity.

LAMBERT, Johann Heinrich (1728–77).   Of Alsatian origin, he was largely self-taught, and led a wandering life as tutor and savant, before settling in Berlin as a member of the academy there. He published extensively on cosmology, physical measurement, logic, mathematics and philosophical method; was the first to measure light-intensity, and to prove the irrationality of π and e; and is remembered also as a pioneer of non-Euclidean geometry, and a much-esteemed correspondent of Immanuel Kant.

LA METHERIE, Jean-Claude de (1743–1817).   A doctor turned natural philosopher, he became editor (1785) of the *Journal de physique* and professor of mineralogy at the Collège de France. A believer in phlogiston, and a four-element chemistry, he was a vitalist in physics, a mechanist in biology, an opponent of Lavoisier, and altogether a rather unenlightened member of the Enlightenment.

LAVOISIER, Antoine-Laurent (1743–94).   The father of modern chemistry and chief demolisher of the phlogiston theory of combustion, he was the first to name oxygen and nitrogen as constituents of the air, and a major reformer in the use both of accurate quantitative methods and a precise chemical nomenclature. A member of the French Academy from 1768, his independent wealth, numerous public services, and connections with tax-farming led to his arrest and execution under the revolutionary Terror, an act of stupidity and injustice which many of his scientific colleagues did their best to prevent.

LE SAGE, Georges-Louis (1724–1803).   A native of Switzerland, he turned from medicine to physics, and evolved a now-forgotten mechanical theory of gravitation, in which attraction, chemical affinity and cohesion are explained by the buffetings of Lucretian atoms. In 1758 he published an *Essai de chimie méchanique,* and he became a corresponding member of the Paris Academy in 1761.

LICHTENBERG, Georg Christoph (1742–99).   German physicist, also well known as a satirical writer, Anglophile and philosophical aphorist, he became professor at Göttingen in 1769, where he wrote on vulcanology, the shape of the earth, electricity and the lightning-rod. He was a sceptical critic of the parallel postulate, the ether, and even – for a time – Lavoisier's chemistry. He was also one of the first to propose a particle-and-wave theory of light.

LINK, Heinrich Friedrich (1767–1851).   A medical man from Göttingen, who taught chemistry, geology and biology at Rostock and Breslau, before becoming professor of botany at Berlin (1815). A supporter of Lavoisier, he rejected both phlogiston and the atomic theory; in philosophy, his preference was for Kant, in opposition to the nature-philosophy of Schelling. His *Über Naturphilosophie* was published in 1806.

MACQUER, Pierre Joseph (1718–84). A Parisian doctor who turned to chemistry, becoming a member of the Academy in 1745, and professor at the Jardin du Roi in 1777. Originally an exponent of the traditional four-element chemistry, he later moved close to the views of Lavoisier. He was the discoverer of potassium arsenate, and contributed to the study of dye-stuffs. His *Elements of the Theory and Practice of Chemistry* (1758) and *Dictionary of Chemistry* (1771) were both translated into English.

MARUM, Martinus van (1750–1837). Dutch plant physiologist, and museum director at Haarlem. Becoming interested in electricity, he built a large electrostatic machine, adopted the single-fluid theory of Franklin, and demonstrated the identity of static and galvanic electricity. In chemistry he was a follower of Lavoisier, discovered carbon monoxide, and was the first to condense ammonia. He later took to palaeontology, and was, in general, an effective disseminator of the scientific knowledge of his day.

MONS, Jean Baptiste van (1765–1842). Professor of chemistry at Louvain, and an opponent of the phlogiston theory, he also took Franklin's side in the dispute about positive and negative electricity. As an authority on fruit-growing, he was active in promoting and publicizing Achard's sugar-beet process.

PICTET, Marc-Auguste (1752–1825). A Swiss-born protégé and disciple of Saussure, whom he succeeded at the Academy of Geneva. His *Essai sur le feu* of 1790 still adheres to the belief in caloric, and lacks originality. In chemistry he was a follower of Lavoisier, and continued the work of DeLuc. He became editor of the *Journal de Genève* and of the *Bibliothèque britannique* (later *Bibliothèque universelle*).

PRÉVOST, Pierre (1751–1839). Like Pictet, a pupil of Saussure at Geneva, where he became professor of philosophy and general physics. His *Origine des forces magnétiques* was published in 1788. He also shared Pictet's interest in the study of thermal equilibrium, though preferring the corpuscular viewpoint. He translated works by Adam Smith, Dugald Stewart, Malthus and Blair, as well as the plays of Euripides.

PRIESTLEY, Joseph (1733–1804). Dissenting minister, political radical and experimental chemist, he was a materialist in philosophy, and in ethics a forerunner of Bentham. By use of the pneumatic trough he was able to isolate a number of gases, most notably oxygen (1774). The discovery led Lavoisier to the true theory of combustion, but Priestley himself remained a believer in phlogiston. With assistance from Franklin, he suggested the inverse square law of electrical force, and published a *History of Electricity* in 1767, to be followed (1774–86) by his six-volume *Experiments and Observations on Different Kinds of Air*. Unpopular for his support of the French Revolution, he lost his house to an incendiary mob, and spent his final years in the United States.

RICHTER, Jeremias Benjamin (1762–1807). A military engineer from Silesia (and allegedly a pupil of Kant's), he became a self-employed chemist.

Believing (unlike Kant) that chemistry could be a mathematical science, he made contributions to stoichiometry, wrote on oxygen and light, and discovered the laws of neutrality and equivalent proportion. Under the influence of Girtanner, he became a hesitant convert to the antiphlogistical point of view. His *Anfangsgründe der Chemie* was published, in three volumes, from 1792 to 1794.

RITTER, Johann Wilhelm (1776–1810). A contemporary and sometime friend of Schelling, and a protégé of Humboldt, he taught at Jena before removing, in 1804, to the Bavarian Academy in Munich. He did reputable work on galvanism, built the first dry cell, and a primitive accumulator, and discovered ultra-violet radiation. His scientific standing was later somewhat clouded by excursions into water-divining, and by his espousal of such Schellingian causes as the world-soul, the omnipresence of polarity in nature, etc.

RUMFORD, Benjamin Thompson, Count (1753–1814). American-born soldier of fortune, engineer, administrator and philanthropist, he spent a colourful career in military and governmental service, first in England, and later in Bavaria, before retiring to Paris, where he entered into an unsuccessful second marriage with Lavoisier's widow. Elected FRS in 1779, and a cofounder of the Royal Institution (1799), he created numerous endowments for scientific research. Apart from many practical inventions, civilian and military, his contributions to science lay mainly in the theory of heat, where he did as much as anyone to overthrow the caloric theory, and to establish the modern (molecular motion) view.

SAUSSURE, Horace Benédict de (1740–99). Swiss physicist and alpinist, he was professor of physics and philosophy at Geneva, and a lifelong student of the botany, geology, mineralogy and meteorology of the region. He was the first (not a guide) to ascend Mont Blanc (1787), and many other peaks. He was also active in devising and improving scientific instruments, notably the hair hygrometer. His main works are the four-volume *Voyages dans les Alpes* (1779–96) and an *Essai sur l'hygrometrie* (1783).

SCHERER, Alexander Nicolaus (1771–1824). A graduate of Jena, he became professor of physics at Halle, and then Dorpat, before migrating to the St. Petersburg Academy in 1804. An antiphlogistical writer on chemistry, combustion, light and the properties of gases, he founded (among other publications) the *Allgemeiner Journal der Chemie* and the *Allgemeine Nordische Annalen;* he also translated some of the writings of Cavallo.

SCHRÖTER, Johann Hieronymus (1745–1816). A pupil of Kästner at Göttingen, he became a lawyer and magistrate, but a part-time astronomer at the Lilienthal Observatory, where he studied the surfaces of Mars, Venus(!) and the moon. The reputation he gained by his careful, if primitive, observations was subsequently lost because of the extravagant conclusions he chose to draw from them.

SENEBIER, Jean (1742–1809). Swiss pastor, chemist and plant physiologist, he occupied a librarian's post at Geneva, and there published, in 1779, his *Action de la lumière sur la végétation*. Founded upon the earlier researches of

Hales and Ingen-Housz, this work gave the first correct account of plant respiration and photosynthesis. Senebier's writings on observation and experimental method anticipate the views of Claude Bernard.

STEFFENS, Hendrik (1773–1845). A Norwegian-born contemporary and disciple of Schelling, he taught mineralogy and physics at Kiel, Copenhagen, Halle, Breslau and Berlin. His *Beyträge zur innern Naturgeschichte der Erde* (1801) and *Anthropologie* (1822) present a speculative history, on Schellingian lines, of the chemical and geological evolution of the world.

SYMMER, Robert (1707(?)–63). An Edinburgh graduate, he worked as a tutor and civil servant, before retiring in 1757. Having experimented on various frictional materials, he proposed, in opposition to Franklin, a two-fluid theory of electricity resembling that of Du Fay. His views found support, notably from Coulomb and others in France. His "New Experiments and Observations concerning Electricity" appeared in the *Philosophical Transactions* of 1759.

VOLTA, Alessandro Guiseppe Antonio Anastasio (1745–1827). Jesuit-educated, but self-taught as an electrician, he was an early correspondent of Beccaria, with whom he shared a belief in Franklin's single-fluid theory of electricity. From 1778 he was professor of experimental physics at Pavia, where he invented the electrophore and condensator, discovered methane, revived the work of Aepinus, and worked with many leading scientists of the day. His best-known achievements are the refutation of galvanism, as a special form of animal electricity, and the invention (1800) of the voltaic pile, a predecessor of the wet-cell battery, and the first apparatus to generate an electric current.

WHISTON, William (1667–1752). A mathematical clergyman and friend of Newton, in 1701 he succeeded the latter in the Lucasian chair at Cambridge, but was ejected some ten years later for denying the Trinity. In 1696 he published *A New Theory of the Earth,* an attempt to harmonize Newtonian physics with the Mosaic cosmogony. This vein of physico-theological speculation was renewed in many of his later writings, such as *The Astronomical Principles of Religion* (1717).

Index of Names

Index of Subjects

Printed in Poland
by Amazon Fulfillment
Poland Sp. z o.o., Wrocław